For Deborah
from N——

Amherst 1977

Beyond the Crisis

Beyond the Crisis

Edited by

Norman Birnbaum

With essays by

Hans Peter Dreitzel
Serge Moscivici
Richard Sennett
Rudi Supek
Alain Touraine

OXFORD UNIVERSITY PRESS

LONDON   OXFORD   NEW YORK

1977

Copyright © 1977 by Oxford University Press, Inc.

Library of Congress Catalogue Card Number: 76-42637

Printed in the United States of America

Acknowledgments

We owe a very large debt to Professor Gianni Giannotti who, as Consultant to the Giovanni Agnelli Foundation, initially conceived of and secured support for the formation of an international group to study industrial society. We also have to thank the Foundation and its officers for their encouragement and support through most of the phases of our enterprise. When the Foundation's resources were curtailed, we were fortunate enough to receive assistance from the Fondation de la Maison des Sciences de l'Homme and Amherst College. I would also like to record my gratitude to The Institute for Advanced Study where, as a Member 1975-76, I was able to complete my work on the project.

At different times, a number of colleagues participated in our discussions. We regret that none of them could contribute directly to this volume, but we do wish them to know that we appreciate what we learned from them at our meetings. They are: Francesco Alberoni, Thomas Bottomore, Marcello De Cecco, Gianni Giannotti, Leszek Kolakowski, Alberto Martinelli, Edgar Morin, Claus Offe, Alessandro Pizzorno, and Jean Ziegler.

Professor Sara Via translated the essays by MM. Moscivici and Touraine, and Professor Susan Woodward translated the essay by Rudi Supek.

I wish also to express my personal thanks to June McCartney of Amherst College, Catherine Rhubart of The Institute for Advanced Study, and Marisa Torchio of the Agnelli Foundation for invaluable administrative assistance.

Amherst, Massachusetts *Norman Birnbaum*
May, 1977

Preface

As Chairman of the Industrial Society Project Group whose work is presented in this volume, I take considerable satisfaction in noting that it seems to stand the test of time reasonably well. Gianni Giannotti and I initiated the project in 1972, and our first meeting with a larger group was in May of 1973. The oil crisis and severe economic recession in the industrial societies had as yet to make themselves felt. Our work certainly bears the traces of a change in the context of theoretic discussion, but the substance of our discourse was not appreciably altered by these events. We intended to generate the elements of a long-term analysis. The response of the industrial societies of western Europe and the United States to the recent crisis suggests that whatever precise social configurations and political alignments may now arise, their elements are quite unlikely to be very different from those we depicted.

Certain themes, indeed, have become more salient. The critique of an exploitative attitude to nature, the demand for a new sort of technology, have become political issues in a number of countries. The recent surge of votes for an environmental ticket in France, mass protest and judicial action against nuclear power plant construction in Germany, the considerable gestures (at least) to environmental protection made by a new American administration, provide very immediate footnotes to Serge Moscivici's essay. Hans Peter Dreitzel points to new conceptions of personal existence, an enlargement of the sphere of cultural choice. The routinization, even the vulgarization and commercialization, of these ideas suggest that they are constituents of modern culture that cannot simply be dismissed as fads. Desperate efforts to appropriate and incorporate them may be interpreted as attempts to defuse their explosive possibilities. Richard Sennett is, surely, correct in depicting the constriction of public space—and therewith, of the experience of a public sphere—in our societies. A restoration of early modern conditions is impossible, as impossible as a return to the solidity of bourgeois tradition. The creation of a new public dimension requires the delimitation of alternative modes of intimacy, of the inner life itself. When Alain Touraine insists on the politicization of cultural questions, he is accepting the challenge of those who suppose that the bureaucratization and marketing of culture can leave tradition intact. The search for alternative social forms, for collective and communal creations which can enable us to struggle against bureaucracy and the market, must necessarily entail inquiry and even experimentation in culture.

It is our contributor from Yugoslavia, however, who—by example rather than precept—warns us that a politics reduced to the search for identity is no politics at all. Statist socialism's obsession with output, its addiction to minute and tyrannical hierarchy, demonstrate what can happen when the spontaneity of community, the inventiveness of society, are denied. Politics is the effort to find the limits of community, not the effort to replace community by a system of command. Alain Touraine, in depicting a continuing if at times covert revolt against centralization and bureaucratization, indeed reposes a great deal of confidence in the autonomy and purposiveness of self-aware, even self-constituted, human groupings. My own effort to explore the possible social bases of a new politics (new in that it would develop original solutions for some perennial problems) deals in different fashion with the same problem.

Is there a common thread to these very diverse contributions? There is not one, but several. One may appear paradoxical. The crisis of capitalism, banished as a theme of self-respecting analysis in America during two decades of relative affluence, can now be discussed again. We do not do so, not, at any rate, in banal fashion. More precisely, we never doubted that there was such a crisis, and we propose to do what we have always done in our separate works—analyze its cultural, political, and social forms. We do not conceive of the economy as distinct from society and the state, of a structure and a superstructure separated the one from the other. The retrogression of production has accentuated the contours as well as the conflicts of advanced capitalism—not resulted in a regression to more primitive forms of social conflict within capitalism. Another one of our common ideas would be expressed by the historians of the *Annales* school as that of the long term. Processes of historical accumulation in culture, the economy, and politics have brought about a social formation quite distinct from that of early twentieth-century society. Still another theme, finally, is the end of Western domination, or self-sufficiency. We do not for one moment subscribe to the belief that Western culture is either dead, or that it deserves to be put to death as an expression of imperialism. We observe, as a matter of historical fact, that our culture has lost its self-containment: we can no longer think of our history as entirely immanent, apart from that of other civilizations and cultures. What is true of culture, of course, is no less true of politics and the movement of society, generally. The problem, however, is not to suppose that our society has lost its capacity for change: it is to think of these changes as entailing our relationships with the rest of the world.

Four of the six contributors to the volume are Europeans, and the two American authors are not strangers in Europe. How relevant is the discussion to the United States? European thinkers, these days, are likely to be warning one another not to use an outmoded socialist rhetoric That is not a conspicuous American problem. It is curious how, despite the evidence, on each continent otherwise sentient colleagues insist that there are no longer large-scale social conflicts and that we face, instead, a large and unconnected series of small conflicts. In no case did any of us think in exclusively national terms. Even Rudi Supek, whose contribution was prepared in the midst of the cultural and political tensions that led to the suspension of publication of *Praxis* (the libertarian Marxist journal of which he was editor), did not concentrate on Yugoslavia. Rather, he attempted a comparison of the deformations of both state (or statist, in his terms) socialism and corporate capitalism. No one of us believes that our societies can necessarily contain their present conflicts. We do not anticipate, much less hope for, an apocalypse. We do think that a new order of conflict is emerging, and we have attempted to describe its elements. Our readers are well able to decide how to apply these ideas to their own national situations. I'll assert that the period of domestic (and imperial) tranquillity in the United States, 1945-60, will by the end of the century seem far less typical than the decade 1960-70. That, however, is matter for another book. For the moment, we hope that the present one will encourage our readers to reconsider some of the conventional modes of social criticism and social thought.

Norman Birnbaum

Contributors

Norman Birnbaum
Professor of Sociology, Amherst College, and Editorial Consultant, *Partisan Review*. An American who taught for many years in Europe, he was a founding editor of *New Left Review* and now works with the United Automobile Workers. Author of *The Crisis of Industrial Society* and *Toward a Critical Sociology*.

Hans Peter Dreitzel
Professor of Sociology, The Free University of Berlin. A frequent visitor to American universities, his most recent work is *Die Gesellschaftliche Leiden und das Leiden an der Gesellschaft*. In the tradition of critical and philosophical inquiry of German sociology, he has also dealt with concrete aspects of culture and politics and the contemporary psyche. He is Editor of, and a contributor to, *Recent Sociology*, five volumes of which have been published by Macmillan.

Serge Moscivici
Director of Studies (Professor) at the School of Advanced Studies in Social Sciences of Paris, the former Sixth Section of the Ecole Pratique des Hautes Etudes. He has taught in the United States and been a Fellow of the Center for Advanced Studies in the Behavioral Sciences, Palo Alto. A social psychologist, he has extended his inquiry into the area of the history and functions of the concept of nature. Two of his major works have been translated into English, *The Human History of Nature* and *Society Against Nature*.

Richard Sennett
Professor of Sociology and Director of the Center for the Humanities at New York University. Author of *The Hidden Injuries of Class* and *The Uses of Disorder*, his most recent work is *The Fall of Public Man*. His work is at the confluence of psychology, sociology, and the other human sciences.

Rudi Supek
Professor of Sociology at the University of Zagreb. Active in the French Resistance, he is a survivor of Buchenwald. Animator of the suspended journal *Praxis*, an international center of critical Marxism and libertarian socialism. His works are available in the west European languages and he has recently edited (with Branko Horvath and Mihailo Markovic) *Self-Governing Socialism*.

Alain Touraine
Director of Studies (Professor) at the School of Advanced Studies in Social Sciences of Paris. His early work on industrial sociology has been followed by work on industrial society and social theory. Two of his most recent works in French are *La Société invisible* and *Vie et Mort du Chili populaire*. Translations of four others are: *The May Movement, Post-Industrial Society, The Academic System in American Society*, and *The Self-Production of Society*. He is an advisor to the French Socialist Party.

Contents

Acknowledgments v

Preface vii

Contributors xii

Alain Touraine
Introduction
page 3

1
Alain Touraine
Crisis or Transformation?
page 17

2
Rudi Supek
The Visible Hand and the Degradation of Individuality
page 49

3
Hans Peter Dreitzel
On the Political Meaning of Culture
page 83

4
Serge Moscivici
The Reenchantment of the World
page 133

5
Richard Sennett
Destructive Gemeinschaft
page 171

6
Norman Birnbaum
On the Possibility of a New Politics in the West
page 201

Contents

Acknowledgments v

Preface vii

Contributors xii

Alain Touraine
Introduction
page 3

1
Alain Touraine
Crisis or Transformation?
page 17

2
Rudi Supek
The Visible Hand and the Degradation of Individuality
page 49

3
Hans Peter Dreitzel
On the Political Meaning of Culture
page 83

4
Serge Moscivici
The Reenchantment of the World
page 133

5
Richard Sennett
Destructive Gemeinschaft
page 171

6
Norman Birnbaum
On the Possibility of a New Politics in the West
page 201

Beyond the Crisis

Introduction

by Alain Touraine

The sum of accidents and uncertainties which we call the *crisis* has rid us of the pallid promises of new discoveries the greater wealth, education, and leisure which future-peddlers have tried to sell us. But by confronting us with the most pressing difficulties of unemployment, inflation, and imbalances in international trade and by drawing governments into politics of short-term situations without a vision of the desired evolution of societies and economies, the crisis places us in a contradictory intellectual situation. On the one hand, it appears risky to make predictions beyond the very short term; is not the principal objective one of "emerging from the crisis" and reestablishing conditions of activity analogous to those which existed before the oil crisis or the crisis of the dollar? On the other hand, we are more or less aware that the most fundamental categories of our social, cultural, and political experience no longer correspond to the evolution of today's world and that we are left without ruler or compass in our evaluation of changes which resemble crises more than transformations. Should we not envisage going beyond crisis, breaking equally with hazardous extrapolations and blind pragmatism, attempting rather to reestablish modes of reflection that will lead from basic socio-cultural transformations to political and economic "problems" to the choices and decisions confronting individuals and states, social movements and institutions alike?

The group that has been meeting these last three years in Turin and Paris has chosen, in reaction to the obsession with the present moment, to defend the notion that crises and change can be fully comprehended only in the perspective of a vast social mutation characterized simultaneously by decadence and breakdown and by emergence and creation.

It is a questionable choice. It might have been preferable to analyze the economic crisis itself, seeking its deep causes and its possible outcomes. But this kind of effort is widespread and inevitably encounters the problems of defining a "new growth" without digging deeper, without going below the workings of economic systems and their principles to the very categories which organize our collective experience. We have also come to think that one of the principal transformations of our time lies in questioning the governing role of the economy in society. Following the first decades of the nineteenth-century Industrial Revolution, industrial societies struggled to regain a measure of control over their economic activity, particularly through the formation of workers' movements and through governmental intervention. After thirty years of exceptional growth in industrialized countries, do we not feel again the necessity of regaining control both theoretically and practically? Are we not already persuaded that the economy is indeed political and that we cannot separate the logic of a system from the behavior of its actors?

This attitude could have led us to considerations of the entire planet: the domination of the Third World by rich nations, the confrontation of imperialist strategies on all continents, the role of oil-rich countries in recent economic developments. Everything indicated that we should not limit our analysis to industrialized countries alone. Yet our choice goes counter to these indications; our considerations here will bear only upon industrialized countries, not for purely theoretical reasons but because today we find it ill-timed and out of place to speak for the rest of the world as if the privilege of birth and wealth granted us a monopoly on analysis. This book represents the effort of each of us to bring criticism upon himself even more than upon a "situation." Therefore, a sense of our involvement in our own analysis, rather than indifference, leads us to limit our scrutiny to industrialized countries. This double limitation has had the advantage of orienting us entirely toward the hypothesis of a change in society. Rather than speak of an accident, of a crisis born of the limits of a kind of society, we have elected to raise the question of the birth of a new culture and a new society.

But this is a dangerous formulation. New culture? Undoubtedly, for the image of the relationship of society to its environment, the image of nature, of techniques, of needs has been sufficiently transformed for the general public to be already aware of this change. But can we speak of a new society? Cultural change today is so violent that it is almost an overthrow. In a few years we have moved from the notion of a limited human effort exploiting limitless natural resources to the image of a human power capable of devouring, consuming, and destroying the patrimony of a finite nature.

As a reaction against industrial hubris and the philosophy of history by which it seeks to justify its claims, many today wish to value equilibrium above progress and solidarity above accumulation. All reject the notion of society as a machine whose power increases as the difference in level between opposite poles increases: as modernity destroys tradition, cities take over the country, reason destroys feeling, the mother-country dominates its colonies, and man crushes woman. Nothing must attenuate this break with ethnocentric progressivism in whose name cultures have been destroyed, domination by the most powerful greatly increased, exclusions and enclosures multiplied: the reign of rules, norms, and modernity. The vertical, hierarchical image of the world must be abandoned: everywhere claims are argued from nature, those of men like those of nature itself, refusing dressage, uniformity, discipline and searching for specificity instead of accepting imitation. Urban decomposition and violence, the uprisings of women and other colonized groups, anxiety at the threats weighing upon the genetic patrimony and the eco-system have put an end to the reign of reason and an end to the triumphant evolutionism which has animated the culture of industrialization, whether socialist or capitalist.

Our societies are too powerful to be situated within history: they have devoured history, and perhaps they will die of it, or perhaps they will transform it into the capacity to manifest themselves in historicity. Cultural mutation is an inadequate means of defining what our lived experience will be. Such a formulation describes the field that societies are to cultivate. But are societies transforming themselves as profoundly as the problems they must resolve?

Nothing is less obvious. The vast socialist world, despite the new struggle between China and the USSR, is developing within the confines of already outmoded political theory and practice. And in industrialized capitalist countries, the growing importance of multinational businesses, the intervention of the government, and the influence of a unionism increasingly accepted by both management and government do no more than follow tendencies almost a century old. In no way do these developments oblige us to speak of a change in society. Social science is in disarray. No strong movement is replacing the revolutionary labor worker movement. Protests and utopias are countless, but none of them appears to have a central role to play. The idea of a transformation in social relationships, class relationships, political systems, and social movements is upheld by several of the members of our group. One may even think that this is the principal intellectual stake of this book: to gain acceptance for the idea that a social mutation is taking place. But the reader who opens this work cannot initially accept this idea as a given; on the contrary he has many reasons, some of them very strong, for regarding it with suspicion. I wish therefore to stress the points of difference so as to better expose the central question of this book.

Had I to plead the case against the thesis of the birth of a new society, I would say this: we have just lived through a succession of "historical" societies combining structure and evolution. Are we not now entering into societies of pure change, without structure or nature, purely political societies which, at any given moment, are nothing more than the sum of antecedents and consequences of their decisions? For a century or two we have talked of industrial society, capitalism, rationalizing, or secularizing. Should we not speak exclusively of development, to identify a multiplicity of "paths" defined more politically than socially rather than to reconstruct the stages of modernization? Who cares to ask about the nature of socialism at a time when historical reality urges us to understand why China opposes the USSR or what distinguishes Syria from Iraq? Do we not ask ourselves frequently whether Germany, Italy, Great Britain, and France will still figure in the first ranks twenty-five years from now? Since Bandoung the notion of a Third World has paled before the acceleration of diverse situations and politics there. Even in a more limited area like Latin America, the idea of a general analysis of the continent meets with strong resistance because the evolutions of Chile, Peru, Brazil, and Argentina are so dissimilar. How far away is the time when we perceived international confrontations as the projection of social struggles! It is true that the USSR often supports "progressive" regimes, just as the United States backs conservative governments. But is the struggle between the USSR and the United States the clash of socialism with capitalism, or is it rather the clash of liberty with despotism? Since the Vietnam War and the invasion of Czechoslovakia, who dares to use such terms? We are witnessing the confrontation of empires whose only superiority over the rest of the world is military in nature. What would the USSR count for without its potential for thermo-nuclear destruction? Who can still believe that the United States is the model of modernity opposed to the archaism of the rest of the world?

War seems to dictate politics. Does not the politics of a state determine its society? We have inherited from the previous generation the notion that political events are but the surface manifestations of a history whose great movements are those of the economy. In the age of Hitler, Stalin, Mao, and Nasser who can accept that claim? Who can believe that the essential is the impersonal and that societies are like buildings solidly fixed on their foundations, while their inhabitants may, without real consequences, devote themselves to the decoration or superstructure of their apartments?

But let us return to questions bearing more directly on concrete analyses. Are we not at the beginning of societies defined by their modes of change rather than their civilization or mode of production? This would mean that the great questions of the nineteenth century, those of Comte, Spencer, or Durkheim, like those of Marx or Weber, no longer concern our present experience, which would be better understood in the light of political science than of sociology. Or, more specifically, are we not emerging from societies dominated by class relationships into an era dominated by the problem of the state and, as a complementary problem, the defense of citizens' liberties against the state? Is this not the message carried by those voices speaking from countries where the state calls itself socialist? In the course of our discussions as we attempted to clarify our own positions, we found to our surprise that we all identify ourselves as "liberals." And since there is no question that each of us is clearly "on the left" in his own country, this word obviously does not express a defense of free enterprise, but rather a conviction that the struggle for liberty against the growing fusion of economic exploitation, political hegemony, and cultural power has become the first article of any program of opposition to all forms of domination.

We thus arrived at a precise formulation of our method of posing the problem. Cultural paradigms are changing; we are already in a world dominated by multiplicity of policies and "routes" of development and thus also by rivalries among states. Does something still exist between culture and state which one might call society, or is the social scene nothing more than the political scene, a world of actors, "forces," and decisions rather than a network of social relationships defined in larger terms than the consciousness and the gestures of the actors?

This increasing invasion by the state still reminds many people of the triumph of an enlightened central power over local notables and over the agents of transmission of cultural traditions. In France, particularly, it recalls the victory of the republican state over Catholic conservatism. But are we not already far beyond this progressivism? The technocratic state destroys the web of social relations, protecting only a private life reduced to consumerism and to intimacy defined by the absence of social ties. Is the triumph of sexuality really more than a withdrawal from eroticism perceived as both desire and connection? Do not communities, so quick to present themselves as locales of intense social exchanges, really attract us to the degree that they have no objectives, and are stifled in immediacy? Public life, *Öffentlichkeit*, as Habermas says, is in crisis. Symbolic systems are decomposing and being replaced by a confused appeal to energy, to the body seen not as an agent of communication but as a reserve of extra-societal strength. We rapidly reach the point at which cultural protest is merely a fearful retreat facilitated and protected by the centralized power.

Even if it seems excessive to speak of the dissolution of society into the political process, can we not say that the world of tomorrow will be dominated by collectivities under the direction of a conquering state, or one able to exercise sovereignty over all its functions? Four of the six authors of this book are Europeans. Does not doubting the existence of a new society include for them a painful awareness of the inevitable decay of European national states East and West and, consequently, the dissolution of European societies at the very moment that from all sides empires, national states, and simple centers of political pressure are converging in a tightening network of rapid changes? And the American uneasiness is perhaps explainable also in terms of the loss of hegemony of the country whose economic and military power has represented the triumph of "modernity" and industrial society for an entire generation of men [not excepting Soviet leaders]. How strange is the situation of powerful countries whose wealth dazzles and offends the poverty of the world they pillaged, whose wastefulness insults the famine of Asia and Africa, and who nevertheless are losing their place as national states or cultures—countries where getting rich is so closely allied to decadence!

Is it accidental that social thought today seems so confused and disoriented? The great constructions that were the pride of American sociology have been falling into ruin for more than ten years. Marxism lives again in Western countries but more as ideology than as a way of knowing; its claim to scientific status is less and less often affirmed. The only intellectual current to have attracted a real audience is, characteristically, an idea formulated fifty years ago in answer to an earlier crisis, a critical current formed by Western Marxism. But this idea has had repercussions only as it has become, through the Frankfurt School, more pessimistic and more critical. From Sartre to Marcuse, is it not the destruction of the illusions of reason, undertaken in the name of philosophy and not of a class or a party, which has most profoundly stirred young thinkers?

We have chosen to look beyond the crisis. When we do we discover "the end of society," not the end of the world but of a certain type of society. We know that we are very far from societies defined by their mechanisms of reproduction of exchanges, from "anthropological" societies. Are we not at this moment emerging from "historical" societies which must be studied in their being and action, in their structure and origin? Or, to go even further, are we not experiencing the shattering of a concrete correspondence within a single country between political collectivities, culture, society, and the state?

Shall we not begin to speak of a new planetary culture, the rivalry of empires, and the multiplication of partial societies—grouped by age, sex, ethnicity, and proximity—foreign to the mass media they consume as to the pressures they undergo? If this were accurate, those of us brought up in the ancient traditions of a profoundly different situation would have to speak of crisis rather than transformation.

It is not difficult to look beyond the accidents of situations, however serious and revealing they may be. The real choice, however, presented as theoretical but charged with practical consequences, is between the idea of going beyond the historical era, of breaking with this very long period and returning to societies characterized by equilibrium and externally induced changes which are the successors to societies of production and accumulation largely motivated by internal changes; and on the other hand, going forward into new societies beyond the industrial ones. This does not obviate either qualitative changes or a breaking off, but these new societies will be even more production-accumulation-oriented than the preceding ones have been.

If we accept the vague term "post-industrial societies," should we conceive of them as anti-industrial or as hyperindustrial? The following essays contain a variety of opinions on this fundamental but unanswerable question. I believe the contributors to this book have all taken a position against the technocratic pragmatism that reduces society's function to a series of adaptations to a changing environment and to internal political situations in a permanent state of renegotiation.

Society has no more autonomy of existence; it is no longer any more than the product of its acts. But the capacity of industrialized societies to produce themselves, instead of dissolving conflicts and ideologies, broadens the domain of politics. In every sector of social life, it creates opposition between management apparatus seeking to impose its monopoly on change-making, and popular forces defending their biological, psychological, and social selves against power. These forces struggle to protect autonomous exchange and relationship against hierarchical and mechanized order, against rules and categories, and against integration and exclusion. Such is our shared position, which does not, however, exclude certain divergences in opinion. Once again there appears a distance between two modes of analysis of industrialized societies. For one the essential problem is their mode of change. If those who think this way are "on the right" they trust to mechanisms of apprenticeships and adaptation; if they are "on the left" they fear an all-powerful state and consider that the principal issue is the humanist defense of liberties. In the other mode of analysis, the structural problems of society and thus the relationships of classes take priority without denigrating the seriousness of modes of change. In this framework right-wing thought will exalt the role of multinational societies or of a great technocratic *apparatus* able to extend its actions far into space and time; leftist thought, on the other hand, will examine new forms of domination and class conflict and seek to understand as rapidly as possible the nature of new social movements as they evolve in the midst of present confusion. Let us not totally oppose those who think particularly for or against statism and those who think principally for or against technocracy—but let us not confuse them either, for their choices also correspond to different historical situations. In large capitalist countries which still occupy a dominant position and where changes are above all endogenous, the problems of structure and social classes are probably more important than those concerning development and the state. On the contrary, countries which came late to capitalism or whose economic or colonial dependence and politico-cultural apparatus were overturned by a voluntary act, either national or revolutionary, have as their leading agent the state and as their principal preoccupation the defense of liberties. Every country partakes of these two worlds but in variable proportion. This explains both our community of views and the relative sensitivity of each of us to one or the other of these problems. Whatever the ideas propounded, it seems to me that all the texts collected here are linked by a "desire for society."

All of them manifest at the least a refusal of the so-called objective view of history, as if a society were defined by its place in an evolution or by a central mechanism. All are dissatisfied with what could be called a humanist, ethical, or utopian criticism that would place, in opposition to society, in general a conception of freedom or of desire, or indeed a people or a working class defined as extraterritorial, as an absolute. It was normal that the time of utopias should follow, in the East as in the West, upon the illusions of abundance. This was creative in that it made social problems reappear; but it is no longer creative when, mingling cultural transformation and social conflicts, it keeps us from recognizing in society connections between power and private domination which will be the focus of new conflicts.

How can we fail to judge critically this "moral" interpretation of crisis which easily eliminates social analyses, rejects society categorically in the name of an anti-societal principle that often remains religious in nature and which strikes out in search of an identity defined outside social relationships? When unemployment spreads does the rejection of work maintain the same liberating force it had in the abundant years? Ours is perhaps the moment at which economic crisis reveals the limits of an analysis that is too exclusively cultural and forces us to reanalyze society, to ask in new ways the important questions: Where is the ruling class? What is the state? This means looking at society from the inside, in its social relationships, powers, and inequalities. The themes introduced by the counter-culture will not disappear, but they will be transformed by becoming instruments of social criticism. The appeal to identity can perhaps be merely the defensive aspect of a movement whose true nature will appear only when an offensive action is launched against the technocratic apparatus.

It would be an error to choose hastily one response or another, for cultural criticism frees us from worn-out analyses of old social problems. However, if we accept it complacently for too long, we risk both not seeing the formation of new social problems and according permanent importance to sensitivities closely bound to the actual moment of mutation rather than a new type of society. But this slow pace may prepare us to answer more clearly the fundamental question: Are we entering upon a new society? Certain people say yes, and I am one of them; others find this too cautious and think that the very notion of society is in question today. Both attitudes are represented here by those who feel the need to produce a social life instead of drifting with the winds of chance in the hands of opportunists and local traders who lack both hope and imagination.

We must speak of crisis if our societies have become incapable of conceiving of themselves, of knowing what they are and what they are making themselves be. Economic crisis has exposed, behind the mask of growth, the seductive and terrible visage of decadence. Until recently we would have declared, somewhat fatuously given our audience of starving nations, that we had to choose our future course, much like the promising young man who hesitates between Polytechnique and Ecole Nationale d'Administration. But now the question is not which form of growth to choose, but whether we accept death or wish to live.

Not one of us has failed to experience the crisis of recent years as a warning. The American intelligentsia suffer from having been identified with the powers of napalm and the dollar; Germany feels uneasy confronting its triumphant and repressive clear conscience bought by money; Italy, England, and France stand giddy on the edge of a precipice. Which of these societies does not feel glittering death leaning over it as it sleeps?

Within these very pages a voice from the East speaks to us of the dead hopes of socialism stifled and deported by a state which cannot even be called Stalinist any longer. We do not set out for a new world like champions exalted by having broken every record. We have neither maps nor navigators, and we no longer believe in astrologers and prophets. Fear of death, untamed imagination, and the desire that goes beyond every object alone can lead us, without a plan but moved by passionate feeling, beyond crisis toward the uncertain goal of inventing a new society.

This book is neither scientific nor partisan. We are at the same time committed and disengaged, in an effort to distance ourselves not merely from a society but, more painfully, from a mode of knowing, from a language which still forces us to say what we no longer feel when we try to communicate. It bears also a hope for the rebirth of social action. A new cultural backdrop is in place; now it is time for the stage to come alive, for a new drama to be played in both life and knowledge. We are not setting out at twilight to tell stories and to judge them, but rather at the hour when waking gestures are still rooted in dreams and objects are still shaped by our visions of them.

I

Alain
Touraine

*Crisis or
Transformation?*

Introduction

There is mounting criticism concerning the state of society in the rich nations, thus creating a general feeling of crisis. This feeling is provoking a wide discussion of the inevitable or desirable changes, but it is also leading to much confusion. In fact it is tempting to oppose, in general terms, two civilizations, one of affluence and the other of crisis, or even to oppose Zero Growth to an exceptional progress in history. On closer examination these brilliant oppositions do not have a clear meaning, for in some cases we oppose a hundred and fifty years of capitalist, or of noncapitalist, industrialization to a new society, which would find its state of equilibrium in a new plateau after a steep climb. Sometimes, on the contrary, it is a question of bringing to an end a wasteful consumer society which, in rich Europe, has been in existence for only one generation. Finally, it is sometimes the end of the "historical period" which is being announced and which heralds a return to societies which may be termed anthropological.

Instead of regrouping these into a single opposition and trying thus to name the general crisis which we are supposedly experiencing at this moment, it seems better to separate what is being mixed up and to understand, first, the nature of the changes and the questions which are temporarily being superimposed. Before doing this the reason for such an approach must be clearly indicated. There are two objectives: a theoretical one and a practical one.

1. It is wrong to analyze the essence of present problems as a crisis. A crisis is an accident in the evolution of a given society. There are certainly elements of crisis at the present time, but their importance is related to changes in the structure of society. The spectacular increase in oil prices or even the sudden acceleration of inflation in almost all capitalist industrial countries should not lead us to give greater importance to short-term accidents than to long-term transformations.

Let us acknowledge that we are simultaneously experiencing the instability created by the "energy crisis," the very profound disturbances linked to the crisis of the hegemony of the dollar, a redistribution of the division of labor and economic power at the international level—a new phase in the loss of leadership by the oldest industrial nations—and finally, a transformation of society which affects these industrialized nations above all, but which nevertheless gives them a chance to avoid decadence and introduces new forms of power and social struggles. Since our attention has been focused mainly on the most immediate and the most visible transformations, it seems useful—and this will be our aim here—to shift our attention to the more profound mutations and the long-term transformations of our society.

2. Whether we speak primarily of crisis or of transformation is not merely an intellectual choice; it implies different manners of defining causes of the present situation and, above all, of imagining the evolution of our societies. My idea is that an analysis, undertaken in terms of crisis, leads to a search for a plan to rescue our planet, conceived of as a vast social system, at the center of which one would find a central authority, or simply a coherent will, proposing reasonable solutions, that is, solutions which would be both good for humanity as a whole and technically feasible. If we cry "Fire!" it is because we expect the firemen to come. In other words, an analysis in terms of crisis, which eliminates real social actors and the real relationships between them and which speaks indeterminately in the name of humanity as a whole, can only serve as an ideological instrument. Such an instrument permits the rise to power of new ruling classes, or rather of new ruling elites, that is, of new social categories which control the transformation of one society into another, and which set up new ruling forces. On the other hand, to speak of transformation of society is to place in the foreground the transformations of a culture and of social relations, particularly of power relations, which find their meaning only within the context of real social systems, that is, when defined by institutions and ruling forces.

Thus, a new critical outlook on society is arising. During a first phase, characterized by the pronounced growth and zenith of the American empire, by the great economic, cultural, and military expansionism of the Kennedy era, the image of the future was most often that of a hyperindustrial society, becoming increasingly richer, more flexible, and more integrated. The utmost in terms of utopia was the idea of a society whose central value would be change and whose internal conflicts would consist only of permanent, increasingly institutionalized adaptations to continual changes. We were supposed to experience the transition from the secondary to the tertiary, from goods to services, from work to pleasure, from the governing of men to the administration of things. Then some voices were raised against this conquering optimism. They tried to imagine the new forms of social classes and their conflicts, the new forms of power and of exclusion. They were not often heard, since it was so easy to be carried away by the sweet winds of extrapolation toward the enchanting shores of the year 2000.

Despite my personal efforts, the idea of a post-industrial society, introduced by Daniel Bell, has maintained the meaning which he gave it. It is seen as a society guided by knowledge, capable of continual adjustments, and freed from fundamental conflicts. Herman Kahn, in a more superficial manner, announced our arrival at a horizon where new arms were being discovered to conquer the universe; however, he never considered the nature of the social field in which such innovations would arise.

But we must also add that in response to this conservative image of the future, one could only hear an echo of the old social problems, which had increasingly become ideological themes as their practical importance diminished. Between the exegeses of the texts of the past and the prophets of enrichment, there could not be much room for those who wished from that moment on to imagine the society of the future, not merely the technology of the future—in other words, for those who wished to recognize the new forms of power and social struggle.

This period has long been over, even though chronologically it is still very near. It was only eight years ago that *The American Challenge* by Jean-Jacques Servan-Schreiber—a hymn to modernization, Americanization, and affluence—was the greatest European best-seller. Enrichment was so rapid and great during this period, and it presupposed such an increase in inequalities at the international level, that rich societies had to learn once again to speak of crisis and to rediscover doubt before being able to return to analysis. We have just been through a decade in which the thunderbolts have come one after the other in all the domains of social life; finally, the idea of a general crisis appeared. The protests of dependent countries did not disturb the good conscience of the dominant countries. The misery and famine in the Sahel and in Calcutta were repressed into the unconscious in the name of the hopes placed on the Green Revolution and on development in general. It was finally the student movements in Japan, the United States, Germany, and France which made the rich countries uneasy for the first time. Even those who referred to these movements as the actions of a few extremists did not entirely believe this.

Then came the Vietnam War, which in turn brought a long American political crisis. At the same time, the invasion of Czechoslovakia and the persecution of the Jews and the intellectuals in the Soviet Union accelerated the decline of the other model of society, which had dominated the 1950s. The United States and the Soviet Union were no longer used as references; consequently, the ideological juxtaposition of capitalism and socialism represented nothing more than the rivalry between two superpowers and no longer furnished formulas for social struggles. Then came the crisis of the dollar and the increase of inflation. Finally, as a consequence of the preceding, came the brutal rise in the price of oil and the great panic of 1974.

This panic is beginning to be dispelled. It is no longer possible to believe that the rich world is in danger of succumbing to the blows of unchained "barbarians," as at the end of the Roman Empire. Very great industrial countries, such as the Federal Republic of Germany and Japan, increasingly are bringing their inflation under control. In Europe, at least, anxieties of all kinds no longer seem to be joining forces to produce the maddening wait for the final catastrophe. At the same time the richest capitalist countries are discovering their own weaknesses, the seriousness of the threats of recession, and the weak dynamics of certain national economies. Not long ago one only worried about excessive growth. The time has come to widen our vision and ask ourselves whether the industrialization of new countries, the revolt of the poor countries, and the transition of industrialized countries to post-industrial society form a historical whole of which we should be aware. The uneasiness and the moral protests of the rich countries represented a last attempt to defend their privileges. These countries were asking their citizens to reform their behavior so that their organization and its consequences should not be called into question. Criticism today should be more radical and more concrete. Let us forget our dreams of Zero Growth, since the United States has just experienced Minus Four Growth, that is, the rise of unemployment to eight or ten million. The time has come to replace utopias and good intentions with a social analysis of the mutations under way.

I believe it will be useful to distinguish five elements which lead to a rupture of the present image of society. They must be read in a certain order: social crisis→cultural crisis→cultural mutation→social mutation→political debate. First, the previous type of society and culture is questioned; only then can we outline the image of a different future. The central moment of this evolution is the transition from the consciousness of a cultural crisis to the idea of a necessary cultural mutation. We are now speaking at this moment. That explains my insistence on progressing to the next phase, that is, the reintroduction of social personages onto a scene whose decor has been changed. We must put aside political debate which, although constantly present, deals more with the manner of administering change than with the actual content of such change. Let us specify the content of each of these "crises."

The Phases of Transformation

1—Social crisis

How can it be possible not to mention the idea of *The Great Transformation* as outlined by K. Polanyi in his description of industrialization during the last century? Economic growth has escaped social control. Instead of being guided by society, growth has become an end in itself, that is, an instrument of profit. A crisis is being declared on all sides: by the defenders of the capitalist economy, themselves uneasy as they see the sources of capitalist industrialization—the propensity to sound long-term investment in productive activities and the stability of currency—threatened by a consumer society, that is, a consuming society; and in a more spectacular manner, by those who oppose unsatisfied real demands to over-satisfied, artificially stimulated demands. The latter ask, How can one not be sensitive to a crisis in societies that respond to needs only when such responses increase profits? The profit-makers are interested in maintaining an unequal society, because those who receive the highest incomes are those who consume the greatest number of new products, which are indicators of high social status. They are also interested in giving priority to those needs expressed in the most individual manner, that is, those needs which most threaten the community's control over growth. Since our society is one of change, the fundamental crisis has become inflation. It is a result of the constant rivalry among social groups as they pursue relative advantages—a rivalry in which the weakest always lose. It is also a result of the unlimited investments of enterprises extending credit in order to impose new products that increase their profits.

As during the last century, the time has come in which moderate and radical movements have demanded that society recover control over its own growth. First, the dominant ideology, which falsely asserted that enrichment would lead to an equalization of situations and opportunities, had to be criticized and overthrown. The discoveries that social inequalities had not diminished, that American society in particular was supporting a large percentage of "poor people," that mass education, even at the college level, had not been accompanied by a decrease in the inequality of opportunity, prepared the way for more general and active protest movements. These movements rejected the exclusive reign of profit, rehabilitated ways of life which had nothing to do with consumer frenzy, and questioned the military and cultural crimes, the genocides and ethnocides, and all forms of social, cultural, and, generally speaking, colonial domination exerted by societies which like to refer to themselves only in terms of enrichment and well-being. At another level this criticism has been expressed, although with greater difficulty, in the so-called socialist countries. Here also, particularly in Yugoslavia, Poland, and Hungary, intellectuals and workers have fought against the disappearance of society's control over its own growth and against the absolute concentration of the instruments and the products of growth in the hands of the party-technocracy. The differences between the capitalist consumer societies and the state-industrialized societies should not hide the crisis they have in common: the "wild," uncontrolled character of growth and the absence of all social and cultural criteria for the evaluation of the Gross National Product.

2—Cultural crisis
Even more radical from many points of view was the denunciation of a cultural crisis. The Club of Rome was not the only agent of this denunciation, but it was the most active and the most effective. Because I present here a very different point of view, I must first recognize the importance of its contribution. The culture of industrial society is based on evolutionism, that is, on the idea that societies follow one another in sequence, each society being more diversified and instrumental than the preceding one. These were

the ideas of Auguste Comte, Spencer, Durkheim, and Tönnies; they have, fairly recently, been taken up in a more systematic form by Talcott Parsons. This evolution is characterized by the growing triumph of man over nature and by the Promethean energy—fire and work—drawing resources from nature, the bottomless reservoir, to build a "spiritual" and "cultural" world, as opposed to a natural world. It is essential to link two affirmations: (1) social action is directed by a movement which transcends man and which does not lead to a world of order, as in the case of divine intervention or of the prince's law, but to progress, thanks to freedom of movement and initiative; (2) the humanization of society is equivalent to its denaturalization, and consequently all social struggles are the work of spiritual forces opposing themselves to natural forces—civilized men against savages, the bourgeoisie against the people, reason against feeling, men against women, adults against children.

This evolutionism, which was both optimistic and aggressive, had been submitted to such severe trials in Europe that it has never been able to recover the strength it had at the time of Renan. Two world wars, a severe crisis of capitalism, and above all, Nazism and Stalinism—in other words, the disruption of a continent whose main problem was no longer poverty but concentration camps—made it impossible to believe in progress and the attainment of a world both rich and free. The United States, however, despite the great depression of the 1930s, had kept herself away from the great wars and the political catastrophes. Instead she showed an extraordinary inventive vigor and a capacity for international domination, which led her concretely to consider herself the vanguard of humanity, the best example of modernity. This was the era in which Rostow defined the stages of economic growth and in which Lipset told Latin American and other underdeveloped countries about the difficult beginnings of American democracy, letting them thus understand: we have been as you are now; if you behave, you will some day be like us.

What was thrust upon us by the reflections of the Club of Rome, based on calculations by MIT—little does it matter that these calculations are debatable—was that the idea of unlimited growth had to be abandoned, that its limits had to be acknowledged, that a continuation of the trends of the last few years could no longer be imagined. The time is nearing when such growth will become self-destructive, when the growth of population in particular will lead to mass starvation.

The decline of the culture of the industrial period faces some resistance. Those who are beginning to take part in mass consumption, who have the feeling that they are no longer being excluded and can now have access to available goods, whether these be college education or automobiles, will not easily permit that enrichment to be criticized just when they are beginning to take part. This is why the Soviet Union and the Communist parties in the West are the political forces most attached to the continuation of industrial society. This, in itself not to be criticized, reminds us that it is the privileged classes who first become conscious of mutations. But one must also bear in mind that those who demand a simple enlargement of the former type of society lose the opportunity of initiating historical change; they demand only the role which had once been that of the republican petty bourgeoisie at the beginning of the twentieth century.

3—Cultural transformation

This criticism, which was also a result of the social protest against growth conceived of as an end in itself, naturally led to the production of utopias, to a search for equilibrium and order which would replace growth and movement, and to a withdrawal into primary groups and community life so as to escape mass society. These are important and creative utopias. We need only mention the efficacy of Illich's critique of the school system and of the illusion of equalization through schooling, of the hospital system and the partiality of the assumption which identifies it with public health, and so forth. But these utopias are, as always, important not so much in themselves but as a critique of the dominant ideology and as the first expression of protest movements which are not yet organized, both because they are repressed and because they are subjected to old forces of opposition. Moreover, the present cultural crisis cannot be separated from the creation of a new culture and of a new image of the relations between society and its environment. For the two principles of industrial society which I mentioned above, we can substitute two very different principles:

1. Social facts are not controlled by a superior order of any kind—religious, political, or economic. They are but the product of social actions and thus of social relations. Society is the product of its own making. It is not situated in an evolutionary movement or in history; it produces its own history. This has led me to introduce, at the heart of sociological analysis, the concept of *historicity*, the self-production of society.

2. Thus deprived of its link with a transcendental world, society discovers that it is a part of nature and is thus subjected to natural laws. This new naturalism is not opposed to a consciousness of historicity. Rather, historicity is the other facet of the new naturalism: human societies have the capacity to modify their environment; ecology does not delineate an order in which man must simply find his niche but rather analyzes interactions between the equilibrium of the environment and cultural initiative.

We must pause for a moment to consider the definition of this new cultural field. The domain of social action has been trapped between a transcendental order and the natural laws which govern, within society itself, the equilibrium of the population, the systems of exchange, and particularly the kinship systems. The growth of society's capacity to act on itself has not led to a secularized, instrumental society rid of both its gods and devils and rid of transcendence and nature. Rather, it has led social action to interiorize both creativity, which had until then been relegated to a transcendental order, and nature, which had until then been considered a resource external to man. This double transformation has been carried out on the one hand by Marxist thinking, which reduces the economic, political, or religious order to social relations, and on the other hand by the Freudian school, which discovers sexuality and the language of the unconscious behind the façade of the ego.

What has been destroyed by this cultural crisis, which we will continue to experience for a long time, is precisely the illusion that a society is entirely defined by its own change and its own instrumentality and that a society has no values and thus no absolute power or fundamental conflicts. This illusion is both liberal and ethnocentric, optimistic and conquering. We are rediscovering the fact that social organization is the product of social relations, centered on society's capacity to act on itself, thus centered on cultural and economic orientations. We are also discovering that social action is subjected to restrictions imposed by resources, coming from the environment or from the brain and the whole body, even though social action is the result of cultural orientations.

4—Social transformations

Later we will analyze the new forms which social relations will take in this new cultural field. Let us now note only that in the present historical period, social conflicts have reappeared and social actors have been progressively redefined. The social scene, which for a moment was empty with the departure of the old actors, is being filled up once again with new personages. It is at this point that our analysis encounters its greatest barriers. We easily accept the idea of a socially undetermined crisis; this idea can cause great fear, but it does not lead us to change many of our opinions concerning daily experience. However, we do not wish to stop naming the principal personages of social history as we did formerly, because we would consequently have to change our ideology.

However, we must have the courage to question the ideas we have inherited. A long industrialization period, which has not even come to an end in such countries as Italy and France and even less so along the greatest part of the Mediterranean coast, has given us the habit of considering the labor movement as the main actor of social history. Today, the importance of the labor movement, and particularly of trade-unionism in social organization and in public and private decision-making mechanisms, has been steadily increasing and will continue to grow for a long time. But we must accept that the labor movement today is no longer the agent of basic issues, despite the continued existence of some active centers of working-class "fundamentalism." The struggle between capital and labor was a struggle between something that went beyond social action, that is, the market and the enterprising spirit, and something that pertained to nature, that is, the labor force. Therefore, this struggle could not be separated from a culture in which social action was limited both by a transcendental order and by a natural order. In other words the fundamental struggle between the capitalist class and the working class could not be reduced to relations of production, because it opposed the privileges of a class which declared itself to be superior, naturally and culturally, to a class which defended its own social and cultural organization also transmitted despite extreme proletarianization. Student movements, particularly those in Japan and France, have been the principal agents of a rediscovery of fundamental social conflicts in a society undergoing rapid transformation, even though they often deliberately linked themselves to the ideology of the labor movement. It is true, at the same time, that we have observed, above all in Italy and in England but also in France, a new type of radicalization of trade unions. But "radical reformism" must not be confused with a revolutionary movement. The rigidity of decision-making systems, archaic ideologies and customs, or a difficult economic situation can lead a movement, whose main objectives are to modify the conditions of work and exert greater influence on decision-making, to take on more radical forms and utilize revolutionary means to obtain reforms. This is certainly not the same as pursuing revolution through reforms, as was the strategy of the labor movement at the height of capitalist industrialization.

Do not misunderstand me. I am not saying that the labor movement is on the decline throughout the world; I am saying that it will not be the central social movement specific to post-industrial societies. However, its role as a social movement will continue to grow in countries undergoing industrialization, such as Latin America and other parts of the Third World. It may also be a determining factor in those countries presently considered industrial, which may fail to pass to a post-industrial phase; in this case, the labor movement would be, above all, defensive and would take part in the general decomposition of a society torn by internal struggles aggravated by national decadence.

If I refer in a limited way to the "decline" of the labor movement or simply to an increasing institutionalization under violent pressure of labor conflicts in the most industrialized societies, it is certainly not in order to assert that this change is leading us toward a society without fundamental social conflicts. My argument is exactly the opposite. If we maintain that a labor movement is by nature the bearer of fundamental issues, it is difficult not to conclude that in the United States, both Germanies, the Soviet Union, and many other countries, we have reached a phase of relative peace. Attachment to images of the past inevitably prevents one from seeing the new actors and struggles appearing today. Even if, as is often the case, the new social movements use the language of the labor movement, just as the labor movement used the language of the French revolution, it is important to realize that new social conflicts are entering the social scene, although still in a confused manner. I will try to define them. For the moment, however, let us simply take for granted that the social actors have changed.

5—Political debate

Cultural crises and social conflicts may lead to ruptures but also to a new policy of change. Such is the last aspect of the social transformations which span the present period. About ten years ago, one spoke of depoliticization. Those who understood the term to mean the end of social antagonisms were wrong; but one did in fact observe a weakening of political institutions. This weakening of political institutions has worsened in the United States. In France social problems seem constantly to be overflowing from political institutions which, according to many observers, are paralyzed. This is also the case in Italy but for different reasons. In England the tensions within the Labor Party and the transgression of collective agreements at the factory level have been steadily increasing. Even in Sweden and Norway, the large social-democratic parties are weakening.

If we admit that one of the fundamental aspects of the present crisis is that industrialized countries, or at least some of them, are entering post-industrial society, this entrance necessarily leads, on the one hand, to the creation or strengthening of a ruling elite with considerable capacity to undertake large investments, and on the other hand, to new forms of mobilization and popular demands. Between these two opposing forces, the mechanisms of political negotiation seem overloaded. We ask ourselves if some new type of political participation exists, which would avoid the polarization of society into powerful technocratic groups on the one hand and movements of withdrawal and violence on the other.

The Liquidation of the Legacy

It is difficult to reduce social conflicts to cultural changes as if the main social problem were a return to equilibrium after an excessive emphasis on movement. It is also difficult to describe at this moment the great social conflicts which will hold sway over the future. We are living in an intermediary situation in which cultural transformations and social conflicts are so completely intertwined that we can no longer separate them. What seems to be a major conflict ends up being nothing more than a modernization crisis and vice versa. Therefore, we must try first of all to recognize the cultural changes related to present mutations and realize that they cannot be identified as social conflicts and that they are, for the most part, politically ambiguous. It was in this way that the struggle against privileges in revolutionary France was led both by a new ruling class and by the people.

1—From social classes to class relations

The more a society defines itself by its own action rather than its subjection to natural laws or to a transcendental order, the more will the real social categories, based on these non-social foundations, tend to disappear. The most important example of this is the example of social classes. In the past social classes were defined both by a relation of economic domination and by reference to a transcendental order. The distance between the dominant class and the exploited class was always measured not only by the appropriation and the management of the means of production, but also by an appearance of purity or impurity, by participation or lack of participation in civil rights, and by the enterprising spirit or survival needs. It has always been useless to ask oneself if classes should be defined economically, culturally, or politically. They have always been defined in all three manners, and they have always been groups for the production of influence and for reproduction.

Now society has ceased to call upon a transcendental order of any kind. At the same time, social classes, even though they have not become purely economic groups, have become entirely definable at the levels of social relations and society's self-production. They cease being real groups which transmit heritage. This does not mean that there has been progress toward equality. On the contrary this process has become a part of a more general transformation, first perceived in a clear way by D. Riesman: the transition from a vertical to a horizontal society, from a society of fathers to a society of brothers, from a society of time to a society of space, from internal moral controls to external controls exerted by public opinion. To this I immediately add: the transition from a society of discrimination to a society of segregation. The ruling class, which controls the large apparatus of social production, is no longer a real group based on legally recognized symbols and mechanisms. It must therefore create a physical distance to replace the social and cultural distance which has disappeared.

For a whole generation the triumph of consumer society had put critical social thinking upside down. Marxist ideology in Europe has strongly produced the image of present-day society as the ideological practice of the dominant class, exercised directly or through the state apparatus. What this amounts to, in fact, is defining and analyzing class relations at the level of consumption, culture, and symbols, rather than the level of the relations of production. It is in fact a critical version of functionalism. American functionalism presents society as a personage guided by values and regulating a complex system of norms and roles. Marxist ideology, in a parallel way, presents society as a demon manipulating all social mechanisms in its own interest. There is a difference of tone but not of method.

The time has come to overthrow these analyses; studying great Marxist analysts, such as Gramsci, may contribute to this. Is it not strange that we refer only to heritage and reproduction when speaking of a historical period which has undergone the most profound disruptions, at the height of which economic power was concentrated in the hands of a few dozen multinational corporations, in which the state has intervened more often than ever before in social and economic organization, and in which employment has been profoundly modified? Let us put society back on its feet by affirming the necessity—more absolute than ever before—of analyzing society through class relations. Instead of dissolving class relations in social inequalities and their transmission—no less real though surely more limited than they were two centuries ago—one should give up considering classes as real groups and recognize the reality of class relations. In other words, we should recognize the reality of the conflicts between those who have the power to control values, norms, and policies and those who struggle against the private appropriation of the instruments and the products of cultural orientations and economic investments.

2—From sex-defined groups to body relationships
The disappearance of classes as real groups is related to the disappearance of groups defined by sex; the strengthening of class relations is related to the growing importance of relations between the sexes and, more generally, to the body. For, as we have already mentioned, social action invades simultaneously the transcendental and the natural domains. How can we fail to notice that the same development is taking place in two kinds of facts: the decline of reproduction and the progress of production? Woman was established as a "natural" category, submitted to males' control of productive work and symbolic systems. This domination is constantly linked to that of social classes, because it is not only the masculine group which has dominated the feminine group; it is also the males of the upper class who have most completely dominated the females of the popular classes, using them as breeders, nurses, servants, and for all kinds of personal services.

We see thus the importance of the women's struggle today. It is not strictly speaking a social struggle, but it does destroy cultural practices and their social consequences firmly implanted in our society, even though it is not our society that produced them. This gradual disappearance of the "feminine condition" is related to a decrease in that part of a woman's life spent bearing and raising children and to the pressure of consumerism which pushes the potential labor force to take on salaried employment. Thus, discrimination is reduced to mere inequality. This development is accompanied by an active movement, which can appropriately be termed "feminist," that is, a movement which breaks off women's relations to men. The most important real social practice of the women's movement, besides the very effective ideological critique, is the homosexual withdrawal, the affirmation of an identity acquired by breaking off with dependency. This clearly indicates that the social relation must be broken, not overthrown, and that women wish to be liberated from private, materially based models and practices. The biological differences between men and women will not prevent the feminine and masculine roles from disappearing. This is another aspect, just as important as the preceding one, of the liquidation of society's heritage.

The decline of sex-defined groups leads, in a spectacular manner, to the growing importance of social relations to sex. We can all feel this when we see how advertisements have taken hold of the sexual theme. Whether it be the conquering theme of performance and "fun" or the more conformist theme of the body as bearer of the signs of social status and thus the means of communication between equals (usually young, vigorous, well-fed, happy, white, fashionable, and so forth), the ruling class is imposing its own interpretation of sexuality. This is done with all the more vigor as the traditional domination of men over women declines; otherwise, the dominant class would risk losing control over an important part of behavior. We can observe, on the opposite side, the appearance either of defensive attitudes, best defined by the theme of love, that is, of sameness and of community, or of counteroffensive attitudes, that is, a demand for sexual "relationships," in other words, the desire to free interpersonal social relations from alienation and domination. The women's movement joins in this demand for liberated interpersonal relations and desires.

3—From the nation-state to national struggles
Just as in the case of the economic and the cultural spheres, the political sphere has experienced a disintegration of its heritage and

the accelerated decline of reproduction mechanisms to the benefit of production mechanisms. Just as "historical" societies have expanded at the expense of "anthropological" societies, today sociological societies are increasingly prevailing over historical societies, those which we used to call civilizations.

Sometimes this transition is brutal. Nowhere has this been so much so as in popular China, where Mao's thought and the Communist party's apparatus are shaping a society and fighting for an extensive and thorough cultural revolution against Chinese "civilization," epitomized in the teachings of Confucius. But the direction which change is taking is the same everywhere. Which of today's sociologists would unhesitatingly refer to French or Italian civilization when we all know how much the cultural heritage of a national political community is weakening? In even more concrete terms, the growing multinationalization of economic power is associated to an infranationalization of social and cultural organization. Switzerland has long been an association of local societies with an international economy. Belgium is composed of two communities which each day are coming closer to a confederate relationship. The French state, the best example of a nation-state, fortified by almost three and a half centuries of existence, is itself being called into question, either by international entrepreneurs, who have become impatient with the state's bureaucratic restraints, or by regional leaders who, because of their abandonment by the state, have been relegated to marginality and deprived of their culture. This therefore signifies the cultural, economic, and sometimes political decline of the nation-state.

At the same time in many parts of the world and sometimes even in industrialized countries, movements and policies of national independence are being developed in response to the strengthened domination of empires over a large part of the world. For example, the national or regional community is called upon to fight Soviet techno-bureaucracy; in Western countries it is also called upon to fight for the national control of trade and economic production and against the domination exerted by large multinational corporations and their political supporters.

4—Desocialization

This triple decomposition of the social, cultural, and political heritage necessarily entails a decline of the social agencies which transmit norms, symbols, and techniques. It is wrong to speak of a generation gap as if a conflict existed between young people and adults, a fact which has not been upheld by research on student movements; however, it is necessary to recognize that a socialization crisis exists and that it is becoming impossible to define education in terms of socialization. The most spectacular decline has been that of churches, particularly the Catholic church, since churches were related to a type of society in which social action was subjected to a transcendental religious order as well as to traditional community rules and customs. This decline has led to two kinds of consequences. On the one hand, religion has been reduced to morality, and morality to an instrument of social control and stratification. This degradation of religion and morality, whose origins go far back, has been accelerating. A call to moral education, whether lay or religious, is increasingly becoming the middle class's means of defending itself. The disappearance of the ruling class as a real and stable group inevitably induces the ruling apparatus to create zones of social and cultural defense. The more impersonal and distant the apparatus, the greater the need for a middle class, defined by its morality, to hide the real ruling forces.

On the other hand, a private religious feeling without ecclesiastical content is spreading throughout society. Sometimes this feeling attaches itself to political or social movements, giving them a messianic, eschatological, or sectarian touch. Sometimes it does not attach itself to a social object; rather, it invests itself in desire and in transcending all identity. It is the experience of creativity rather than production in society and demand and revolt rather than a category of social practice.

What has just been said of churches can also be said of schools and even more so of new forms of education, whether they be vocational training for adults or sex education. References to values and images of man are being replaced by adjustment to social needs, and integration into groups. Reproduction of cultural heritage is subordinated to production of a meritocratic society. To adapt, to integrate, to standardize—in all of these cases the will to these ends is more and more imposed. The aim is to replace respect for the law by attachment to the norm, to internalize authority. It is a form of moral control all the more constraining because the dominant cultural, economic, and political elites increasingly overlap. Each, moreover, has its own unity and a larger monopoly. We live in societies held together by chains which are increasingly fine, where the signs of what are supposed to be good and bad behaviors are increasingly evident, where sanctions are increasingly applied by the peer group.

At the same time, creativity is desocialized, drifts away from social norms, is linked with revolt. This leads to the creation of new types of primary groups, which are weakly institutionalized and yet strongly integrated. These groups are trying to go beyond the juxtaposition of revolt and moralization by "technicizing" themselves (practicing sports or learning about cinema) and by "politicizing" themselves, that is, by defining themselves in a social relation of opposition, either experienced in fact or in their imagination (solidarity movement, underground networks, self-managed groups).

Apparatus and Legacy

These phenomena of crisis and cultural innovation are the most visible ones. They normally precede the appearance of new social conflicts at the moment in which a new society is being formed. It is even more difficult to grasp these phenomena when the conflicts peculiar to an industrial society, even in those places where they have been institutionalized, occupy the front of the scene. But my idea is not to describe the social problems of such and such a country; I wish only to grasp future trends. Was it not useful, during the first half of the nineteenth century, to realize that a labor movement was being formed, even though at the time, particularly in 1830, "political" and not "social" movements were in the foreground?

1—A pure social conflict
If we admit that today a ruling class can no longer be defined by its identification with an order governing the social order, whether this be a religious, political, or economic order, its position can only be understood as an identification with society's action on itself and, more precisely, with its capacity to produce itself. The ruling class is the identification of scientific and technological production with an apparatus which monopolizes one type of information. Class domination consists of administrating the community

in a manner which strengthens the apparatus. The best term to designate this class is technocratic, since it is a ruling and a technological apparatus. No one, in fact, can use the term technocratic to mean government by technicians; this would be absurd, since a technician controls the means and not the ends. The existence of a technocracy appears when a system of means is transformed into ends for the sake of their own maximization; that gives to such a system a dominating, manipulating, and repressing role. As in all class relations, the dominant position cannot be defined by itself: it can only be defined in terms of the opposition between the categories of ruling and ruled. In this case, the ruled category is the community itself, inasmuch as it constitutes a "territory" which can be irrigated by a certain type of scientific and technical knowledge. The ruling and the ruled categories are, as always, opposed to each other and yet interdependent. The apparatus—that is, the ruling class—accumulates the necessary resources for creation and investment, but it utilizes the means and the products of this investment to strengthen its position and its control over the territory. As for the territory it tries, on the one hand, to protect itself from the domination of the apparatus and, on the other, to collectively reappropriate the technical means of intervention, usually produced by the apparatus. The common stake for both adversaries is neither transcendence nor nature, but the self-producing and self-transforming capacity of society. This capacity requires, in fact, both concentration of investments and extensive social participation.

This central social conflict differs from that which dominated industrial society, that is, the conflict between employers and workers, in that it is no longer situated inside an organization at the place of work. Class domination in industrial society consists of controlling labor organization, the keyword in industrial capitalism from Saint-Simon to Taylor and Ford. Class conflict, therefore, is placed at this level. It is the system of division of labor, authority, and demands linked to production which directly manifests class domination. The factory, or rather the workshop, is the cradle of the class struggle. When investment is no longer limited to the distribution of products, as in the market economy, or to the organization of labor, as in industrial society, but transforms production itself—thanks to scientific and technical progress, including the capacity to administer complex communication networks—it is then the organizations which become, as sociology has long pointed out, the dominant actors. The main conflict takes place between these organizations and their social environment, between the apparatus of production and the territory of consumption.

Inside these large organizations, there are many conflicts which, however, are not fundamental, because they do not question the system of production and social domination; consequently, they can be taken care of by sectorial or local reforms. Whereas in the traditional factory, class relations are immediately present at the place of work, we now observe that problems concerning the organization of labor, and even problems concerning decision-making in a corporation, are rapidly acquiring autonomy from fundamental conflicts. The more modern organizations, far from being more monolithic than the others, have on the contrary a more autonomous political system and a greater flexibility in their forms of organizing labor. However, they exercise a more brutal domination over their territory. This evolution explains the evolution of the labor movement, which we mentioned above. Its influence increases; its importance diminishes. It is a political force of increasing importance; it is less and less a social movement. However, it may remain a place in which new forms of protest are manifested.

2—*Generalized social conflicts*

By placing the organization rather than the business enterprise at the center of our analysis, we are clearly indicating that there is no longer a privileged area for social conflicts. The existence of such areas proceeds from the idea that social action is subject both to a transcendental order and to nature, considered as independent from social action. It is in this way that social struggles had, as their privileged areas, religious beliefs and cultural communities, then political rights and territorial communities—peoples and nations—and finally, the ownership of the means and the forces of production. Today a pure social conflict is taking shape whose only basis is society's action on itself; consequently, it is appearing in all the areas in which society intervenes in its own activity.

It is wrong to say that problems are shifting from the sphere of production to that of consumption, from the economic sphere to the cultural sphere; on the contrary, they are appearing in every place in which the opposition apparatus-territory is formed, that is, increasingly in all the spheres of social life. The first such area is, of course, that of economic activity, in which the techno-structures predominate, whose logic was best understood by Galbraith. But we also find problems in the areas of health, education, and research, and even as we have already mentioned, in an area as unexpected as sexuality. We must also add the military sphere. Let us briefly consider these different cases.

The area of health is probably where we find the greatest ideological obstacles to an acknowledgment of the conflict. It was Illich's utopian thought which first had the strength to attack this sanctuary. To do it, he was forced to throw all its weight against hospital domination, thus somewhat losing sight of the complex relations which exist between a dominating yet creative apparatus and a contesting yet traditional territory. Thanks to these attacks, we do realize today that the power of the hospital system and the state of public health are not synonymous. The concentration of resources in modern hospital equipment is often associated with a weak interest in the improvement of public health, which depends much more on safety measures at work, on the struggle against social isolation, on action against epidemics following the example of Pasteur, or on literacy.

It is, of course, indispensable to recall that many health care measures demanded by the territory are made possible by the discoveries of the medical apparatus; it is also indispensable to remember that the doctors and the researchers of the hospital apparatus do not necessarily identify themselves with this apparatus and may behave like "scientists," trying to separate scientific production from the forms of social control. This is a phenomenon whose importance is growing rapidly. But what is essential is to realize that social conflicts are being formed in an area in which profit is not king.

The same analysis can be applied to research as a whole. Researchers, particularly in the United States and more recently in Europe, have become conscious of the fact that we can no longer naïvely identify a university with the search for knowledge, as if the professors were outside and above society.

This same general type of class conflict can be found in military life. Now that nuclear terror is making international wars retreat to the background, confrontations are developing between the apparatus and the territory, which are clearly taking on the appearance of a social struggle. The Vietnam War is the best example of this. In more general terms, the guerrillas and popular wars are associating armed and social struggle more and more directly. The guerrilla defends the independence of a territory against a domination, which utilizes the territory's resources and controls the best part of its internal market.

Those who no longer find in the contemporary world the equivalent of the great labor struggles of the turn of the century would be wrong to conclude that fundamental conflict no longer exists in highly industrialized societies. On the contrary, the conflagration is everywhere.

3—Self-managed conflicts

It is correct to speak of mass society where a greater and greater part of that society is reached by decisions, policies, and informations. If social conflicts may appear anywhere in society, then social movements are less and less subordinated to the intervention of ideological and political mediators. Let us consider the traditional example of nineteenth-century peasant Russia. Its process of change led to the formation of revolutionary groups made up of intellectuals. We are reminded of the immense distance which separated and still separates in many parts of the world political activities and ideologues from the base in whose name they act. In industrial Europe itself, not only the Social-Democrats, but also the Leninists consider the labor movement as an actor enclosed in the capitalist system, which can be superseded by reform or revolution only if there is a political agent, a party. Our political life is still largely dominated by this autonomous intervention of politicized intellectuals or professional politicians. The distance between the base and the agents of intervention recently seemed to be widening, since the first protests came from students, who are quite distant from the most brutally dominant "masses."

However, the opposite trend is much more important. Protest movements today are increasingly demanding the right to define the meaning of their own action and to produce their own policies and their own ideology, instead of leaving this up to mediators. This is the reason for the lasting crisis of the intelligentsia and doctrinaire parties. The spontaneity of the masses is often opposed to the coldness of the apparatus; however, this formulation is incorrect. It is not a question of spontaneity—a vague, almost irrational notion—but of the social movement's capacity for self-management. What formerly would have been nothing more than a grievance or a pressure group is now becoming more clearly a social movement; it tries to control power.

The objective of self-management raised great hopes for the

future of the Soviet revolution; later, it was almost identified with the Yugoslavian regime. Today, self-management is being demanded by forces of increasing importance in many large industrial countries. We must nevertheless distinguish two opposite meanings of this catchword. The first is strictly utopian and analogous to the populist dream of maintaining the social and cultural identity of a community throughout a period of economic transformations. The deeper the changes and the more rapidly they take place, the greater the extension of the myth of "change with continuity." Even though this meaning entails greater mobilization, it is not the most important one. The theme of self-management expresses the desire of social actors to control directly the meaning of their action instead of receiving it from the state, church, or political parties and claiming a monopoly over the orientation of collective action. The theme of self-management has been seen during recent years as the social movement's declaration of independence from parties. This has been reinforced by the intervention of groups of religious origin, which have been liberating themselves from ecclesiastical organization. Often this desire for independence merely leads to the formation of new interest groups, which exert direct influence on the political game. This is particularly true in the case of peasants' cooperatives as well as of groups of citizens, which are being formed almost everywhere at the local level. But these grassroots movements also clearly call into question either the social or the cultural organization of their society. This brings Europe closer to an American tradition and, at least in some aspects, to the attacks of the Red Guards against the "headquarters" during the Cultural Revolution.

4—Protest and deviance

There is another side to this expansion and growing independence of social movements. The greater the power of the apparatus and, consequently, the greater the identification of "rationality" and power, the greater the displacement and the marginalization of the forces of opposition. This explains the importance of Marcuse's idea: in this integrated, manipulated, uni-dimensional society, only those who are rejected and marginalized are able to protest.

This idea was successful, above all, at the historical moment in which it was formulated; this was the period during which reigned the dominant technocratic ideology of affluence, of the growing rationality of our society, and of the decline of ideologies. Confronted with this dominant ideology, only "marginal" groups could make the utopian voice of protest heard. It is thus normal that the expansion of these protest movements led to criticism of the pessimism of this thesis; even Marcuse himself modified his positions after his discussions with protesting students in 1968.

It is certainly not possible to confuse social movements in the strictest sense of the term with liberal, and even libertarian extreme left, public opinion campaigns against social exclusion, "labeling," and total institutions. Nor is it possible to confuse them with the community of dropouts enclosed in religious utopias of equilibrium or in drugs. But it is also not possible to separate them completely when social domination defines itself as rational and "positive"; protest movements must be based on negation and withdrawal. All social movements have also a counteroffensive policy; they attempt to collectively reappropriate the means of self-production of society, and all of them try to defend a social and cultural territory that protects them against the grasp of the dominant order. The more traditions and communities wane, the greater the tendency for these defensive forces to become forces of negation and refusal. What was the revolt of a few intellectuals at the end of the First World War, in Switzerland, France, and Germany, that is, the period of Dadaism and surrealism, is increasingly becoming widespread behavior. Protest supposes, in the first place, a scandal, a breach with the ideological and institutional guarantees of the dominant order. This breach leads to the formation of primary protest groups; such groups may exist as sects, prophetic movements, or simply as collective desocialization.

In all these cases, it is impossible to draw a clear line between protest and what the dominant order labels and organizes as deviance or marginality.

The radical black movements in the United States, such as the Black Panthers, clearly show the arbitrary aspects of the traditional separation between the proletariat and the lumpen-proletariat. This is partly because of the violent police repression, which from the beginning gave them their social image. But this lack of distinction is an evident cause of the weakening of social movements, because their roots attach them to a particular area of social exclusion and thus prevent them from forming coalitions and acquiring the strength necessary to fight the central apparatus.

5—*The aims of social struggles*

In order that social movements be formed in any type of society, it is not enough that populations defend themselves from the grasp of a dominant group or order. They must proceed to a counteroffensive attack, that is, try to recover control over the forces of development, appropriated by the ruling class. The labor movement has fought capitalism backed by the idea that with labor in power, there would be a rational progress of the forces of production, which would finally get rid of waste, speculation, and irrational individual profits. What is thus today the aim of the collective reappropriation of the forces of development? Or should we give up the search for it, thus admitting that only the ruling elite is able to initiate an integrated action?

Only real political life can bring an answer to this question. Then, we will be able to say that a new type of society has been entirely created and that it actively experiences its fundamental problems. Today, we can only furnish an abstract answer to this question, that is, an answer which cannot yet be formulated directly in terms of social practices. We can say that the aim of a popular counteroffensive attack can only be the liberation of social relations and the existence of a society which defines itself as a communications network instead of as an energy-consuming machine. When women refuse to be objects which are consumed or which reproduce, when workers refuse to be subjected to the logic of profit or power, when city inhabitants protest that their cities are being overrun by automobiles and office buildings, they are demanding the right to a social relation, the right not to be treated as raw material or instruments.

Is this any more vague than the demand for freedom, which sums up the specifically political demands and the demands for justice that symbolize the labor struggles against capitalist exploitation? Today, social movements can have no other aim than the very existence of social life against the growing technocratization of society and against the system of rules, decisions, and information which leave no room for exchange, discussion, and communication, because they permit the concentration of power within the apparatus.

It seems difficult to all of us who are still under the sway of the social problems of the great industrialization period—which we are only now beginning to leave behind—not to define social struggles in relation to economic systems, their logic, and their laws of evolution.

In fact, the central idea expressed in the preceding remarks is this: we are entering class struggles without "real" classes, class heritage, or transcendental stakes—either religious, political, or economic. All is action. Some still try to define a class situation without specifying class relations and class action. This is an illusion from our past. In a society which makes itself, classes can only be actors which fight to control society's self-production. Powerholders everywhere object to the study of social relations and social action, because this sociology of action threatens the status quo by showing men that society has no value and principles, is nothing but social relations, and that therefore, everything can be changed through action.

Once again, it is the Chinese Cultural Revolution which best illustrates the nature of class relations, even though the Chinese situation is evidently neither an example of post-industrial society, nor a model of general validity. Class struggle in China is no longer defined by the opposition of class situations, but by each class's relation to the means of social and political action. All over the world the popular class is the collectivity for whose sake actions are directed against the technocratic apparatus. A class can no longer be defined without referring to class consciousness, that is, to a consciousness of class relations and thus of antagonistic actions. This does not mean that the class struggle no longer has an objective basis. It means only that class action transforms a class category into a real group. This is not a new idea, but it is opposed to the idea which dominated the industrial period, according to which the meaning of class action came from the outside, from the political intelligentsia. I am asserting, on the contrary, that class consciousness can be produced by the class actors themselves.

In some societies this involves an open struggle, but in most societies the struggle is controlled by a political system of either representative institutions or an absolute power. But it is precisely the conflict of classes and class consciousnesses that dominates those societies which act most strongly on themselves, conflict that the dominant order tries to hide under its positivity. This is true both for those countries controlled by communist parties as well as for capitalist countries.

Conclusions

1—From consciousness of a crisis to behaviors of social transformation

Crisis is a state of consciousness. It is important because it manifests the end of a civilization, the growing difficulty of finding a meaning for that which loses its unity. Of course the traditional discourse of the last century, concerning the supreme virtues of the market economy or the central role of the working class in social movements, will continue to be heard for a long time; but it is becoming less and less capable of accounting for observable social or economic facts.

It is preferable to accept a calling into question of former categories. Intellectuals, revolutionary protest movements, "experts," and even political and economic leaders are little by little destroying our confidence in the solidity and the eternity of "Western civilization." Most probably, there is also considerable doubt concerning the modernity of the Soviet type of industrialization.

But the time has come to surpass these interpretations of present changes in terms of crisis, for if we are experiencing a mere crisis, the only solution would be the appearance of a new principle of political and moral integration, of an all-powerful leader such as Pisistratus or Cincinnatus, an enlightened prince, or, more modestly, wise men backed by unquestionable computers. This can only lead—and this is the main ideological function of the notion of crisis—to a strengthening of a new ruling elite, acting both in the name of rationality and the common interest. We may feel that such should be the case; or on the contrary we may desire another type of change. But we must first realize that the notion of crisis is part of the ideology of the ruling forces: it therefore implies a reorganization of society from the top down.

If we analyze a social situation without referring to social and political relations, we are acting as did the bourgeoisie during the nineteenth century: it was always careful in analyzing society to hide its own role and the social relations of domination which defined this role. To say that there are rich people and poor people in the world is the best way of not saying that one part of the world dominates and exploits the other. There are necessarily two opposing manners of analyzing present problems. When we speak of crisis, we are looking at society from the point of view of the ruling forces; when we speak of transformation, we imply that we are studying the formation of a new cultural field, new relations, and new social conflicts. This directs our attention not only to the birth of new social movements but also to the shaping of new forms of power.

2—Generalized politics

Social relations and social conflicts can be found at all levels. At the local level, citizen committees intervene to save trees and fight detrimental conditions in their environment. At an almost worldwide level, a negotiation is being organized between great Western industrial powers and oil-producing countries; the latter are understandably requiring that the demands of the sellers of raw materials also be heard. We can no longer listen to the disgusting appeals for helping the Third World, appeals which hide a massive looting of the resources of dependent societies. Conflicts, confrontations, and negotiations are being set up everywhere.

We realize the dramatic importance of what is at stake: starvation, overpopulation, and abuse of limited natural resources, such as the atmosphere. Such problems can only be overcome by increasing society's capacity to act; in other words, by increasing the mobilization of the real social and political actors. The overpopulation of a part of Asia will not be controlled unless a political capacity to overthrow social structures having destructive effects is acquired. The development of Latin America presupposes a strengthening of political action, which would develop and integrate the internal market by diminishing forms of external and internal domination that disconnect and separate economy and society. The industrialized countries themselves can only respond to a necessary redistribution of industrial capacity at an international level by taking a step forward. This implies both technical and economic progress, as well as broadening social participation in societies which have been maintained in archaic social and cultural conditions so that ruling groups could accumulate power and wealth in their own hands.

The main problem is not whether in twenty or fifty years we will have enough of such and such a raw material at our disposal, but whether in the months and years to come, those nations which waste and dominate, as well as those buried in poverty or subject to paralyzing forms of social domination, will be capable of massively increasing their "political production," their capacity to act. This presupposes a strengthening of both popular pressures and the initiative of the ruling elites; consequently, this means an increase in the level of conflict.

We must speak of crisis when we see some populations abandoned to hunger and death, while others speak only of relaxation, identity, and pleasure. These preoccupations, which do not seem to be related, do have in common the fact that they are beyond any possible action, that they are the product of a dramatic lack of political action. The world seems to be made up of nations abandoned either to misery or to affluence. As long as we do not go beyond such a description, as long as we do not reveal the nature of the actors and the social dramas, we will not be able to prevent this crisis from increasing the strength of the ruling forces, the inequalities, and the domination. If it is necessary to realize the limits of industrial growth, it is even more necessary to expand the field of political action. In the rich societies in which we live, the ruling forces no longer assert themselves by using prohibitions, naked violence, and respect for the sacred. Instead, they dissolve protest by using persuasion and dependent participation. Social struggles have always encountered considerable obstacles; they have been diverted and divided by the defenses of the social order. These defenses were strong enough to have enclosed protest for thousands of years in night and silence, and today they are vigorous enough to fragment, weaken, and seduce protest.

But what is the future of societies no longer guided by an active democracy? There is a great risk that they will become decadent. We are therefore correct to refer to a crisis. We are being threatened with the loss of our capacity to imagine, prepare, and build the future. A crisis is not a situation; it is an incapacity to act. To come out of a crisis, we must learn to recognize the new lands in which we find empires being built and forces to fight them. So many voices are trying to convince us that we must wait for better days, for a change of wind, as if we were on a drifting raft with nothing but hope for survival. We must rid ourselves of this false wisdom and learn once again to analyze society with its issues and its conflicts so we can help society feel responsible for its own choices.

2

Rudi Supek

The Visible Hand and the Degradation of Individuality

Although the supporters of convergence theory are probably mistaken in their prognosis, it is hard to dispute the similarities in current trends of the two dominant systems. Thus, there is no question that the roles of the state and of executive power, acting as the representative of "general social interests," have grown equally more powerful under capitalism and contemporary forms of socialism because of the appropriation of economic functions by the state. Under organized capitalism this appropriation is shared with powerful corporations and thus is partial, while under statist socialism this appropriation is total. Furthermore, both refer to the increasing need for planning economic growth and insuring the buying power of their citizens, regardless of the fact that this is done in the names of "the welfare state" under capitalism and "relative poverty" under socialism. The leitmotif of these lovely promises for a "brighter future," even though in both systems the exploitation of man and nature has become an increasingly obvious fact, is the scientific-technological revolution. The idea of economic progress and continuous growth in material goods is the underlying legitimation of the rulers' policy, and both systems contemplate with horror the day when its citizens will say: "We are rich enough; let's see whether we are living the life man deserves." Both have defined the meaning of life according to the logic of their system, but that system decreasingly feels the necessity to consult its citizens about the future. In one case decision-making about the future will be left by experts to computers alone through programmed development (democracy becomes superfluous, as Schelsky says, because machines are more precise than humans); in the other case, "wise leadership" acts according to "objective laws of history," once again making the consultation of its citizens unnecessary. In fact both systems defend the status quo and view development only through the prism of gradual reforms originating from technology rather than people, while their "Weltanschauung," in spite of futurological excursions, is essentially statistical and positivistic, tied to the prevailing order. They wish to preserve it and smuggle it into the future by means of insignificant changes on the surface of the system rather than in its principles, especially not in the name of that which it negates at base—the human personality. ("Man is dead, long live the System!" shouts contemporary positivism—structuralism.) Both systems degrade individual personality, as an autonomous and unique totality, reducing it to an element of the system, a part of the machine, a particle of the mass. Thus, criticizing the technocratic vision of society, Donald N. Michael says about the cybernetization of society:

> Electronic computers are particularly suited to treating social situations which relate to people in the mass, as is the case with traffic control, financial transactions, mass demand for consumer goods, the allocation of resources, etc. . . . In fact, the entire tendency toward cybernetization can be seen as an effort to deny the variety in the behavior of a man at work and in his needs outside of work which complicates production and consumption because of his non-statistical nature. And so, somewhere on that path, the idea of the individual can be completely lost in a statistic.[1]

Stalin—future theoretician of socialist statism—expressed a similar judgment: "The cornerstone of anarchism is the *personality*, whose liberation, according to this view, is the main condition for the liberation of the mass, the collectivity. . . . The cornerstone of Marxism is the *mass*, whose liberation, according to this view, is the main condition for the liberation of the personality."[2]

Accordingly, both systems by making use of means of political coercion and appropriate socialization in order to maintain the system—American behaviorism as well as Pavlovian theories of conditioned response equally treat means of conditioning human reactions "externally, as a product of the environment" as omnipotent—consider that in this way they will degrade the human personality, depriving it of the right to responsibility and decision-making, both in the field of production and in the life of the community. In particular to do so they will tickle man's stomach with a variety of products and entertain his eyes with an unending line of spectacles. Technocrats act as if the use of political force in such an undertaking is unnecessary, even though it demonstrates, every day in an ever more striking way, increasingly powerful means of coercion. Marxists, for their part, also trust in economic determinism and have no suitable theory concerning the role of force in the shaping of society. We are necessarily confronted with the question: Can such an undertaking succeed? Will man as producer and man as citizen capitulate in the face of advances offered him,

---

1. Donald N. Michael, *Cybernation: The Silent Conquest* (Santa Barbara, Cal.: Center for the Study of Democratic Institutions, 1962).
2. J. Stalin, *Anarhizam i socijalizam* (*Anarchism and Socialism*) (Belgrade: Kultura, 1949).

even if in a deceptive and skillful manner, as man the consumer? Will man, as laboring man, allow others to decide his work and his fate, in the name of some personal or impersonal system?

Rationalism and Bourgeois Society

Bourgeois society has developed productive forces and the productivity of human labor to the greatest extent, above all because capitalism succeeded in subjecting rational technology to economic goals. For example, with the smallest expenditure of energy, an ever greater result is achieved in some effect on nature or with the least expenditure of human labor, the greatest profit is made. It is understandable that this "control over nature" (Bacon), and thus over human nature as well, would prove to be, directly because of its efficiency in individual processes, harmful and even catastrophic—as the contemporary technological crisis shows—in relation to nature as a whole and thus also in relation to man as a whole personality. Indeed, just as science sought to establish certain general relations or a general measure for quantifying natural processes, so political economy sought to channel concrete, individual, human labor into some general measure. It found this measure in the working time of a general or "abstract human labor," stripped of its individual traits, but which could be easily followed in the processes of exchange when it is transformed into commercial value. Working time, in the form of "abstract labor," made it possible to view human products as equivalent. However, the equivalence of human labor, taken in its entirety, is important only for the sphere of the circulation of value, while in the work process itself, in relation to a concrete worker, it had to correspond to an "ideal worker," whom Frederick Taylor, as we know, placed clearly above the average worker, being guided by the principle that the "worker is inclined to laziness." This measurement of work processes according to time led also to a fracturing of human labor into component parts, to a transformation of a living man into a dead mechanism which is increasingly adapted to the needs of the machine. (Consider the "time and motion study" in which psychotechnicians engaged intensively according to the model of Frederick Taylor and his wife Gilbreth.) It is obvious that this kind of "rationalization" suited the irrational needs of the capitalist market, where competition signified the struggle for subsistence and every advance in improving technology meant at the same time facilitating the process in which the "large fish devour the little fish." In addition, it meant the crippling of human nature, also an irrational motive, which equally affected the intensity of exploitation and the preservation of domination by the exploiters of human labor.

The citizen attempted to apply the same type of rationality to the political sphere, where citizens obtained the right to be "equivalent" in the expression of their will in the sphere of legislative power or public political life. Here this equivalence was expressed quantitatively in "electoral votes" or "ballots," and the citizen had the illusion that he was expressing his own sovereign will. As in the economic sphere, so in the political, we find the individual as an "abstract individual," that is, isolated, separated from his natural community, as if it satisfied certain general rules of social transaction. Marx warned that the bourgeois revolution gave freedom to individuals in these transactions, in contractual relations, but at the same time, by means of that freedom, it abandoned them to an egotistical mechanism, transforming one man into the instrument of another. "Out of the act of exchange itself, the individual, each one of them, is reflected in himself as its exclusive and dominant (determinant) subject. With that, then, the complete freedom of the individual is posited: voluntary transaction; no force on either side; positing of the self as means, or as serving, only as means, in order to posit the self as end in itself, as dominant and primary; finally, the self-seeking interest . . ." (K. Marx).[3]

It is significant that this principle of "instrumental rationality" (Horkheimer), translated from technology into production, calls forth the alienation of man as producer, but when translated from production into politics, it leads to the isolation of the individual from his natural community. We can say concisely that the exchange of goods leads to an intensification of the division of labor, which in turn leads to the disintegration of the social community. Hence, the capitalist system itself produces not only more and more goods but also simultaneously a larger and larger number of

3. K. Marx, *Grundrisse: Foundations of the Critique of Political Economy*, tr. Martin Nicolaus (Harmondsworth, Eng.: Penguin, 1973), p. 254.

alienated and lonely individuals, individuals who are guided by their own selfish interests and serve as instruments of their own or someone else's interests. Marx emphasized that the "human community" is a single "productive force" and that the "disintegration of community" is also a "productive force" which corresponds to the Weberian Protestant Ethic as its sociological substructure.

Bourgeois liberalism believed strongly that it is easy to reconcile the rationalism of production with the irrationality of human goals and the competition of the struggle for subsistence. Behind selfish interests, which collide in the market, it sees the activity of an "Invisible Hand" (A. Smith), which leads them to a higher harmony, reestablishes equilibrium after temporary crises, and positively ensures *general progress through the free entrepreneurship of individuals*. The results of individual actions are, in their effects, the opposite of particularistic intentions. That is the force "which always wishes evil but does good" (F. Nietzsche). Nonetheless, in the course of eternal development, capitalism has betrayed the expectations of its liberal supporters. Thus, for example, the freedom of entrepreneurship, which is given to all people (to the worker to sell his own labor and to the capitalist to sell capital), has had the role of leading to a natural selection of the most capable. In the meantime, it has led gradually to a drastic diminishing of any entrepreneurial role, because gigantic national and multinational corporations have taken over. Thus, also, has the attempt to preserve political liberty by a balance of the three forms of power (legislative, executive, and judicial) led to an actual domination by executive power. And public opinion, as the guardian of this balance, has become, thanks to the control of the mass media (the press, radio, and television), only an instrument for shaping human thought and needs in harmony with the prevailing system. The natural selection of talents and capable people through the struggle for subsistence has been replaced by the parasitism of bureaucracy and the propertied classes. The responsibility of the citizen in public affairs, in "matters of the general interest," has been replaced by short-term and long-term plans of social development, worked out by rulers or corporation experts, assuring citizens that in "the technical state" or in the "technotronic age" every form of democracy "dies a natural death." All remaining liberties of the citizen (association, speech, and thought) continue in force, although in practice one can only use them in one's "free time," for example, in choosing a favorite hobby or turning the television dial. The citizen has given up production to "private interests," and now corporations and the state demonstrate to him that his public life is also only *their* private interest.

Hierarchical and exploitative relations in production have necessarily developed (as a consequence of the development of the social division of labor, the concentration of capital, and the ever greater role of technology) in all spheres of social life, carrying with it loneliness and indifference. If anyone today wishes once again to develop a man as Citoyen, then one ought to say to every well-meaning liberal that it is worth beginning the task with man as producer, that is, to transform hired labor into free production with the aid of "associations of free producers." Although this old phrase sounds strange, it has obtained today quite a specific meaning and one which is radical.

Hierarchy and Alienation

Technology, in fact, is not only the scientific application of production methods aimed at the optimal use of natural resources. It does not possess the autonomy of some natural science and its application in a laboratory. Indeed, it does not develop solely according to the logic of its own laws on the principle of efficiency (J. Ellul). The truth is, however, that it assumes a whole, rationally established plan in which the parts are strictly subordinated to the whole and that whole must function according to a single "established order." As such, it is an autonomous force and an intellectual discipline but one which is simultaneously found associated with other forces, even in their service. Above all, under the control and logic of that economy itself, it is geared to efficiency or productivity, that is, to a maximal extraction of profit from a single production process. That common nature of a (capitalist) economy and technology allow one to speak about capitalist economy in the language of technology and to speak about technology in the language of the capitalist economy.

G. Lukàc's statement in criticism of Bukharin's Historical Materialism of 1925 that social conditions precede modern technology in its contemporary perspective seems accurate:

The *social* precondition of modern mechanized techniques thus arose first; they were the product of a hundred-year social revolution. The technique is the consummation of modern capitalism, not its initial cause. It only appeared after the establishment of its social prerequisites, when the dialectical contradictions of the primitive forms of manufacture had been resolved, when "At a given stage of its development, the narrow technical base on which manufacture rested came into conflict with requirements of production that were created by manufacture itself." (*Capital*, I) It goes without saying that technical development is thereby extraordinarily accelerated. But this *reciprocal interaction* by no means surpasses the real historical and methodological primacy of the economy over technique.[4]

A century earlier Edward B. Taylor had already considered technology as part of a particular culture, that is, the fundamental attitudes and values of a society toward production in general. As technology relates equally to the organization of human labor and the arrangement or regulation of machines, so the acceptance of social demands stamped production with the spirit of a single authoritarian and hierarchical organization. We find this already in Adam Smith's description of the technological division of labor, where the arrangement of people and their behavior is far more significant than the operation of the machine itself (the production of pins, for example). Thus, it is no wonder that a modern author, William Leiss, defines technology completely in the spirit of the Frankfurt School "as an authoritative method of organizing human labor for the ultimate satisfaction of human needs" (Postscript to *The Domination of Nature*, 1973).[5]

The division of labor has evolved in the direction of the scientific analysis of motion of F. Taylor or Gilbreth, which attempts to see how much the human body can be "transformed into a mechanism" and at the same time be easily controlled by the managerial hierarchy. Giedion warns that the ideal of "the scientific organization of work" would be a militaristic organization in which "every man in the organization must accept orders directly from the superior who stands immediately above him. The main superintendent communicates his orders to the worker on tickets or written notes with the help of various employees in the same manner as some general who commands a division communicates

---

4. G. Lukàcs, *Marxism and Human Liberation*, p. 56, quoted by Frederic J. Fleron, *Technology and Communist Culture*, Bellagio Conference, 1975.
5. Quoted by F. J. Fleron.

his orders" (Giedion, *Mechanization Takes Command*, p. 99).[6] Taylorism has become the model of "scientific organization" in socialist statism, and this method of management by means of the "principle of command" demonstrates that his model was in fact that of militaristic organization.

Technological rationalization in capitalism presumes a "separation of means and ends, of work activities and products; the fragmentation of knowledge, the separation of intellectual and manual labor, man's domination over nature; efficiency defined in nonhuman terms; hierarchical control of production and, at the base of all this, the assumption of the priority and inexhaustibility of human material desires" (Fleron, p. 25).

This kind of organization of work leads necessarily to various forms of alienation on the job, which are equally linked with the estrangement of human products as parts of "his objective world." The objectivization of labor is made manifest by the realization of the worker that his products no longer belong to him but rather to some foreign force who distributes them to him. It leads to the impoverishment of his sensory-subjective activities, because the more complex the product, the simpler, poorer, less powerful is his work. It also leads to work which is coerced activity for the worker, since it belongs to someone else and because for man, as social animal, work distances him further from other men rather than brings him closer. Describing this form of alienation in work, Marx pays particular attention to that form which is associated with the *versatility of human nature* and the one-sidedness of work alone, and he dramatically stressses, as a "question of life or death," that the "partial individual, who is responsible for only one partial social function, replaces the universally developed individual, for whom various social functions are the methods of activities which are successively exchanged." (Marx, *Capital*, I) Marx had equally in mind all those functions which are linked to the production process itself (planning, production, control, and distribution) as well as the universal education of the worker as social animal. Of course this "versatility at the work place" is not achieved simply by job enlargement, as Charles Walker thought, although it is also important to take that into account, but rather, above all, by introducing the worker "successively," in time slots, that is, in various time periods, to all those tasks which make man a producer in the

---

6. Quoted by F. J. Fleron.

full sense. And that means performing not only productive but also managerial functions.

Even growth of the division of labor proceeded increasingly in the direction of the impoverishment of the worker, culminating in assembly-line production, and thus, as empirical research has demonstrated, in the physical and psychological degradation of the worker as an alienated being. Empirical research (Bottazzi, Seeman, Blauner, and so forth) has shown, thus, that for a person both as worker and employee in production, we can identify a feeling of senselessness, isolation, self-estrangement, when he is alienated from his own role and works only for wages, and powerlessness, a sensation which the personality feels because it is "manipulated and controlled by other persons or by some impersonal system (such as technology) and when he cannot be verified as a subject who is in a position to change or modify that domination" (R. Blauner).[7]

It is understandable that the perception of this person as worker and employee does not depend alone on his immediate position on the job or in the work collective but rather on the entire system which encircles him, and thus not even partial measures in the sense of "humanization" or "democratization" (various forms of participation) essentially change this feeling of estrangement. While personal relations between the employer and worker predominated in the early phase of the development of capitalism, now relations are becoming increasingly impersonal, although that does not also mean less oppressive. Progress in rationalization increasingly imposes diverse external controls. "The impersonality of these constraints in industrial society leads to a great extent to a feeling of powerlessness. If the sole source of oppressive control is a totalitarian leader, one can attack him. If the source is an entire way of life, revolution is a less efficacious response. The idea that 'you can't beat the system' expresses the impotence of people against a rationalized and impersonal system of control" (William A. Faunce).[8]

Research has also shown that a certain intercorrelation or interaction exists between authoritarian organization and the "authoritarian personality" (T. Adorno), which is characterized by an in-

---

7. R. Blauner, *Alienation and Freedom* (Chicago: University of Chicago Press, 1964).
8. William A. Faunce, *Problems of an Industrial Society* (New York: McGraw-Hill, 1968).

clination toward excessive conformity, a need for rigid rules and strict discipline on the job (M. Aiken and J. Hage, 1966). There also exists a certain correlation between an overly simple task and "anomic" or "alienated personalities," since technology regularly forces a gap between the technical complexity of instruments and the ultimate simplicity of operating them. (It creates "a boat built by genius which idiots will pilot.") Charles Hampden-Turner warns that· "the further one goes down the hierarchy within a system, the greater the simplicity of the system and the lack of fulfillment of the needs of the workers, who suffer from alienation, anomie, and fatalism." Chris Argyris has arrived at the same conclusion, and A. Kornhauser as well, in his well-known study on the mental health of workers in the automobile industry in Detroit, has shown that the less skilled are subject to a greater extent to mental injury.[9] The dangers which follow from an exaggerated specialization of labor, at all levels, are already generally known phenomena. But technology desires such simplicity, lessening the insecurity and indefiniteness of procedures by means of the isolation, estimation, calculation, and reduction of the unexpected.

The technological mode of thought and the mentality of technocrats reveal similar features of the simplified approach to human situations. Social processes and human relations are looked upon as something mechanical, akin to nonliving concepts, and particularly as stripped of those profound dimensions by which man seeks in another man what is unique, his alone, original, and individual. An individual is treated only as an element of a single mass or system. He is no longer a *sui generis* totality which stands with equal right against the social totality and which that social totality ought to serve.

Technocratic scientism under the influence of the "scientific-technological revolution" and the ever wider use of cybernetics, computers, various forms of programming economic, and other, processes, is inclined to interpret the well-known Saint-Simonian thesis that the "management of people should be replaced by the management of things" as the thesis that "the rule of people becomes superfluous if one succeeds in managing them as things."

There is no doubt whatsoever that the advance of technology in production of the capitalist type has had the effect of an ever greater division of labor and so also has led to an ever greater sepa-

---

9. Charles M. Hampden-Turner, *The Radical Man* (New York: Anchor Books, 1971).

ration of man from his products and from the productive process, that in mechanized labor his craft has been completely destroyed, reducing him to several stereotypical work operations, to work of the "spinal type" (L. Walther, G. Friedmann). There is also no doubt that both control and hierarchy on the job grew simultaneously, that man was less and less the productive subject of his own activity. Even where the traditional form of social hierarchy was weakening at work places, economic and technical hierarchy was being strengthened, as expressed in planning bureaus and professional staffs which decided the type of products and their use and thus also the economic security of the worker himself. Although the working class, through the class struggle, was subdued for a generation in exchange for more secure work and pay, at the same time it lost more and more control over the production process as such, because the hierarchical pyramid was shifted upwards to the summit of the corporation and the state itself.

Feelings of impotence among workers and employees were not conditioned only by their immediate position at work but also by their perception of the entire organization of social production which exhibits a hierarchical and bureaucratic character to a greater extent even than relations inside the firm. Instructions to the worker to seek a sense of his life in his "free time" may have strengthened these feelings of meaninglessness and impotence even more but not the manner in which he is compensated. In addition the entire "mass culture" in contemporary society is calculated on passive and hedonistic enjoyment, not on an active and engaged role of the individual. For that reason the revolt against the prevailing "mass culture" has become as important and revolutionary a factor as the revolt at the work place. The encouraging symptoms of this revolt are as much the demands by workers which aim at "workers' control" or workers' self-management, as is their refusal to work on an assembly line. The first strikes which take the form of a revolt against mechanized labor foretell the rejection of an entire culture which sacrificed the wholeness of human personality to the efficiency of production. Indeed, it is important to add immediately that this "efficiency" today is beginning to show clearly its exploitative face not only in relation to man but also to nature in general.

What is worrisome, however, is the fact that in countries which call themselves socialist, and this means those countries with the system of socialist statism, technology is above all viewed as a neutral tool of the "scientific-technological revolution" and as a source of material prosperity, rather than a source of alienation or the crippling of human personality. What is more, socialist statism, in accepting Taylorism and authoritarian organization in the firm, has even surpassed capitalism in terms of hierarchical and bureaucratic organization. In particular such organization of the firm is known to support an analogous organization in the entire sector of production (state-administrative and centralized production) and, as authoritarian an organization in the form of a political party, the true holders of social power and overseers of social norms of behavior. Marx has said that under capitalism, enterprises are ruled by "despotism" but the society and market are ruled by "anarchy." Organized capitalism has already partially refuted this statement by Marx at the expense of liberal capitalism, but it has been even more thoroughly butchered by socialist statism itself, which has pitted a triple "despotism" against man, three times as authoritarian and rigidly hierarchical, monolithic, and centralized an organization: in the firm, in the state, and in the party. It is worth adding further that unfortunately these three factors in statism do not go in a decrescendo but rather in a crescendo.

Technocracy and Statism

When we look at social development from the perspective of our work place, somewhere at the bottom of the social pyramid, we are inclined to accept that it is moving in the direction of technocracy. However, if we view it from the top of the social pyramid where major decisions are made, then it becomes clear to us that it actually is moving in the direction of statism rather than technocracy, and we note that technology is utopia and statism is reality. Late or organized capitalism already illustrates all the developmental tendencies in terms of the concentration of power and the strengthening of social hierarchy which will come to expression in statism as well. Above all, the role of the state becomes much more significant, because it directly intervenes in the developmental problems of capital, financing the greatest portion of scientific-technological research, giving credits to the most important productive branches (particularly those which are important for armaments), removing cyclical crises and recessions (Keynesian doctrine), creating necessary experts (by the school system), stabilizing the buying power of the work force and citizens in general (with the doctrines of "full employment" or "the welfare state"), constructing an infrastructure for the circulation of capital (transport, communications, mass media, public works, urbanization, and so forth), in the struggle on the world market, without regard to the fact that capitalism increasingly takes the form of multinational and transnational companies, fleeing from the taxes of their own country but seeking its protection in all competitive conflicts with other countries. Their own state attempts not only to maintain the buying power of its own citizens, but it also labors to obtain the cheapest raw materials for its national capital and their distribution on a world scale as profitably as possible. And here it is prepared to use military means. (This is illustrated by the threats of the American Secretary of Defense, during the "petroleum crisis," that even "one turn of the faucet" by the Arabs could cause a "third world war" even more brutal than the second.)

The state is prepared to take into its own hands those branches of production with low capital accumulation or those which have a deficit by nationalization (particularly in the field of energy and raw material industries—coal mining, electrical supply, and so forth). By defending the stability of consumer power and a certain economic security for producers—don't forget that to a capitalist, a worker who works for another capitalist is above all a consumer—it claims itself as the defender of the "general interest," as a force which acts in the interest of the entire society, particularly in the sphere of distribution, even though statistical analyses show that there has been no great change in the distribution of national income in the last one hundred years. That is, it has remained equally unequal at the expense of the working strata, just as it was before the appearance of the "welfare state" (J. Kalecki, p. 10).[10] Although the means of coercion in the modern state have in fact expanded—the police often has at its disposal weaponry as devel-

---

10. M. Kalecki in *Essays in the Theory of Economic Fluctuations* (Allen and Unwin, 1939) shows that in the distribution of national income in Great Britain between 1880, when wages in production amounted to 41.8%, and 1935, when it was 41.8%, hardly anything had changed. Similar results have been obtained for the period between 1950 and 1970 (36.6% to 42.6%), while the main source of fluctuation was not syndical (trade-union) action but rather the market environment.

oped as that of the army, while modern means of controlling the life of the citizenry have long ago made a mockery of the rule that "private life is sacred"—its coercive character is even more a result of its economic role. Guaranteeing to its citizens various social and economic rights (employment, schooling, health) in "the name of social justice and the equality of all citizens" and oftentimes in the name of the welfare "state" or "national socialism," its tendency is to turn all the citizens into some form of "state official" or "hired worker" increasingly dependent on various bureaucrats' windows and cashiers' offices. The disease of monopolistic capitalism—inflation—favors this tendency so that the "small savers," at one time the buttress of the state and social order, disappear because inflation dissolves their savings into nothing, and a man with debts or "open credit" is always richer than the man with savings. The petty entrepreneur more and more begrudges the petty official his economic security, even though the salaries of these officials fall below the income of highly skilled workers. Economic security, even at a low income, becomes the obsession of the citizens of "organized capitalism," while economic risk and entrepreneurship is a matter for only the highest levels of managers.

A strengthening of the state's economic and social functions speaks in favor of technocracy. At the same time, the *strengthening of state executive power* at the expense of legislative power (that is, an ever larger role for the state apparatus or bureaucracy, and a less and less significant role for the citizen) speaks against it. Many political scientists speak of parliament as a place where fine speeches are made, but its role has been reduced for the most part to that of a "chatter box" because its real business and decisions are made on the basis of expert staffs of the state administration who alone have access to the reliable analyses and statistical and planning services which make it possible to set the main directions of development policy. In addition, the modern state possesses powerful means for pressure in its army and police which guarantee that a certain amount of economic security will unavoidably be accompanied by a lessening of that liberty and responsibility for which the citizen was so proud in the liberal phase.

One may say that the organization of the state displays a structure as obviously hierarchical as the firm itself, in which the decisive role in making key decisions is taken by those at the top. (Samuel Brittan has shown that in Great Britain, in the period from 1951 to 1964, of some 650,000 civil servants only some 2,500 individuals in the highest positions had "real decision-making power."[11]) The influence of some high functionaries is greater than that of many ministers because they enjoy a more stable position in the administration and represent a kind of "permanent politician" (Donald Kingsley). Along with their knowledge as experts, they regularly come from the highest social strata and enjoy a large salary in addition to various privileges and other more or less illegal sources of income. (In Italy a public scandal broke out in 1975 when several newspapers announced that the highest officials in parliament receive a monthly pay of up to 1,600,000 lira, while the average worker's pay amounted to 270,000 lira!) Although the state claims to be the defender and representative of the "general interest," in fact it increasingly represents its own "special interests," the interests of the state and military apparatus.

We have drawn attention to these statist tendencies in "late" or "organized capitalism," because they are resurrected in socialist statism not simply as tendencies but rather as a faithfully executed system. In statism the state takes on total control of production by means of nationalization of the means of production, primarily in industry. But this is not done in order to entrust the management of the nationalized economy to experts or managers, that is, to some form of "depoliticized state" (this very concept is actually a contradiction), but rather, on the contrary, it brings an even greater concentration of executive and political power to the state and the political party which controls the work of the state apparatus from its summit. This leads to a dual concentration of power at the very top of society, speaking once again in favor of the thesis that technology remains heteronymous, subordinated to the economy, and through the economy to state and political power. Democracy does not die out because *there is nothing* for people to decide since science has taken it over, as Schelsky and others think, but rather people *cannot* decide because they are subjects of a centralized and monopolistic social power.

Statism, as a specific and faithfully executed social system, exists today only in countries which were socially and economically backward when they began the socialist revolution and turned it toward statism. Do they as such represent only one "historical aberration" (see F. Marek, *The Philosophy of the World Revolution*), contrary to Marx's predictions or only one "historical stage," even

11. Samuel Brittan, *The Treasury Under the Tories, 1951-1964* (Harmondsworth, Eng.: Penguin, 1964).

though the most well defined and powerful among them—the Soviet Union—insists that it has already left "the phase of socialism and entered the phase of communism"? Or do they represent an original and lasting (in the sense of preserving rather than overcoming the present order) socioeconomic creation, as some Yugoslav authors think (S. Stojanović, B. Horvat)? One thing is certain, that it is a tenacious and coherent system (of course with strong internal contradictions, as every social system until now has displayed), where the principles of a statist organization of society are consistently carried out and which necessarily presents an explicitly political rather than socialist society. It is a society where the factors of social power play an essential role directly on the political rather than the economic plane, one that seeks a new interpretation of Marxist theory in terms of the factors of power.

Statism as Political Society

In East European countries after the October Revolution, a statism developed which displays the following essential characteristics:

1) The state, by means of the nationalization of the means of production, has placed all industrial production and the distribution of goods under its control and management. Centralized, administrative, and planning management of production replaced individual or corporate entrepreneurship and a competitive market. The "visible hand" replaced the "invisible hand" in harmonizing economic growth with the economic interests of all of the people.

2) The main goal of state concern and of all social activities became production and constant economic growth in order to amass material wealth as the precondition of "communist society." Under conditions of social backwardness and relative poverty, production is also the main means in the "contest with the more developed, capitalist states."

3) The merger of state administration with production and distribution led to an extraordinary strengthening of the organs of executive power at the expense of legislative power and public opinion, which lose not only basic but also every autonomous

meaning. This led to a crisis in the structure of power, since executive power is not responsible to the legislative authority but rather to the party leadership.

4) The government and the state apparatus (with the organized means of state coercion—courts, army, and police) are under the direct control of the political party which represents the real center of social power and decision-making.

5) The state and the political party which governs it are organized as single, rigidly centralized, monolithic, and hierarchical creations, such that they belong by type to monarchical executive bureaucracies.

6) The ultimate concentration of social power in the political party, centralized leadership of social affairs from above, with the assistance of the state and political apparatus, give an expressly political character to the entire society and the role of essential integrator of society to the political party and control. Every opposition to the party is viewed as an attack on social integrity, an act of the "enemy."

7) The subordination of the legislative power to the executive, and public opinion to the political party, noticeably lessens the role of the citizen as *citoyen* and leads to his marked privatization, in spite of the political pressure for constant participation in society.

Statism equates the nationalization of the means of production with socialism as such, since it concerns the expropriation of the capitalist. Furthermore, statism performs this nationalization in relation to the working class as well, because where workers' councils had already taken over the factories and placed them under their own control, they are compelled to transfer them to the management of state organs—to planning commissions and directors whom the government nominates and who are the sole superiors and the sole ones responsible. Statism abandons Engels's thesis that nationalization of the means of production means the transformation of the state into an "ideal general capitalist," which also means that the workers and people in that system become only an "ideal general proletariat," hired labor of the state. However, one achieves socialism only with the *socialization of the means of production*, as K. Korsch clearly understood on the basis of his experience with the October Revolution, that is, by means of a negation of a negation (socialization of nationalization). This corresponds to Engels's formulation that "the first act in which the state really acts as the representative of the entire society—taking into its own possession the means of production in the name of society—is simultaneously (and must be) also its final independent act as a state." The socialization of the means of production or their transfer to management by work collectives, "by free associations of producers," (Marx) in fact deprives the state of one of its essential functions and sources of power—control over production. It is not in vain that the revolutionary workers' movement as early as the nineteenth century warned that nationalization could only establish the state as an "even more powerful and baser master of the private person."

With the aid of planning commissions, the government establishes a production plan (usually in the form of Five-Year Plans) and controls the plan's fulfillment directly out of its own offices. ("The telephone is the most important instrument of planning," said Kidrič, Yugoslav leader during the statist period in Yugoslav socialism.) The management of production flows from the top, from the ministry on down to the director as the government's executive organ. The plan has the force of law. Its lack of fulfillment is accompanied by legal and political sanctions and may be interpreted not only as an expression of poor organization but also as insufficient personal dedication and even as "enemy sabotage." It is well known that legal and political sanctions, which are taken in the name of the "general interest," usually strike people harder than do economic sanctions, which are seen as an expression of "particular interests," so that such centralized planning leadership is associated with far greater pressures on people. Such centralized administrative rule has its own expressly dysfunctional side (a clumsiness due to the volume of production with more than a million "planned products," the clumsiness of an administrative apparatus with bureaucratic parasitism, disproportionate investment, a large stock of surplus products, a poor assortment, and so forth), while the principle of "command" in administration stifles every initiative from below (such that one of the most fundamental laws of the dialectic is abrogated—the lack of uniformity in development, which presupposes independent initiative or a new, accelerated pace in particular sectors), and there is a constant need for intervention with sanctions from above. That leads to those bureaucratic diseases about which Marx had already warned, namely that "higher and lower circles mutually deceive each other" and systematically swindle each other, because the "lower circles" become skilled at "discovering loopholes" in the laws and plans in order to make their own task as easy as possible. It is well known that the very application of "administrative zeal," the repeal of any spontaneous, creative dedication on the part of each individual is one form of "strike" (rules strike). Hence, centralized planning proves successful during the phase of primitive accumulation and massive investments, but it regularly fails under a more developed division of labor and production (P. Wiles, B. Horvat).

The principle of rigidly hierarchical, vertical lines of decision-making is associated with a Tayloristic organization of the firm, in favor of which Lenin argued after the October Revolution, seeing in it the "scientific organization of work." Thus, an authoritarian organization at the level of the global economy coincides with the authoritarian organization of the firm, and both contribute to the authoritarian organization of the party as well so that the worker constantly encounters a three-fold hierarchy in his own behavior. Theoreticians of statism think that this type of organization suits socialist conceptions, but they defend it with classical principles of representative democracy! Thus, for example, A. Rumjancev in a polemic against the idea of workers' self-management, says:

Members of ruling organs in the economy, as it is well known, are elected on a mandate from the working class, can be recalled and are obliged to be accountable to the masses. The organs of the State are under the control of the vanguard of the workers—the Communist Party—as are the trade unions and other social organizations. The material process of work, by its very nature, seeks to subordinate the will of all to the will of one authorized by socialist society and responsible to it. This suits the interests of all workers. And sensible workers cannot but submit themselves to that which represents the general interest.[12]

This is the classical formulation of the process of alienation at work, but as socialist statism considers the theory of alienation a youthful delusion of Marx, it looks at work with the spirit of traditional bourgeois relations between "lord and servant," or rather "work morals"; thus, good workers are lavishly rewarded with public recognition like good students in school, because work signifies above all the disciplined execution of orders which come from above. No form whatsoever of responsibility, individual or

12. A. Rumjancev, "Socijalistička stvarnost i teorije druga Kardelja" ("Socialist Reality and the Theories of Comrade Kardelj"), *Komunist*, Moskva, 18 (1956).

collective, comes into consideration in the management of production by the work collective. The worker does not even have the right to protest since strikes are forbidden as "antisocial."

Since workers have neither their own class organizations nor the right to strike, every workers' movement under statism necessarily takes on the form of social protest, as the workers' movements in the GDR, Hungary, Poland, and Czechoslovakia between 1956 and 1968 illustrate. In these revolts the workers did not limit themselves to demands for better pay but rather took over factories and created workers' councils, proving in that way that they cared as much about responsibility and freedom as they did about their material position. Under such pressure from the workers, the Polish Party leader Gomulka at first permitted the organization of the workers' councils, only later to liquidate them gradually using a typical statist argument:

The Director and other managers, as part of the administration, are representatives of the socialist State, and thus of the State of the working class: these are people whom the State has trusted to manage the socialist enterprise in its name, and thus in the name of the working class. The workers and the administration are not two opposed sides of the personnel, they are two sides of one, united organism, sides on which its functioning depends.[13]

What characterizes statism most profoundly is that this authoritarian bureaucratic organization multiplies itself and is mutually reinforced at various social levels and sectors of life. Thus man as producer will encounter the organization first in his own enterprise, only to encounter it as an authoritarian state as a citizen in public life, and, as a member of the party, or as a nonmember, experience it in the form of a centralistic and monolithic party. All these organizations teach him that society is actually a "New Factory." (Stalin emphasized that it is most important for a country to become a "land of metal, a land of automobilization, a land of tractorization," that the ideal is to "take control of the USSR by automobile and of a peasant by tractor."[14])

However, this multiplication of authoritarian organization appears not to be sufficiently efficacious ideologically, for the system

---

13. Cited in Paul Barton, ed., *Misère et révolte de l'ouvrier polonais*, Force ouvrière (Paris, 1971).

14. J. Stalin, *Pitanja lenjinizma* (*Questions of Leninism*), (Belgrade: Kultura, 1946).

had to depend more and more on the material incentive of persons working in production. The original revolutionary desire to equalize personal income is condemned as "levelling" and as a reactionary attitude. (He who is "for levelling in the area of income . . . he breaks with Leninism and Marxism," stressed Stalin.) It is up to the leading cadre especially to provide incentives. ("The cadres decide!"—Stalin) Thus differences grew in incomes from 1 : 1.8 after the revolution in 1920 to 1 : 40 and 50 in 1950 (S. Ossovski).[15]

The ruling party possesses a political monopoly, so its managerial function is above its ownership function in the state when it comes to the means of production. Stalin, whose undoubted historical service was to channel "Marxism-Leninism" with highly simplified formulas into the proportions of statism, found fault with the Paris Commune because it had not introduced a "total and unyielding dictatorship" as it had not been ruled by a single party. Therefore the "true dictatorship" of the proletariat is that which is composed "of directives from the party plus the execution of those directives by mass organizations of the proletariat plus their animation by the population." The party as the real director of social administration in all fields is defined by the spirit of a maximum concentration of social power. Stalin defines the style of the party by a contrast with spontaneous and democratic movement: 1) as the "vanguard of the working class," it "leads the proletariat along after it" instead of its being dragged by "the tail of a spontaneous movement"; 2) in place of waverers (professors, high school students, nihilists), it is an "organized division"; 3) instead of diverse organizations (trade unions, corporations, and so forth), it is the "highest form of class organization"; 4) in contrast to petty bourgeois elements, it—as "the instrument of the dictatorship of the proletariat"—brings to the masses a "spirit of discipline and organization"; 5) "The Party, as a single will, unconnected to existing fractions," distinguishes itself by an "iron discipline" which "does not exclude but rather presupposes awareness and voluntary subordination"; 6) "The Party is fortified by cleansing it of opportunistic elements." (Cited by N. Popov, unpub. ms.) It is worth noting here that what is to us a certain "laïcization" or rationalization of the abovementioned attitudes about the "monolithic nature of the party" can lead to the same form of "monolith" which a rigidly rational technical organization requires. The very nature of the

---

15. S. Ossovski, *Class Structure in the Social Consciousness* (London: Routledge and Kegan Paul, 1963), p. 116.

ideology which is used by such a party speaks on its behalf, although, as is well known, it is one type of dogmatic, positivistic (the subjugation of individuals to the system) and pseudoscientistic (rule in the name of "objective laws of social movement") ideology. It is interesting that someone so familiar with bourgeois functionalism as Alvin Gouldner has noted that the differences between the American functionalism of Talcott Parsons and Soviet Marxism are more terminological than of any fundamental nature.[16]

That this ideology is profoundly irrationally based is shown not only by its dogmatic character and the immutability of its basic positions (often radically contrary to Marx's, for example, his theory of reflexes and the rejection of his theory of alienation) but also by its role of hatred for every intellectual movement in the sphere of public life, of public opinion, of the citizen's role in legislative power (parliament has truly been diverted into an "information center," and not toward the expression and formation of the "will of the people"). All this arises from the simple fact that social authority is uninterested in any progress whatsoever or in input in the sphere of public opinion and humanistic concerns, since only technological input and the technical intelligentsia, linked into production, are decisive for the system. Thus the intelligentsia under statism displays a peculiar dichotomy or "schizophrenia," namely that the humanistic intelligentsia is told to concern itself primarily with the past (socialist realism as a typical, encompassing doctrine in addition to its apologetic role), while the technical intelligentsia is directed to concern itself with the future, with progress and advancement. While "innovations" in the field of humanistic science and art are a "deadly sin" against the regime, thus far they have been obligatory for the technical intelligentsia. Thence comes, of course, also a certain liberal position toward an occasional critical attitude on the part of natural scientists and an extremely intolerant attitude toward every attempt at criticism by the humanistic intelligentsia.[17]

So as not to prolong this description of statism any longer, we will conclude with a comparison between capitalism and statism which B. Horvat has formulated as follows:

16. Alvin Gouldner, *Coming Crisis in Western Sociology* (New York: Basic Books, 1970).
17. See R. Supek, "The Statist and Self-managing Models of Socialism." In *Opinion-Making Elites in Yugoslavia*, ed. by A. H. Barton (New York: Praeger, 1973).

In capitalism political power is primarily derived from economic power. In statism this relationship is reversed. In the former society the state is in the last analysis ruled by plutocracy, in the latter one the economy is ruled by politocracy. In capitalism, income is mostly derived from one's place in the economic hierarchy. In governing the society, the capitalist ruling class uses primarily economic coercion, which is accompanied by an ideology forcing the minds into conformity, and, finally, by political coercion. In statism, ideological coercion is followed by political coercion with economic coercion occupying the last position in the sequence. Since political coercion is personal, it is felt as more oppressive than the impersonal economic coercion and so statism looks more repressive than capitalism. As a consequence of the differing importance of various types of coercion, capitalism is characterized by economic insecurity, statism by political insecurity. These two insecurities have been the main organizational devices for establishing and maintaining stratified social orders in the two systems.[18]

Revolutionary Charisma, Bureaucratization of Utopia, and Degradation of the Personality

Even though statism appears to many as a highly coherent and ideal system in terms of the organization of production and distribution, its greatest weakness is nevertheless that it cannot function without political force and political socialization which penetrates in an authoritarian and externally imposed manner into all pores of society. However, its greatest "systematic weakness"—no matter how much its adherents have drawn attention to the fact as an *ultima ratio* that it "functions successfully"—is that it rests entirely on a single, unsystematic, and what is worse, anti-systematic moment, that is, on a single historical event, a moment in the distant past, which is simultaneously and constantly present as a promise and hope of its future—on the socialist revolution. Although it seems to an outsider that the latter is present particularly as a façade for society with its ubiquitous emblems, red flags, and slogans, nonetheless the socialist revolution gives legitimacy to

18. Branko Horvat, "Capitalism, Etatism, Socialism," unpublished paper.

statism. It dupes the working man into making continual sacrifice and consoles the citizens with the belief that the promised future, filled with wealth and freedom, will arrive very soon. Revolutionary charisma is still a source of respectability and power for the political leadership, and there is no suggestion that some purely technocratic conception could replace it. The dying out or rejection of revolutionary charisma would mean only the beginning of a process of open crisis, where all social contradictions would gush to the surface and above all the question of civil liberties—estranged now in the form of "the general interest of the proletariat" represented by the state and party leadership—would be placed on the agenda.

Revolutionary charisma, as with every organism, is vulnerable to the ravages of time and a natural decay. Thus statism endeavors to prolong the manipulation of social consciousness skillfully by stressing that "its own revolution was the only authentic one" and as such is necessarily the direction for all others in the future, that those which have already taken place in another form are "ordinary revisions." Statism imprisons its own people and working class in tightly closed borders of its own past, which is constantly and inexhaustibly resurrected in an uninterrupted series of diverse jubilees and even dead heroes of the revolution. Statism also imprisons its own bureaucratic control within geographic borders so that internationalism has become only a lovely slogan. Furthermore, statism prolongs the manipulation of social consciousness in the myth of the "vanguard of the proletariat" which carries a fateful responsibility for the world revolution, in spite of the well-known principle of "one's own road to socialism" for diverse nations; in the dogmatism of a single ideology to which its founders have given a definite form; in teachings about the "infallibility of the party," whose policy is founded on "objective laws" and which acts with the security of illusion or of fate; and in the constant struggle against "enemies," who work not only from the outside but also from within. It is believed each individual carries within himself the potential to be an enemy, since by now even the greatest revolutionaries have been exposed as "enemies and traitors to the revolution." "Hostility," just as Manichean Evil, is implanted in every individual, and therefore measures of vigilance taken by the political leadership are never excessive but can only be insufficient.

Every revolution has its internal dynamic: a phase of totalization, when individual will and consciousness coincide most with collective action, and the phase of detotalization, when this conscience begins to withdraw from collective action or at least from those who speak for it. In the totalization phase, the future seems very close to the present as do people to one another; in the detotalization phase, the future begins to move away from the present along an ever more distant horizon and so do people from each other. Every individual who holds some utopian vision of the future begins to behave critically toward promises and hopes which have not been met. At that moment political organization intervenes in order to preserve its own unity as well as the unity of the movement. A. Hegedus has described the division of former revolutionaries into those who become skeptical and disappointed with that which is done "in the name of the revolution" and those who begin to monopolize the revolution and utopian consciousness as the only legitimate interpreters. Using various means, from ideology to open terror, the political bureaucracy expropriates this utopian consciousness in the name of its own "vanguardism" and attempts to silence all those who wish to speak independently in its name. Even though this utopian consciousness, in the sense of the "real utopia" of Ernst Bloch, is an intimate possession of every individual, the idea by which an individual defines himself as a "social animal" or "communal animal" (*Gemeinwesen*, Marx), is something ideally and morally unalienable. Nonetheless, the political leadership arrogates the utopian consciousness exclusively for itself and reduces it to the level of political pragmatism, of its own daily activity.

The political leadership has imposed its own political methods to justify its own vision of the future, and it is increasingly compelled to prove every political action as a "step forward," a series of "constant successes" which will lead ever closer to a realization of ideals. With this unrestrained optimism, the political leadership begins increasingly to equate the future with the present, the feasible with what exists, and the desirable with the real. In this way the leadership bureaucratizes the utopian conscience. Thus one day the citizens discover, by means of a decree, that they are on the threshold of communism, since it was decreed that "socialism had already been built," even though they had not noticed how it had happened and what social signs told of such a passing from one historical phase to another!

The humanistic intelligentsia, in the name of this same utopian consciousness and following the same political practice, have become less and less optimistic and ever more skeptically see the future being moved further from the present. Out of this arose the conflict between the political bureaucracy and the humanistic intelligentsia, a conflict which in the revolutionary period, unfortunately for a very short period, had been a subject for dialogue but rapidly became a cause for social sanctions and suppression of the humanistic intelligentsia. The latter retreated into privatization or, as the bureaucracy puts it, into the "political underground." A natural developmental contradiction between social practice and social aspirations became the subject of social coercion and silence. Progress on the basis of the "general interest" and "general welfare" simultaneously meant both retrogression and defeat in the sphere of "particular interests" and "individual freedoms." Every attempt to complete the dialectic of "class against class" with the dialectic of "individual and society" is considered "abstract humanism" by statism. However, this situation is not new; Marx spoke of it more than one hundred years ago in connection with "true socialism" in Prussia. Marx reproached the "true socialists," who rejected civil liberty in the name of absolute rule with the following:

By this, the long wished for opportunity was offered to "true" socialism of confronting the political movement with the socialist demands, of hurling the traditional anathemas against liberalism, against representative government, against bourgeois competition, bourgeois freedom of the press, bourgeois legislation, bourgeois liberty and equality, and of preaching to the masses that they had nothing to lose and everything to gain, by this bourgeois movement, German socialism forgot, in the nick of time, that the French criticism whose silly echo it was, presupposed the existence of modern bourgeois society, with its corresponding economic conditions of existence, and the political constitution adapted thereto, the very things whose attainment was the object of the pending struggle in Germany.[19]

This civil society with "human rights and freedoms" is the essential precondition for the socialist revolution to be able to replace civil class society and to do so by that order where "in place of classes and class contradictions arrives one association, in which the

19. K. Marx and F. Engels, *Manifesto of the Communist Party*. In *Basic Writings on Politics and Philosophy*, ed. by Lewis Feuer (New York: Anchor, 1959), p. 34.

free development of each individual is the precondition for the free development of all" (*Communist Manifesto*).

Since under statism a new state has arisen in place of workers' associations or councils, the situation has been perverted; "the free subjugation of the individual has become the precondition for the [un]free development of all the others." A dogmatized official ideology has deprived him of the right to express himself creatively in a social sense or even in art (socialist realism as a static and encompassing theory). Thus the individual has been forced to withdraw more and more into his own private life, and privatization has become one of the stabilizing moments of the system itself, to the same extent that activism of party militants is. S. Strumilin, one of first investigators of leisure time, gives comparative figures for the USSR in 1925 and in 1959, that is, for an interval of twenty-five years. These data speak clearly of the progressive privatization of citizens. Thus, for example, the Soviet worker spent, on the average, 109 hours for "social activities" in 1925 but only 17 hours in 1959, in other words, six times less. Even the "reading of newspapers, books" has fallen from 453 to 329 hours in spite of the eradication of illiteracy. However, all those activities which today characterize a privatized mass culture, such as attending the cinema, the theater, and other spectacles where man appears as a "public" rather than an "association," have clearly grown (from 42 hours in 1925 to 374 hours in 1959). According to these data, cultural activities, such as going to the cinema, the theater, the circus, and sports events have grown, while activities in social organizations, social leisure activities, and general relaxation, have fallen. In addition, for men even "free time" itself has decreased; the worker has less of it today than earlier, and the less skilled worker and the professions have less of it than the more highly skilled.[20]

As we can see, while statism deprives each man as producer of every responsibility on the job and, as citizen, of the right to express his opinions freely and influence legislation, it deprives him as a consumer of the right to take advantage of his "free time" in an original, free, and social way because creative originality is a "sin." At the same time passive leisure, that is, the reception of impressions sent to each citizen from outside according to the logic of "conditioned reactions," is the single freedom at his disposal. In

---

20. S. Strumilin, "Les problèmes du socialisme et du communisme en URSS." In *Recherche Internationale à la lumière du Marxisme*, 18 (1960), ed. Nouvelle Critique, Paris.

order to know how he ought to behave in society, he is forced continuously to direct his eyes to the social summit, which stereotypically appears as several dull faces on the pages of newspapers or on the television screen and who constantly try to convince the citizen how to look after his own welfare in the best way. This monopolization of responsibility at the social summit on the part of a single elite has led in fact to an "organized irresponsibility," as C. Wright Mills would say, to a minority which takes advantage of "political channels" for vertical mobility and a majority which passively watches how far individual "climbers" advance.

How to Overcome Statism and Technocracy?

From the standpoint of the socialist revolution, statism represents a historical aberration. From the standpoint of technocracy, it represents a system which is worth improving by lessening its political coercion and above all its ideological dogmatism and political voluntarism. From the viewpoint of statism itself, a strengthening of technocracy means a real advance, because it wants to replace social integration on the basis of bureaucratic-political control with "objective, neutral, scientific" methods. However, from the standpoint of socialism itself, the improvement of a historical aberration means only replacing voluntaristic or "subjective coercion" with scientific or "objective coercion" and giving to human activity an objective, external, impersonal character. Accordingly, socialism longs for the simultaneous negation of both statism and technocratism. Which tendencies in contemporary society today act against one or the other? We will now point to these.

1) Marx's retort against "true socialists," as we have seen, means simply that a social revolution or radical change in a social system of progressive character cannot endure, if at the same time it does not signify a *widening of individual freedom*. The class struggle of the proletariat for its own liberation from exploitation necessarily includes a demand for the general emancipation of all people from various forms of alienation, from inhuman social relations. Social revolutions which carry with them a lessening or restriction of

personal freedoms can have only a reactionary and regressive character, and they have no right to call themselves socialist. This is not only a matter of freedoms from various forms of oppression and bondage but also of "freedoms to," since man is by nature a "social animal." Therefore, these freedoms find expression in the creation of new forms of human community (productive, territorial, and so forth). However, as the individual bears the responsibility for the quality of his sovereign totality and in a similar way for the various forms of social association, then the social community can only be a "free form of alliance or association," that is, one into which an individual freely enters and from which he is equally free to leave. Every form of totalitarianism or sectarianism is foreign to socialism and communism, since no community can really be measured to fit the individual, as it restricts his creative disposition.

In fact, however, when the limited bourgeois form is stripped away, what is wealth other than the universality of human needs, capacities, pleasures, productive forces, etc. created through universal exchange? The full development of human mastery over the forces of nature, those of so-called nature as well as of humanity's own nature? The absolute working out of his creative potentialities, with no presupposition other than the previous historic development, i.e. the development of all human powers as such the end in itself, not as measured on a predetermined yardstick? (K. Marx, *Grundrisse*, p. 488).

The universality of human needs demands a universality also of human forms of association, which can in no way be exhausted by one or more given forms of social community. The individual will always transcend every form of social community, simply because of his own social and communitarian nature.

2) When the subject is socialism and the socialist revolution, then the extension of human freedoms relates *above all to industrial democracy*, to the rights of man as producer, to the self-determination of man at work, and further to the right of workers' self-management. Man as producer must have the full right to decide autonomously on his own productivity in its entirety, from planning and its realization to control and distribution of the completed products of his labor. The precondition for that is, as we know, the socialization of the means of production, and in this socialism differs radically from statism, whether it calls itself socialist or something else. K. Korsch had already come to the conclusion following the October Revolution that nationalization,

which corresponds to the "state-socialist conception of social-democracy, ought to be distinguished from socialization by which workers will become rightful participants in production."[21]

3) Bureaucratic-statist ideology has imposed an incorrect interpretation on the "transitional period between capitalism and socialism" or the "dictatorship of the proletariat" in the sense of a single totalitarian authority. Instead, what makes that period "transitional," regardless of what one calls it, is precisely the fact that it involves a *dual or contradictory organization of power:* one power taken over from the former society in the form of the state and political parties is pitted against the second power in the form of workers' councils or workers' self-management. While the first is destined to disappear or "wither away" (according to the theory of Marx and Lenin), the second is destined to grow stronger. Thus the power of workers' councils gains its own politico-territorial form in communes. While the first type of power belongs to representative democracy, the second type belongs to direct or delegated democracy. Marx expressed the duality of this power in that formula that "the proletariat does not need a social revolution with a political spirit but rather a political revolution with a social spirit," which means that the political instruments of the revolution (the state, the political party) must surrender to the new forms of social integration in the form of workers' self-management and the communal system. In this case social integration is not accomplished by political means from above (Stalin's theory of the strengthening of the state under socialism and further even under communism), but it is accomplished by forms of social association and management from below, from the very bottom toward the top. Such a way leads to socialist democracy, whose realization is a rather long historical process with a series of social changes, among which is the constant decline of that "mutual exploitation" which P. Naville has analyzed in statist socialism, and the development of self-management socialism between workers' self-managed collectives.[22] Only with the transformation of society in the direction of socialist democracy does the proletariat appear historically as the "emancipator of the entire society."

4) The socialization of the means of production refers to *the decentralization of decision-making and management in the econ-*

---

21. K. Korsch, *Schriften zur Sozialisierung (1919)* (Frankfurt: Europeische Verlag sanstalt, 1969), p. 55.
22. See P. Naville, "Les salaires socialiste," *Le Nouveau Leviathan* 2, vol. 1.

omy and, accordingly, the abolition of the main source of power of the state and the bureaucracy. (Aleksandra Kolontaj: "Bureaucracy—that is where others decide your fate.") Decentralized management means at the same time the extension of market exchange of manufactured goods. Here we encounter the problem about which there is much discussion in contemporary economic theory, namely, whether or not a market economy and a planned economy are mutually exclusive, particularly if one takes into account that a market goods economy is an essential characteristic of capitalism, while a planned economy characterizes socialism. J. Proudhon discussed this problem in his theory of mutualism and suggested that the society intervene periodically in the market mechanism in order to remove inequalities which may accumulate from time to time. The Spanish Republic met this problem in a practical way in the 1930s during the civil war, because it introduced workers' councils and one of the theoreticians of "libertarian socialism," Diego Abad de Santillan, first attempted to reconcile decentralized management of enterprises with planned economic production. Contemporary theory finds—in cybernetics (M. Shubik) as well as in the so-called "labor-managed" or "participatory economy" (B. Ward, J. Vanek, B. Horvat)—that decentralization and the plan are not necessarily mutually exclusive. It is interesting that Marx thought that a planned economy and "free associations of producers" would go perfectly together and contain no contradictions, such as have been found in practice in Yugoslav society. Thus Marx in one of his later manuscripts from 1872 says in one place:

Agriculture, mining, industry—briefly, all the branches of production—will be gradually organized in the most useful way. The national centralization of the means of production will become the natural basis of a society made up of associations of free and equal, consciously active producers—working according to a common and rational plan. That is the end to which the great economic movement of the nineteenth century tends.[23]

5) In the contemporary workers' movement there is an increasing conflict between two contradictory conceptions, one of which leans toward the statist model of socialism and the other toward self-managing socialism. The center of gravity of the first still rests

23. K. Marx and F. Engels, *Marx-Engels Werke* (Berlin: Dietz, 1962, Bd. 18), p. 62.

on pauperization or "quantitative demands" (the struggle to raise wages). The second emphasizes "qualitative demands," which in addition to wages relate particularly to workers' control, the extension of "workers' power" in relation to the process of decision-making over working conditions and various aspects of business policy in general. The first saw the main ally of the working class in the peasantry as "an element of spontaneity in the revolution"; the second saw it in the technical staffs and "hired intelligentsia" (employees, cultural workers, scientific-research staffs, students, and so forth), whose significance becomes all the greater in a more developed society as a consequence of the expansion of tertiary activities and the disappearance of the peasantry. The higher level of socio-economic development this type of society has, and the more individual categories of working people are organized and experienced in a longer tradition of struggle for democratic and social rights, then the same strategy in the struggle for radical socialist change becomes all the more complex, and the role of ideology or the consciousness factor the more decisive. This is even more understandable since in a developed society the working class together with the progressive strata of society no longer share "physical poverty" as much as "moral and civil poverty," that is, vulnerability to the same hired relations within a single authoritarian and hierarchical organization. If the material conditions of life on the average have improved, the work position of man has become all the worse, and it is more and more subject to exploitation by personal and impersonal forces which make him "helpless" and his work "meaningless." The center of gravity of human resistance and revolt remains necessarily in the sphere of production, in terms of the role of man as producer, while all the manipulation of human needs in the sphere of consumption and a distribution which has preserved a traditional inequality, take on a somewhat secondary importance. Its significance is secondary not so much in relation to the immediate situation as in relation to the image of the future with regard to the society we desire and whose image hovers before our eyes.

3

Hans Peter Dreitzel

On the Political Meaning of Culture

Today any general statement about the variety of phenomena which we usually consider to be part of the culture of a society runs a high risk of immediately being falsified by one contradictory element or another. The fads and fashions of the cultural scene seem to come and go so quickly that any attempt to gain an overview easily ends up in breathless confusion. The present essay will therefore concentrate on certain developments within the culture of Western industrialized societies which are or will be of political consequence. Hence, this essay casts a selective view on cultural phenomena from a sociological perspective. The question of the extent to which observable changes in our norms and values, symbols and interpretations reorganize our social structure according to the pressing problems and needs of our time will serve as a guideline for this perspective. After having clarified some conceptual problems, I will follow this guideline beginning with a description of the functional crisis of culture, continuing with an analysis of the development of the present counter-cultures. I will then present a rough model of the relationship between culture and society today and conclude with remarks on the present issues and future prospects of cultural developments in regard to their potential social and political impact.

Concepts and Caveats

The difficulties that arise in putting cultural phenomena in a sociological perspective are partly of methodological, partly of historical, nature. A critical sociological analysis of cultural phenomena, on the one hand, will have to take into account the dialectical character of the relation between culture and the economic-political system and, on the other hand, the dialectical character of the relation between critical and apologetic elements within the culture. By dialectical character I do not simply mean the mutual influence which various elements of a society exert upon each other but, more specifically, the phenomenon that developmental trends frequently bear the seeds of their own negation. Thus, for instance, the development of the economic and political domination of the bourgeoisie has gradually undermined the very educational privileges of this class. The industrialization of culture did not only serve to spread bourgeois values throughout society but has also blurred the limits between high culture and folk culture.

The concept of culture which I will use must be distinguished from a more traditional bourgeois concept of culture: it does not refer to the high culture which, in its various forms in art, literature, philosophy, and history, has been the reserve of a quantitatively small educated bourgeoisie and its social correlate, the *bourgeoise bohème*. Neither does it refer to that concept of mass culture which lives from its opposite, the high culture of bourgeois educational elites, and has defensive ideological connotations. Instead I am using here a notion of culture which has originated from American cultural anthropology and comprises aspects of high culture as well as the mores, norms, and life styles of a society. Of course, in modern society we find considerable differences between the cultural styles and symbolizations of different social classes, ethnic groups, and national traditions. This particular use of the concept of culture is justified by the fact that the dialectics of the bourgeois culture—"high culture" as against "mass culture"—has produced a general industrial culture the essential characteristic of which is the continuous production and consumption of cultural symbols, values, norms, and life styles at all levels of sophistication and educational differentiation. In fact, the very frequency of the use of such terms as "subculture," "counter-culture," "ethnic culture," and "national culture" inherently demonstrates the necessity to emphasize the remaining (and occasionally rejuvenated) specificity of certain cultural traditions against the overwhelming impact of the general industrial culture.

The new dialectics of culture consists of the fact that subcultural orientations have become optional for more and more groups within the society while at the same time the industrial mode of production of cultural symbols works for a continuous integration of such interpretations into the cultural market of the society at large. This situation was first analyzed in *The Dialectics of Enlightenment*, by M. Horkheimer and T. W. Adorno, first published in 1947 and still unsurpassed in the field of cultural sociology. What has changed is not the contradictory character of culture but the nature of the contradictions: bourgeois culture, too, has had a dialectical structure—it was at once pure ideology, rigid legitimation of bourgeois forms of domination, and their unmasking in art and literature, philosophy and the critique of political economy. Today this dialectical structure is continued in the contradictory unity of established culture and counter-culture.

Of course, the phenomenon of subcultures opposing the dominant bourgeoisie is not a new one: ethnically rooted folk cultures as well as "traditional" working-class cultures used to be strongholds of resistance against the prevailing bourgeois culture. While the latter can be called "traditional" only from our present point of view, the former were indeed traditional in that their opposition to bourgeois values was rural against urban, manufactural against industrial, ascription-oriented against achievement-oriented; in short, rooted in the mode of production and the set of values characteristic of the preindustrial period. The working-class culture, on the other hand, was progressive in its political goals against the domination of the ruling bourgeoisie, yet also progressive in regard to the emerging industrial civilization, sharing the bourgeois optimism toward the technological development. The present counter-culture has certainly retained some aspects of these earlier subcultures, namely the egalitarianism of the working-class culture and the anti-technological attitude embodied in the folk cultures. However, it is much more rooted in the bohemian tradition of bourgeois culture itself: the counter-cultural rejection of the values of the established culture has a long history which began with romanticism, led to symbolism, art nouveau, and dada, and has not ended with the fascination of structuralists today for the *pensée sauvage*. Culture in the "age of its reproducibility," to paraphrase Walter Benjamin, is still determined by the contradictions of bourgeois culture. This is true even for the industrialized socialist countries: they, too, live more or less on the bourgeois values of achievement orientation, economic growth, and a rationalistic interpretation of nature. In spite of the fact that a *Kulturkrise* has been diagnosed time and time again since the end of the last century, we still live by and large on bourgeois traditions of thought and style. The functional crisis of culture, which becomes more apparent today, is but the generalization of the contradictions of bourgeois culture via its industrialization, and maybe it is only a difficult stage in a long process of erosion of bourgeois values and the emergence of a "post-bourgeois" culture. This stage, however, will certainly be accompanied by a continuous struggle of conflicting groups in search of new world views and new identities.

Before I begin to examine this present crisis of culture in some detail, a few caveats are in order. The following analysis rests on three negative assumptions:

(1) that there will be no major war between the superpowers of this world;
(2) that we are not heading for a major economic crisis, not to speak of a breakdown of the capitalist world system;
(3) that there will be no major accidents in the operation of nuclear plants or the transportation of nuclear materials nor any serious attempt at nuclear blackmail by some private or semiprivate party.

The first assumption does not need any elaboration—I will not exhaust my imagination here "to think the unthinkable." The second assumption, however, calls for some comment. I will be very brief here: should a major crisis in the world economy occur in the foreseeable future, my analysis will no longer be valid. I do not think, however, that we are moving toward a crisis comparable to the situation during the thirties which could only be overcome by war economy. It seems to me that we are facing a long-term structural crisis in the allocation of raw materials and labor power within a world market which by now—and that is comparatively new—has to take into account the Third World as a political factor in its own right. Such a crisis would cause much structural unemployment as well as repeated depressions caused by raw material shortages, shifts in the labor market, and temporary lacks of new technologies. I assume that this crisis will slowly aggravate the crisis of political legitimation rather than lead to sudden and radical changes in the political structure of Western societies. It should not be overlooked that much of the present crisis is certainly welcome if not in fact fabricated by political administrations, who are faced with the problem of keeping the flowering separate interests of various economic and status groups under control in the absence of legitimation for the institution of anything but a defensive policy. The third assumption bears in my opinion the greatest danger of falsification. Since the economic exploitation of nuclear power and the world trade in nuclear materials are presently growing exponentially and since, moreover, experts seem to agree that security measures in most countries are far from satisfactory, an accidental nuclear catastrophe is in fact becoming more and more likely. Such a catastrophe would have a deep impact on the prevailing moral values and standards of the Western world. It is difficult to foresee in what direction this impact would go, but it seems clear that the present crisis of culture could only be deepened.

In addition, I will have to neglect the differences in national cultures which—in spite of the tendency of industrial culture toward a certain degree of uniformity—still play a considerable role. The different historical experiences of nations as well as classes and ethnic groups are an important determinant of cultural interpretations, values, standards, and symbols. The *Gleichzeitigkeit des Ungleichzeitigen* (the coexistence of phenomena which belong to different stages of historical development) is a phenomenon always to be taken into account in an analysis of societies which, on the whole, have been subjected to social change at an unprecedented speed over the past two or three generations.

There are four dimensions of cultural and political experience which vary from nation to nation: attitudes toward a centralized state, fascism, scientism, and ethnicity. These dimensions have to be kept in mind especially when discussing differences between the United States and European countries—even though the differences between the European countries as well as between Canada and the United States are important enough in themselves. Roughly speaking, it can be said that the political culture of North America is distinct from that of European societies in that it still contains a deeply rooted mistrust of all centralized state agencies, a fact which, among other factors, has served as a safeguard against any genuine fascist experiences. On the other hand, the belief in the benefits of science and technology is much stronger in America than in Europe. In Europe such belief was the dominant mood of the nineteenth rather than the twentieth century. Ethnicity finally is a factor of varying importance in different regions of Europe as well as America, though in Europe it takes more often the form of regionalism, while in America ethnicity is more a dimension of group affiliations independent of regional traditions. All these factors have to be taken into account when more specific and detailed problems are analyzed than will be dealt with in the following remarks.

The Social Functions of Culture

From a sociological point of view the interest in cultural phenomena involves mainly an analysis of their relationship to the power structure. The culture of a society has typically certain functions for the maintenance of the prevailing modes of production and reproduction. Three such functions can be distinguished:

(1) The culture of a society provides its members with *legitimations* for the existing mode of production and distribution.
(2) Via the accepted socialization procedures and initiation rites, a culture provides the individual with a *motivational structure* that links his *identity* with the prevailing mode of production.
(3) The culture provides members of a society with *symbolic interpretations of the natural boundaries of human life*.

It is my main proposition that industrial societies have reached a point where the cultural system is proving more and more unable to serve any of these functions. This is what permits us to speak of a *crisis* of culture. The notion of a crisis is justified not because industrialized culture lacks creativity and sophistication, nor because it is in many respects a "mass culture" or a "consumer culture," but because our culture (in the broad sense of the term which I use here) has lost the integrative power to lay the psychological and moral foundations for the economic-political system—a system which now faces such pressing problems as new allocation of resources, redistribution of surplus-value, and new ways of handling ecological disturbances. According to Juergen Habermas "crises originate when the structure of a social system allows for less possibilities of problem-solving than are needed for the maintenance of the system."[1] In the current cultural crisis, the traditional value system of the bourgeoisie no longer offers viable solutions for the problems arising at the three levels of legitimation, motivational

1. J. Habermas, *Legitimationsprobleme des Spätkapitalismus* (Frankfurt, 1973), p. 11.

structure, and the interpretation of nature. This situation, of course, not only determines the nature and content of cultural phenomena but also has or will have a marked impact on the economic and political systems. This is not to say that the "superstructure" is now determining the "substructure" but rather that these terms have lost their original meaning in a society in which such factors as the modes of socialization, the educational systems, or the organization of science belong to the "forces of production."

The Crisis of Legitimation

A system of political power is but the expression of the relations of production. The form in which a society appropriates and transforms the resources of nature into means of subsistence and the system of typically unequal distribution of these resources and products calls for a legitimation, that is, an interpretation in which individuals can experience some degree of justification for their own lack of autonomy.

In feudalism this legitimation was provided by a cosmological world view in which the hierarchical structure of society was interpreted as part of the natural order. The overwhelming majority of the populace lived barely on the level of physical subsistence as is the case today in the Third World. Power was still represented—one could almost say incarnated—by concrete visible persons. Even afterward in the long struggles for monopolization of power, which the absolute state won over the feudal landlords, the king was the wordly and personal incarnation of God's own power. His rule had to be legitimized with the help of the church, which was otherwise dependent and powerless.

The secularization process became a political fact only with the advent of bourgeois revolutions. Henceforth, political power had to be legitimized in some *secular* fashion. Since the dream of equality could not be realized under the conditions of rising capitalism and the industrial revolution, all attempts of the Enlightenment to formulate a "rational" basis of legitimation of the political order were doomed to failure: the idea of a "contrât social" between the enlightened citizen of a democratic society degenerated into the abstract ideology of the parliamentary system.

Instead the bourgeois classes found the solution to the problem of secularized legitimacy in the economic basis of its rule. During the era of market capitalism, the main legitimation of bourgeois rule was the idea that everybody would have an equal chance on the market. Perhaps the reason the United States has always been an undeveloped country in regard to establishing a welfare system is to be found in the fact that nowhere else has the dream of an equal chance for everybody come closer to realization. In the United States it was easier to keep the dream as an ideology than to recognize its structural impossibility. But since the development of monopoly capitalism and state interventionism, the *domination of the ruling bourgeoisie and the persisting inequality has been effectively legitimized by a steady augmentation of per capita income*. While the unequal distribution of wealth and income has remained a persistent feature of all industrialized societies, the continuous growth of the economic output guaranteed an absolute rise of the standard of living which even in the lower classes provided each generation with a level of material gratification which far surpassed the experience of the preceding one.

It is interesting to note that capitalism and industrialized socialism do not differ in *this* respect. Both systems function today by varying degrees of state interventionism, economic planning, and the establishment of welfare systems which exist to guarantee attained levels of material subsistence and thereby the political acquiescence of the masses. Doubtless the socialist countries have achieved a higher degree of equality in income distribution and an even higher degree in the distribution of state administered welfare services—but only by paying the high price of a rigidly authoritarian political system. In fact, they are unable to realize their potential, after the expropriation of the bourgeois classes, to reorient their economies toward the satisfaction of the needs of all due to the persistence of bourgeois values and the leviathanic character of their bureaucracies, which serve as barriers to a democratization of their political structure. The persistence of these problems is illustrated by the carefully controlled reintroduction of restricted markets (especially in the GDR) in which the exchange value of products is again the guideline of economic conduct.

If, in comparison with the West, the culture of socialist countries appears to be more rigid, this is because after the abolishment of the capitalist mode of production, any criticism of the system is *directly* confronted with the bureaucratic organization of planning and control. The formal rationality inherent in the industrial mode of production has been liberated from the "irrational" elements of the market system and hence is carried to its extreme with the unexpected result that the limits of the instrumental rationality institutionalized in the formal bureaucracies have become much more visible. In fact, a good case could be made for the hypothesis that economic and political life as well as scientific and technological progress in state socialist societies function better if principles of bureaucratic rationality are enforced less. This may explain why critics from within the system tend to be either liberal technocrats who want to develop the rigid planning bureaucracies in terms of feedback systems, or conservative humanists who completely reject the idea of instrumental rationality as a guiding principle of social organization. In any event the cultural scene in these countries presents a highly ambivalent picture: while cultural products and activities are no longer dependent on their market value (books and records are extremely cheap; museums without entrance fees are crowded; recreational facilities and activities of great variety are state-supported and available for poorer people as well), the creativity of artists and writers is severely impeded by ideological rigidities, and life styles in general tend to be petit-bourgeois.

As for capitalist systems, Marcuse has coined the term "repressive tolerance" for their remarkable ability to either integrate culturally expressed dissent or leave the cultural sphere as an area of compensatory diversion from political issues. In contrast, authoritarian socialist countries have to repress more or less all cultural activities which are neither a direct nor an indirect expression of ideology because the confrontation of the bureaucratic rationality with intellectual criticism is always apt to lead, as in the case of the CSSR, to a direct challenge of the political structure. In this respect the capitalist system seems to be much more flexible. The point is, however, that *both systems have based their legitimacy on the continuous growth of per capita income and both systems are beginning to face a major crisis of legitimation because the limits of growth are gradually becoming visible.*

I will not enter here into the worldwide debate on the limits of growth. Whatever the prospects of further economic growth are, and they are considerable in socialist countries, there can be no doubt that the situation has become much more complex since the time when exploitation of natural resources and application of ever new technologies seemed to guarantee an unlimited augmentation of economic output.

Let me mention some of the problems which increasingly determine the nature of economic and political action. The growth of world population will continue relatively unchecked for the foreseeable future with the overwhelming majority living in the poor countries of the Third World. Together with qualitative changes in war technology, this produces the constant danger of wars of redistribution from which the socialist countries will not be excluded. At the same time, resources of raw materials and forms of energy production which are technologically manageable today are gradually becoming scarce. Moreover, most forms of modern technology begin to create serious environmental problems which call in turn for new technologies to solve them. The combined effect of these problems is or will be sufficient to either decrease the rate of economic growth or decrease its social value to a degree which is beginning to ruin the basis on which the political legitimacy of industrial societies has rested until this day—the steady increase of per capita income.

This means that the inequality of the distribution of the available surplus, which guarantees a tiny fraction of the population from one-fifth to one-quarter of a nation's wealth, will come under attack. Internal wars of redistribution are quite possible but will in my opinion probably be restricted to marginal and seriously deprived groups of society. The working classes will more likely focus their struggles on qualitative changes in their situation. Much depends on whether the political system is able to establish a welfare system which to some extent makes up qualitatively for what is lost quantitatively. "Quality of life" has become a magic political formula for the necessary shift from an emphasis on the increase of private income to an emphasis on dealing with the poverty of the public infrastructure.

In the cultural sector a strangely paradoxical situation occurs: since the social function of the culture industry is to guarantee the political acquiescence of the masses, in the absence of an accepted principle of legitimation, we will probably be served with more ideological cultural products by the mass media. The producers of cultural activities—interpretations, ideological or critical—are, on the other hand, more and more put under the pressures of political control and threatened with the loss of their economic and other privileges. This is because first, apart from the business classes, they are to a large extent the beneficiaries of the unequal distribution of the surplus, and second, because the growing legitimacy gap is forcing the system to tighten its control over potential critics. This will affect all the liberal intelligentsia, including social scientists, as can already be seen in the attempts for tougher control over the educational system, mass media, and research processes in various countries. Yet at the same time, intellectuals are needed just because they are the traditional producers of ideologies and interpretations. Moreover, they cannot be as easily controlled as, for instance, scientists and engineers, because they can still own their most important means of production, pens and books, even though their public influence is largely determined by the publishing business with its market orientation.

But even with tighter control, the ever growing cultural industries will not be able to fill the legitimacy gap. The continuous changes and shifts of cultural fashions and styles make for the uncommitted and "uncommitting" character of the products on the cultural market. The reason for the instability and unreliability of cultural symbols today is—next to the mechanisms of the market—to be found in their mode of production: the cultural consumer is no longer confronted only with the end product, but is made a participant observer of the production process of cultural symbols. The fact that cultural symbols and interpretations are no longer simply given by tradition and either taken for granted or, at most, reinterpreted, but industrially produced and marketed is in itself almost a guarantee for their lack of legitimizing power. In conclusion to these brief remarks, then, we find that in industrial societies the culture is quickly losing its function to legitimize the prevailing modes of production and distribution, that is, the dominating forms of economic and political power.

The Crisis of Identity

Central to any culture are the modes of socialization, that is, the way in which the traditional norms and values of a society are passed on from generation to generation. Socialization serves to produce a feeling of self-identity and group-identity as well as a motivational structure within the individual on which the prevailing mode of production is psychologically based.

The feudal system did not originally have difficulties with socialization: children were in the care of women until about the age of six and were subsequently treated as lesser adults who began to pass through a lifelong series of initiation rites. From a sociological perspective, childhood was a social invention of the early bourgeoisie, while youth as a distinct cultural group in its own right came into existence less than a hundred years ago. Both developments are, of course, a function of certain economic and political imperatives.

Historical evidence points to a functional relationship between the period of original accumulation of capital followed by the industrial revolution and the era of competitive capitalism on the one hand, and a double trend toward the *privatization of childhood experience* and increasing restrictiveness of childrearing practices on the other: children as part of the unfathomable ways of God's cosmos became first the sons and daughters of the absolute king and later simply the offspring of the bourgeois family destined to continue the accumulation of private property. While during the period of extensive exploitation child labor became a market commodity and the working classes were deprived of the opportunity to educate their children, the development of an "inner-directed social character" (D. Riesman) became a necessity for the bourgeoisie. Supported by the Puritanism of the eighteenth and nineteenth centuries, the rigid socialization procedures of the bourgeois family aimed at a psychological foundation of the Protestant Ethic needed for the individualized labor market and entrepreneurship. With the shift in modern capitalism from extensive to intensive exploitation, that is, with the growing demand for highly skilled labor and the rise of the modern white-collar class, the structure of childhood and socialization again underwent a change: while the tendency to conceive of childhood as a social and psychological stage in its own right grew even stronger with the development of the modern school system, this century has seen a continuous trend toward more permissiveness in childrearing practices. Yet both attitudes, permissiveness and punitiveness, are equally present today in the different modes of socialization of the middle classes and the working classes respectively: childrearing patterns in working classes lag behind in the development of permissive attitudes as long as their "embourgeoisement," that is, their privatization as atomized consumers, is not yet fully achieved.

The overall tendency in the development of socialization patterns can, however, be described as an ever *increasing degree of internalization of external constraints*.[2] The more abstract the general character of work becomes, the less transparent the increasing functional dependencies in economic life are, and the less penetrable the institutions of power in the welfare state, the more rigid are the necessary self-constraints in regard to spontaneous emotional expression. The greater permissiveness of socialization patterns in the present middle classes (that is, more permissive in contrast to the old bourgeoisie as well as the working classes today), is but an expression of this general trend. More permissiveness means in fact that external sanctions are replaced by internal sanctions; instead of corporal punishment there is mainly the withdrawal of love. In other words, the internalization of external constraints as a pattern of early childhood socialization is in fact further progressed in the middle classes with the result that feelings of shame, guilt, and embarrassment have become so much a part of the personality structure that civilized patterns of public behavior are not threatened by sexual and other emotional "liberation" processes, but rather reinforced by the general voyeurism of our culture for which Marcuse has coined the term "repressive desublimation."

As it is these new patterns of childrearing should in fact have produced—in direct correspondence to the needs of the economic and political systems—that kind of flexible yet authoritarian social character which guarantees political apathy, instrumental rationality, and economic submission under the consumer culture. Yet it seems that we are heading for a major motivational crisis for two reasons: first, the nuclear family of the bourgeois type no longer functions as the central socialization agency. Reasons are to be found in absentee fatherhood (we live in a "fatherless" society, as A. Mitscherlich has noted) and in the overburdening of the family with emotional needs which are no longer fulfilled in the sphere of work. (This situation has been analyzed extensively and need not be described in more detail here.) As a consequence public institutions are trying to gain control over more and more of the socialization process. This trend is only limited by the fact that the nuclear family is by far the cheapest socialization agency at hand. "Compensatory education" and "resocialization" have become cen-

---

2. This is one of the results of Norbert Elias's great study "Über den Prozess der Zivilisation—Wandlungen des Verhaltens der weltlichen Oberschichten im Abendland" (Basel, 1939).

tral issues in a society in which highly skilled labor in quickly changing strategic areas of the economy is a scarce commodity in spite of unemployment problems. The problem is that these attempts to secure the high level of instrumental rationality, that is, a high degree of physical and emotional control, seem to be counter-effective: they tend to increase rather than decrease the deeply rooted emotional frustrations which lead to the psychological instability of growing numbers of people.

The other reason for the motivational crisis is the existence of youth as a social, economic, and political factor in its own right. To be sure, historical evidence shows that the young have always been the vanguard of social movements, the core group of social disruptions and revolutions. Today, however, even in "normal" times youth is a social group with a distinct subculture of its own. On the one hand, longer and longer educational processes have created a "social-psychological moratorium" during which the young adult is set free from job and family responsibilities. He forms with his peers the real new leisure class, if with somewhat less economic privileges than the international playboy jet-set. On the other hand, the absence of viable persons and objects for identification (in a situation where fathers disappear to do some incomprehensible or meaningless work behind the walls of factories and office buildings and where traditional values to which the older generation may still adhere are day by day made anachronistic by a changing technological environment), the prolonged adolescence is mainly characterized by what E. Erikson has called "identity diffusion."

However, as it becomes gradually clear that personal opportunities for economic achievement are reaching a critical ceiling and even where economic progress takes place, environmental costs increasingly put limitations to the private use of income, *the identity crisis of the young is becoming a general feature of society*. In spite of the present apocalyptic mood, seen in a larger perspective, economic issues become less important than social issues, because social relations are the area in which reorientation is sought. Yet with the remarkable exception of the political factions of the youth movement of the sixties, this does not create social movements on the political level but rather on the cultural level. Even the student radicalism of the sixties has now given way, partially to pragmatic adjustments to the economic situation and partially to a search for identity and authenticity on the personal level. This is to a large extent due to the remarkable capacity of cultural capitalism to transform political movements into cultural movements, the goal of which are free choices traded as privatized attitudes on the cultural markets. In the absence of a cultural market, socialist societies seem to be much more vulnerable in this respect and therefore react with direct repression of such movements. The point is, however, that the effect of both "repressive tolerance" and direct repression is that *social problems more and more appear on the level of psychological problems.*

Recent counter-cultural movements have, of course, long detected this incorporating capacity of "the system" as a new form of alienation for which the term "inauthentic" has become fashionable. In A. Etzioni's definition "a relationship, institution, or society is inauthentic if it provides the appearance of responsiveness while the underlying condition is alienating."[3] In counter-cultural groups such relationships and institutions are felt to be a soft disguise of the old appeasement and adjustment strategies of the bourgeoisie which no longer have an economic basis. Indeed, the values most emphatically expressed by the counter-cultural movements are directly opposed to the prevailing bourgeois value standards. Instead of functional rationality, organic growth is emphasized. The declared goal of the communal movement is the reunification of the private and public spheres of life, the separation of which used to be a basis of bourgeois culture and the precondition of its socialization practices. The counter-culture rejects the temporality of industrial society, the "tyranny of the clock," and stresses instead the timeless "here and now." In regard to the public sphere, we find a rejection of institutions designed to reach compromises between conflicting interests in favor of spontaneous consent; in regard to the private sphere, we find a rejection of life planning and career orientation in favor of letting-go and dropping-out. On the whole a *Gemeinschaft* type of society is preferred to a *Gesellschaft* type, and the emphasis on economic growth is replaced by an emphasis on personal growth.

We need not be concerned here with the fact that as yet such values can only be realized by fractions of the population who live, economically speaking, as parasites on the prevailing system of technological rationality. It is of much greater significance that such values are gradually becoming optional for a much larger part

---

3. A. Etzioni, *The Active Society* (New York: Free Press, 1968), p. 619.

of the population in regard to the *organization of their private everyday lives* and that apparently they can coexist with standards of instrumental rationality much better than either members of the counter-culture or their critics are willing to admit.

One should always be careful to draw only general conclusions from the American (not to say Californian) cultural scene. Yet it is not without significance that in the United States, over a hundred so-called "growth-centers" have come into existence, which offer a variety of psychotherapeutic and consciousness-raising activities; that experts estimate the number of communes in North America today as being about fifty to sixty thousand, involving a transient participant population of over a million people;[4] and that about a million Americans have taken part in encounter groups. And, of course, the spread of religious revitalization movements all over the country is well known. While all this is less visible in Europe, here, too, especially in Protestant countries, the signs clearly point in the same direction. The search for new personal and communal identities, caused by the motivational crisis, is gradually spreading within the middle classes, while in America the new morality has already penetrated fractions of the working-class youth. Much of this development occurs in covert form: the gradual shifts in middle-class value standards are empirically difficult to verify, and the depoliticized counter-culture groups shy away from the strangling publicity of the media to such an extent that some of them have almost acquired the status of secret societies. There is, however, one recent study representative of American youth which clearly shows that liberal sexual standards, a new evaluation of the role of women, and a general emphasis on the value of "self-fulfillment" are absolutely dominant on the campuses of the seventies and have penetrated the working-class youth to a considerable extent as well as the older generation within the middle classes.[5] To quote this study, the "almost total divorce . . . between radical politics and new life-styles," together with the impact of the present economic crisis on the institutions of higher education, easily blinds us to the fact that a growing part of the population is seeking a radical reorganization of their everyday lives.

Habermas has pointed out that formerly only in the arts could

---

4. Judson Jerome, *Families of Eden—Communes and the New Anarchism* (New York: Seabury Press, 1974).

5. D. Yankelovich, *The New Morality—A Profile of American Youth in the 70's* (New York: McGraw-Hill, 1974).

needs be satisfied which had become illegitimate in the context of the material life of the bourgeoisie—the need for spontaneity and fantasy, for communal solidarity and communicative experience, the need, last but not least, for a noninstrumental, aesthetic approach to nature. The systems of morality were closely integrated with the achievement motivation of bourgeois "economic man"; science has long since become a major economic institution of industrial society; and religion and philosophy have been privatized to the point of irrelevance.[6] *Today the youth movement of the sixties has initiated a general search for a new integration of the moral, religious, and aesthetic dimensions of life which threatens the psychological credibility of the industrial system.* And it is by no means sure that the political structure will, in the long run, be able to integrate the emerging new values via their devaluation as cultural products on an inflationary market. This is true for two reasons. First, the political system lacks the economic resources, including the technology, to maintain itself with the establishment of an economically more or less stationary welfare system *without the consent and motivation of a majority for rational bureaucratic behavior*. Second, it is, to use Freud's expression, caught by the "return of the repressed" in that the repression of the lack of legitimacy of the prevailing mode of production and distribution produces incalculable costs in terms of a general *psychic pauperization*.

The Crisis of Instrumental Rationality

In the final analysis, cultural systems define man's relationship to nature, to the external nature of his environment as well as the internal nature of his body. In the case of Western civilization, the general trend has been toward a rationalistic interpretation of nature. Prepared in the long history of the demystification of nature in the Judaic-Christian tradition, *the development of the scientific world view provided the bourgeoisie with the instrumental atti-*

---

6. J. Habermas, *Legitimationsprobleme*, p. 110.

tude toward nature which became the basis of its economic achievements. Nature, stripped from all magical projections, became a mere resource for exploitation. While external natural resources were supposed to be unlimited until quite recently, the physiological resources of labor soon became a scarce means which had to be more carefully handled than during the time of such excessive exploitation as, for instance, child labor.

Today it is difficult to comprehend how the culturally dominant classes of the nineteenth century were satisfied with economic progress as the central goal of their worldly existence. One has to recall the miserable material conditions of life before the industrial revolution as well as the long prevailing strength of traditional values and interpretations. The achievements were enormous: for a period of about a hundred and fifty years every generation could experience a substantial increase of material well-being over the past generation. The moment such compensations become scarce the old problems of how to meaningfully interpret the natural boundaries of life become pertinent again.

It is my thesis that with decreasing growth rates in all industrial societies and with increasing psychological pauperization the future function of culture will be mainly a reinterpretation of our relationship to nature. The beginning of this development can be seen today in the growing ecological consciousness, the increasingly public debate on issues of physical and mental health, and the rise of syncretistic religious movements which emphasize a cosmological equilibrium between nature and consciousness. It seems that the dialectics of our *having* a body and *being* a body at the same time has more dimensions than the mere control of muscle power. The psychological misery, which is the cause of the general search for a new basis of authenticity, is the subtle revenge nature has taken against a culture which has celebrated its purely instrumental relation to nature in the great achievements of scientific medicine and the technological creation of artificial environments.

The natural boundaries of human life have been interpreted in terms of instrumental rationality which appeared then to be progressively expanding and partly accidental. The undeniable facts of death and illness have been publicly banned and privately repressed. Birth and death are natural factors alien to our culture, that is, lacking any viable cultural interpretation. Yet, on the television screen, we participate in the horrors of a "body-count" in the Vietnam War, inspect the distorted victims of a plane crash, or even shrink when confronted with pictures of Nazi crimes—struggling in vain for some adequate emotional reaction. In our culture death is identified exclusively with the evil and the alien. We even expect our own death and that of our friends and relatives to be an event alien to our lives, an event which will most likely take place behind the barren walls and hygienic screens of a hospital as the culminating point of a slowly increasing dependency of the body on medical machinery, as the final ecstasy of instrumental rationality. A culture which has no other interpretation of death than that of the end of a span of time is deeply disturbed in its relationship to nature. This is the reason why, outside of the established churches and denominations, a new religiosity is growing in which nature is something to relate to rather than something to control.

In the nineteenth century emphasis was put on man's domination of nature; today it appears that more domination of man over nature also leads to more domination of man over man. This is an awareness which in pretheoretical terms is expressed in the new religiosity, which is always in danger of relapsing into an apotheosis of nature, into a theologically reified concept of nature, as well as into more superficial cultural trends like the inclination to natural food, home cooking, and back-to-the-country attitudes. All these trends are, of course, also part of a tradition of sentimentality beginning at least as early as romanticism, which has always been an undercurrent of bourgeois culture hostile to the emerging technological civilization. Today the question is whether such attitudes can be integrated with and consoled by instrumental rationality given the basis of pressing ecological problems.

The counter-cultural flight from urban civilization provides no solution, either technologically or culturally. In fact, there are certain dangers inherent in the mere celebration of nature as a vital, yet mystical, life force. This could be learned from the fact that a one-dimensional glorification of nature was a consistent element of fascist ideology, an element which, under the presently fashionable nostalgia, has become acceptable again to some factions of the cultural scene. (A case in point, for instance, is the new acceptability of Leni Riefenstahl's movies and photographs with their glorification of physical strength as the ultimate aesthetics of power.) Antibourgeois attitudes in regard to nature always have had this peculiar ambivalence of conservative and progressive connotations. But the relapse of fascism into a mythological interpretation of blood, earth, race, motherhood, and death may serve as a warning against all simplistic attempts to rehabilitate nature and as a reminder that all interpretations of nature have political consequences. There are, however, distinguishing marks: a sure sign of a fascist element in the glorification of nature is that it is always simultaneously accompanied by puritanical attitudes toward sexuality—and that these are frequently preceded by a taste for decadence.

Notwithstanding these dangers, the crisis of instrumental rationality calls for new interpretations of the natural boundaries of human life. However, whether such tendencies in this direction which we can perceive today will have a positive political impact, in view of the high probability of internal and external struggles for redistribution, is rather doubtful in the immediate future. But there is also a direct influence which the new awareness of the problem of our attitude toward nature exerts on the political scene: *political identities seem to be defined more and more in categories of nature.* While political and economic power is more and more monopolized in huge bureaucratic organizations, the need for political identification is left unsatisfied. Of course, the nation-state still plays a considerable role as an object of collective identification even in economically advanced countries. Yet the kind of nationalism typical of the nineteenth and early twentieth centuries has become obsolete in view of the functional interdependencies of the world market—a message which was visibly brought home via television during the recent "oil crisis." This consciousness will continue to grow as worldwide crises call for an international crisis management. And the reaction, the search for political identities which can be *directly* experienced, will also grow. These, however, are typically defined by natural categories: today, in the absence of tribal or clan affiliations or even stable intergenerational family ties, all kinds of "body politics" are flowering: from ethnic separatism to women's liberation, from gay revolution to the organization of age groups and cooperatives of the mentally ill. And since social movements increasingly enter the scene as cultural movements, such phenomena as the "sexual revolution" (more an attitudinal than a behavioral change thus far) and the human potential movements are part of this picture. Somehow the respective conservative and progressive connotations of ascription and achievement seem to have switched their original meaning: progressive groups are more and more minority groups defined by some ethnic or other natural trait while the "square" majorities still try to follow the conservative achievement motivation.

It seems that in the future increasingly a gap will open between the shattered old and the not yet established new values on the one hand and rationally organized, technologically sophisticated national and international power centers on the other. Instrumental rationality penetrates more and more of our formerly autonomous life spheres—and yet does not produce viable and satisfying values and standards for our everyday life, for the organization of face-to-face relationships and the integration of the natural dimension of life. This is a crisis which can also be characterized by a growing separation of the freely floating subjectivity of individuals and the increasingly reified objectivity of the institutions of power. The basic question then is: *Can we institutionalize our continuous cultural reflection* upon our goals and values and especially on our relation to nature *such that it will be of some political consequence?*

Metamorphoses of the Counter-culture

To redefine the goals and values of our society with some political consequence was, of course, the guiding idea of the New Left radicalism of the past decade, notably the student rebellion. It has often been said that the student movement was, in regard to the social background of its participants as well as in its peculiar blending of symbolic and political strategies and goals, basically a bourgeois movement. This is true to the extent that it was a really new movement on the political scene and that the basic goal as well as the strategy was the politicization of everyday life, which is what defines a cultural-revolutionary movement. Leaving aside the question of the social origin of its participants and the psychological reasoning usually employed by those dealing with this question, the student rebellion may be called a bourgeois movement in the sense that its program was derived from various avant-garde movements within the bourgeois culture, notably symbolism, Dadaism, and psychoanalysis. Alfred Willener, in his study of the May 1968 events in France, remarks that:

What we find, then, is . . . a major characteristic, one more important to the current we are studying here than union politicization is, namely the politicization of oneself, since man is both the objective to be attained (a "fragmented" individual being merely a sub-man) and the source of political strength. ... From this point of view all aspects of life, including sexual relations ... would be constantly connected with political decisions. The fusion between spheres that are usually separated is regarded not only as natural, but also as a source of political strength. All emotion, since it involves the whole person, will play a greater part in this political work, conceived as the creation of self and society. And there is no boundary to pass from this activity of creation to culture. One is there, art will pass into daily life, daily life will become an "art of life," and civilization will be transformed.[7]

Doubtless the May 1968 events in France are a special case which in some respects can only be understood in the context of French political tradition and culture. Yet this brief moment when the expressive aspects of modern life won a short-lived victory over the instrumental aspects in torrents of words and imagination was a moment of historical condensation during which the politics of the counter-cultures of other Western societies also came into focus.

As we have seen, these counter-cultures are distinguished from other subcultures, be they retreatist, delinquent, or ethnic-traditional, by a set of values directly opposed to the dominant culture. Subcultures may offer considerable resistance to the dominant culture but they never challenge aggressively its dominant role—as counter-cultures do. Insofar as the New Left never crystallized as a political organization, yet combined radical life styles with political goals and strategies, it can be called a counter-cultural movement. From the very beginning, sociologists have differed widely in their views on this movement: for those to whom the age of instrumental reason and worldwide crisis management has just begun, the New Left with its sensualizing and anarchistic tendencies was a counter-revolutionary force (notably Aron in France, Scheuch in Germany, and Bell and Brzezinski in America). On the other hand, to those who think that the culture of instrumental rationality has come close to its final collapse, the New Left was the vanguard of the new age of communality (notably Revel and Morin in France and Reich and Roszak in America). Obviously, both theories are guided by unproven assumptions about the future course of history. The underlying theory of history is also the reason why most Marxists are ambivalent about the phenomenon. Since the New Left was basically a bourgeois rather

7. A. Willener, *The Action-Image of Society—On Cultural Politicization* (London: Tavistock, 1976), p. 121.

than a proletarian movement, its final collapse did not come as a surprise to them. Yet the movement was definitely leftist in its political visions, and if it incorporated a fair amount of criticism of the bureaucratic socialism in Eastern European countries, such criticism could not easily be disregarded—especially when, in the same year (1968), Russian imperialism wiped out the "Prague Spring" of democratic socialism in the CSSR.

What seems wrong with all theories of this nature is that they tend to measure the New Left against a postulated next stage of Western history instead of understanding it in terms of the previous stages of our history. In this perspective an alternative argument could be pursued: after all, to the extent that the New Left was a cultural radicalism of some political impact, it is the first time since the French Revolution and its successors in 1848 that the bourgeoisie has produced a leftist radical political movement. In my opinion what for a certain time transformed a number of campus revolts into a social and political movement was the renewed attempt to realize the great goals of the French Revolution: liberty, equality, fraternity. To be sure, in all crisis of legitimation in bourgeois society, these values have been revitalized as political goals. The critical antagonistic factions of bourgeois culture have always been occupied with a critique of the nonrealization of these goals. What was new in the sixties, however, was that such a critique could find a much larger social-political basis, thanks to the industrial production of symbols and life styles as well as the ever increasing number of young people who spend a prolonged adolescence in the extended educational institutions. Also new was the special emphasis on fraternity and communality while simultaneously insisting on the full realization of liberty and equality.

To understand this emphasis, it is important to note that the three goals of the French Revolution have had a different historical fate—in reality as well as in the minds of people. As a political goal liberty no longer seems to be the basic issue since the establishment of democratic civil rights, the codification of civil law, and the institution of relative freedom of job choices. What matters is not to what extent these developments are a political reality, but to what extent people are no longer sufficiently dissatisfied to become susceptible to political mobilization over this issue. In fact the majority of the population display a remarkable amount of apathy toward issues of liberty—with the racial problem in America being the exception rather than the rule.

Although equality has not been achieved and, on the contrary, the gap between the rich and the poor has slightly increased over the past fifty years in capitalist countries (with national variations), this inequality could be effectively legitimized by the ever growing per capita income. State interventionism and public crisis management were seen as dealing effectively with the danger of a major economic catastrophe. The fact that the Great Depression of the thirties was overcome by the institution of war economies seems to have escaped the general public. However, the lack of economic equality will again become a consciously experienced problem for the masses if the limits of growth continue to threaten the classical legitimation of capitalist society. This can be seen already in the new intensification of the class struggle in England, France, and Italy.

What is surprising today is the emphasis on fraternity, that third goal of the bourgeois revolution which has always been overshadowed by the issues of liberty and equality because of the vagueness of its political content. Fraternity was originally seen as either a byproduct of the achievement of the other two goals or as the necessary emotional bond between the revolutionaries during the time of their struggles. Like equality, fraternity became a political slogan of the proletariat after the victory of the bourgeoisie. The early socialists as well as the later social-democrats and communists called each other "comrade" or "Genosse," and the general idea of fraternity was transformed into a norm of solidarity which finally degenerated into an effective instrument of organizational control. However, fraternity as a goal which would finally revolutionize everyday life was ridiculed by the socialist movement and banned as a utopian idea.

It was not until the student movement erupted that the idea of fraternity was again formulated as an immediate political goal. Since this goal can only be realized by the complete politicization of everyday life, its emphasis is the core of cultural radicalism. While freedom and equality appear to be realizable on the level of political institutions, the idea of brotherhood and communality remains a preserve of the counter-culture. It is the focus on this idea which produces the apparent inability of cultural-revolutionary movements to create new institutions. Such movements do not work through institutional procedures but through spontaneous actions. Once institutionalized they lose their cultural-revolutionary impulse and can no longer compete with the traditional political organizations fighting for freedom and equality. Confronted with the enormous complexity of modern political and administrative systems and in the absence of feasible institutional alternatives, the spontaneous attempt to realize the goal of fraternity has had a certain unrealistic if refreshing naïveté. The political function of counter-cultural movements is rather the continuous politicization of the crisis of legitimacy or, in their own terminology, the raising of consciousness.

The problem, then, seems to be one of the goal itself. In the utopian reasoning of the nineteenth century, the physiocratic tradition was still alive: men are essentially good and would become brothers once they had become free and equal. In fact, nobody has more eloquently and enthusiastically expressed this idea than the young Marx himself. Today, after the experience of the mass murders and world wars of the twentieth century, we have become more skeptical. The brutality of the socioeconomic systems and the respective political ideologies have undermined utopian reasoning on the *practical* level. On a *theoretical* level, however, it has been destroyed by Darwin and Freud: the theory of natural selection could hardly be reconciled with the idea of fraternity; and the pessimistic proposition of Freud that there can be no culture and hence no social organization without repression or at least culturally patterned sublimation of libido has been a death blow to any romantic idea of brotherhood. In his *Civilization and Its Discontents* Freud expressly points to the limits of the socialist utopia:

> In abolishing private property we deprive the human love of aggression of one of its instruments, certainly a strong one, though certainly not the strongest; but we have in no way altered the differences in power and influence which are misused by aggressiveness nor have we altered anything in its nature. Aggressiveness was not created by property . . . it forms the basis of every relation of affection or love among people. . . . If we do away with personal rights over material wealth, there still remain prerogatives in the field of sexual relationships, which are bound to become the source of the strongest dislike and the most violent hostility among men who in other respects are on equal footing. If we were to remove this factor, too, by allowing complete freedom of sexual life and thus abolishing the family . . . we cannot, it is true, easily foresee what new paths the development of civilization could take; but one thing we can expect, and that is that this indestructable feature of human nature will follow it there.[8]

8. S. Freud, *Civilization and Its Discontents* (New York: Norton, 1962), pp. 60-61.

Thus, both Darwin and Freud have redefined the political problem of fraternity as a problem of nature: it is no longer property, which could be abolished, that is the real impediment to fraternity but rather aggression, which at best can be domesticated. Nature has become a political problem.

That Freud's theory of culture should not have been developed into a more optimistic philosophy of modern civilization is not so surprising in view of the lack of institutional alternatives to the institutionalized instrumental rationality. It should be noted that, on the contrary, *the utopias of our time* are in direct opposition to Darwin and Freud. Against Darwin a number of biologists and philosophers of history have maintained that the evolution of man will soon reach a stage of cerebralization in which the cycles of culture will come to an end (Arnold Toynbee and Alfred Weber) and the struggles for survival will be rationally controlled (Teilhard de Chardin and Skinner). Against Freud (and quoting him against himself) Freudo-Marxists (Wilhelm Reich and Erich Fromm) and Freudo-Hegelians (Herbert Marcuse and Norman O. Brown) have rejected the theory of the death instinct and claimed the possibility of a society based on the pleasure principle. During the twenties the "Sex-Pol" movement in Germany tried to combine a revolutionary theory of class consciousness with a psychoanalytic theory of genitality. Later during the fifties and early sixties, Marcuse and Brown reversed the Freudian theory of the stages of sexual development in the child so that now the earliest stage, the "polymorphous-perverse" child, appears to be the hidden goal of all history. As Norman O. Brown has written in his *Life Against Death:*

The abolition of repression would abolish the unnatural concentration of libido in certain particular bodily organs, concentration engineered by the negativity of the morbid death instinct, and constituting the bodily base of the neurotic character disorder: in the human ego. . . . The human body would become polymorphously perverse, delighting in that full life of all the body which it now fears.[9]

Thus, the utopias of our time seem to point in two different yet related directions: the *sensualization of reason* and the *spiritualization of nature.*

These ideas have had a considerable impact on the cultural radi-

9. Norman O. Brown, *Life Against Death: The Psychoanalytical Meaning of History* (Middletown, Conn: Wesleyan University Press, 1959), p. 308.

calism of today. Since the political failure of the student movement has become apparent, the political and the cultural elements of the New Left have disintegrated. Those still politically active have formed groups, some of which have gone into an anarchistic underground, while all of them demonstrate a certain sectarianism. Chiliastic movements which have failed do not usually disappear, but change into a more dogmatic body of a cognitive minority which must maintain its belief system against the continuous challenge of the majority's world view with the help of rituals and a group-enforced selective perception of reality. In its great majority, however, the counter-culture has reacted to its political failure by a shift of emphasis from the transformation of society to the transformation of the self. Jerry Rubin, one of the well-known leaders of the American student movement, has recently described this shift in his personal experience which seems to me rather typical:

We, the children of America, had begun to make our own history. Then, suddenly, poof! It all disappeared, almost overnight. Our 1960 dreams of apocalyptic and sudden revolution vanished apocalyptically and suddenly. We had moved with such energy to the brink of life and death itself, seen ourselves beaten in the streets and jailed, that almost as of a single mind, the recognition came upon us that we are not ready now to make the final plunge. . . . Marytrs die and Myths crumble. I wanted to live—and to love. Do the things I never had time to do in the demonstration-packed Sixties. Like discover myself. Meditate. The first realization I made was that I have a body. . . . If the revolution is going to be a process, I am a process, too.[10]

This shift of emphasis is oriented along the two lines of utopian thought: the sensualization of reason was the declared goal of the anti-authoritarian movement and is still the guideline of behavior for all those who participate in the counter-cultural milieu or sympathize with it. At the same time, however, the hedonism of the counter-culture has reinforced the identity crisis typical of a prolonged adolescence. The ensuing search for identity has led initially to a concentration on one's own personal growth physically and psychologically and secondly to a new religiosity. The total transformation of the self can only be achieved by going beyond the sensualization of reason to the spiritualization of (one's own) nature.

However, on the path into one's own self, which now is no

10. Jerry Rubin in an interview in *Harper's* (May 1974).

longer the psychoanalytic path through the history of the ego but rather the freeing of a natural, authentic nucleus of one's personality in the here and now, the idea and maybe the praxis of fraternity is lost again. This tendency can be traced in the psychology of Abraham Maslow and Carl Rogers and the development of the Encounter Movement initiated by them. To a large extent Encounter is simply an acting-out of aggressions against persons to whom one has no personal or social commitment. If the carthartic effect which is sought in this procedure does not satisfy the troubled participant in his search for authenticity, his next step is frequently toward mystical experiences, the nature of which is, by definition, difficult to communicate. Seminal to the psychology of Maslow and Rogers is the idea that human beings have a "real self," an "inner nature," which in healthy persons resists all pressures of social roles. Socialization is seen only as a distortion of this originally positive nature of man, which should now be stripped of all internalized adjustments to society. Hence in this psychology other people exist to repress one's own need for self-realization or to refuse the necessary support and love for this process. Freud's theory of culture is anathema. Change can only come from within because deep in our selves we are already what we want to become. Spontaneity must be emphasized because the authentic ego can only be freed from external constraints in direct self-actualization. If such self-realization becomes a constraint to our fellowmen, this may be ignored, for everybody can lovingly bear the existence of other human beings once he has realized his own potential to "grow." The heavenly goal of liberation lies buried in ourselves. In the final analysis each of us is God.

In many variations, some of them more primitive, some more sophisticated, this "humanistic psychology" is characteristic of the present world view of the counter-culture and, to a lesser degree, of many middle-class people in America and increasingly in Europe, too. What is irritating in the "Human Potential Movement" with its religious overtones is neither its sensualizing nor its spiritualizing tendencies, but rather that it seems unintentionally to carry Western individualism to its extreme. This loss of sociability in the search for authenticity can be even better detected in some of the more extreme formulations of anti-psychiatry, says Ronald D. Laing:

True sanity entails in one way or another the dissolution of the normal ego, that false self completely adjusted to our alienated social reality and the emergence of the inner archetypical mediators of divine power, and through this death a rebirth, and the eventual reestablishment of a new kind of ego-functioning, the ego now being the servant of the divine, no longer its betrayer.[11]

And David Cooper adds:

Madness has in our age become some sort of lost truth. Madness . . . is a way of seizing in extremis the racinating groundwork of the truth that underlies our more specific realization of what we are about. . . . Madness, for instance, is a matter of voicing that I am (or you are) Christ.[12]

The idea that madness is the authentic state of truth is, in view of its popularity among leftist intellectuals, one of the more astounding ideas of our culture. And it is as ambivalent an idea as the counter-culture is an ambivalent social phenomenon. For, as Lionel Trilling has pointed out,[13] on the one hand it presupposes that madness is an attempt to cope with an intolerable social situation. Whether the attempt is successful or not, the illness is itself an act of criticism. On the other hand, however, it also presupposes that madness is a negation of the limiting conditions of life, and hence of society as a whole, a form of personal existence in which autonomy is guaranteed by self-sufficiency. If the authentic state of being human is madness, such a state is not of this world; for this world is a social world, and madness is the total negation of society, the total rejection of all institutionalizations. In fact, it turns out that madness is the modality of the authentic self if authenticity is to mean a state beyond all socialization.

Thus present-day radicalism moves into a direction which once again leaves out the problem of fraternity and thus becomes depoliticized. Might Norman O. Brown be right in the end with his metapsychological suggestion that the society of brothers will disintegrate after the murder of the father, that the sons always begin to quarrel again over the legacy of the father and will not find peace unless they create a new, spiritual father for themselves?[14] Can there be no solidarity except in the face of a task, an emergency, a commitment, even an enemy? Can there be no reconcili-

11. R. D. Laing, *The Bird of Paradise* (London, 1967), p. 119. Quoted from L. Trilling, *Sincerity and Authenticity* (Cambridge: Harvard University Press, 1971).
12. D. Cooper, Introduction to M. Foucault, *Madness and Society*, quoted from L. Trilling, *Sincerity and Authenticity*.
13. Lionell Trilling, *Sincerity and Authenticity*, pp. 167-71.
14. Norman O. Brown, *Love's Body* (New York: Vintage Books, 1966).

ation between nature and society except on the level of the polymorphous-perverse sensuality which Norman O. Brown advocates?

We have to reformulate Freud's theory of civilization on the basis of Marcuse's attempt to distinguish between repressive, that is, unnecessary, and nonrepressive forms of internalization and between aggressive and creative forms of sublimation. There is no way back to a *Gemeinschaft* of children; we must become a *Gesellschaft* of adults. The counter-culture will lose all political dimension if it does not try to overcome the identity crisis in some mode of solidarity, if it does not concentrate on the legitimacy crisis of the political system and seek to suggest and create alternative institutions and alternative values for this society. Otherwise the future might be some IBM-type of economic and political control over a mystified population escaping into occultism. The counter-culture is merely the progressive part of the established culture. Culture and counter-culture are not seperate entities but antagonistic elements of the same phenomenon, and they depend upon each other. Their relationship is a dialectical one in that their mutual negation of each other may have historical results of an unexpected nature. If the counter-culture is in constant danger of being swallowed up by the industrialized bourgeois culture, it is also in constant danger of over-evaluating the culturally repressed and of regressing into a romantic and reactionary individualism. At the present the latter danger appears to be prevailing.

The anti-social attitude of such individualism is rooted in the idea that there is a naked "authentic" self which, devoid of all social roles, can exist in direct relation to some cosmic energy. While such a direct contact with a "separate reality" (Castaneda) may be felt in the mystical experience of ego-dissolution, be this experience of "consciousness expansion" drug-induced or reached by some form of meditation, in the mundane world of our everyday experience there can be no form of human existence outside the identifications with something and somebody. Insofar as man exists only in his social roles, human identity is always an embodiment, an incarnation maybe, of some socially shared value standards, ideas, and group affiliations. We may take role-distance, we may challenge, interpret, modify, even reject the roles and identities which are cuturally imposed on us—but only by making a choice, by choosing some other form of being what we already are and yet can never be beyond some incorporation. "We know from Greek mythology that Proteus was able to change his shape with relative ease—from wild boar to lion to dragon to fire to flood. But what he did find difficult, and would not do unless seized and chained, was to commit himself to a single form, the form most his own, and carry out his function of prophecy. We may say the same of protean man, but we must keep in mind his possibilities as well as his difficulties."[15] Paradoxically, today the possibility for some may be to stop by their own choice and look beyond our normal realm of experience because modern man is compelled to continually adjust himself to the changes of his social and natural environment and thus learns more than ever to take on many different shapes in the course of his life.

Yet to stop at some authentic state of oneself can only lead back to a reflection upon our usual disguises. As a result a new awareness of our sociability, a new sincerity toward our social roles, may still emerge. The point is, as Marshall Berman has remarked, that "our search for authenticity cannot bypass politics, or else politics will make us inauthentic."[16] Today the New Left seems to be dead. It has given way to a depoliticized counter-culture which has, however, as yet not lost its identity by merging with the general youth subculture. In fact, while the public is no longer excited by counter-cultural life styles and hence the media have lost all interest, many experiments of alternative life styles are still carried out: the communal movement, for instance, has actually grown during the early seventies and the Women's Liberation Movement is more popular than ever before. Even more important than this ongoing practical search for new personal and communal identities is the impact the New Left has made on the attitudes of many fractions of the middle classes: there is a new and growing skepticism toward the benefits of instrumental rationality and an increasing inclination toward a reinterpretation of the natural conditions of human life.

The participants, and many observers, of the radicalism of the sixties have gone through an extensive learning experience which will have a lasting effect. New cultural ideas usually emerge in an overstated, sectarian form. When during sudden "moments of madness"[17] the expressive aspects of a culture gain political visibil-

---

15. Robert Jay Lifton, "Protean Man," *Partisan Review* 35 (1968): 17.
16. Marshall Berman, *The Politics of Authenticity—Radical Individualism and the Emergence of Modern Society* (New York: Atheneum, 1970).
17. Aristide Zolberg, "Moments of Madness," in I. Katznelson (ed.), *The Politics and Society Reader* (New York: McKay, 1974), pp. 232-56.

ity, the result is a growing awareness of the larger population toward the dominant forms of control and political organization as well as toward their own repressed needs. Last but not least, one of the results of the political radicalism of the sixties has been a higher degree of participation in single-issue movements and other kinds of grass-roots politics as well as a new availability of formulated and experienced alternatives to the technocratic standards of political life.

Sub-structure and Super-structure Revisited

An increasing number of social scientists would disagree with the above analysis of the counter-culture. They believe that cultural radicalism is a negligible factor because the real problems of the world today appear to be of a demographic, economic, and administrative nature. Since the Club of Rome publicized the limits of growth, since the oil crisis has initiated a shift of power from the industrial countries to the Third World, and since the structural crisis of the world economic system has become apparent, many leading social theorists have fallen prey to an almost apocalyptic mood. Such different authors as Daniel Bell, Herman Kahn, and Robert Heilbronner in America and Knut Borchardt, Konrad Lorenz, and Niklas Luhmann in Germany have claimed *the necessity of more authority and stronger state control* in order to make the public accept the constraints of the stationary welfare economy dictated by the end of growth.

To some extent the analysis on which this prescription is based is undeniably true and is even shared by Marxists for whom the future belongs to the proletariat rather than the technocratic elites. The free market has lost much of its importance as a regulatory mechanism of the economy. The development of state interventionism and the growth of internationally operating corporations have increased the power of political administrations and corporate bureaucracies. Struggles for a redistribution of the surplus are nationally and internationally increasing as economic growth rates shrink and the structural crisis of the forces of production worsens.

As demographic pressure mounts and ecological developments pose planetary problems, international crisis management, supported by the development of new technologies, is pertinent. The conclusions to be drawn from this analysis, however, are far from clear. Theorists of the "post-industrial" society share with dogmatic Marxists a deterministic notion of historical development and a simplistic notion of man as being only motivated by his material needs. But there is no automatic development in history. History is made by people and people tend to act and react relative to the level of their individual and communal autonomy. Once we take the cultural dimension of social life seriously and see man not only as the animal which transforms nature into the means of his material subsistence but also as the creator of his own symbolic environments and situational definitions, a different picture emerges. J. Habermas has pointed out that if more centralized power is needed to manage the "steering problems of late capitalism,"[18] such power also calls for stronger legitimations. As we have seen, however, such legitimations are increasingly missing.

Using a simplified model of the structure of modern society, it can be said that today we experience a sharp hiatus between the sphere of economic and scientific-technological activity on the one hand, and the sphere of personal life and interaction on the other. While, to use Max Weber's distinction, the first is characterized by instrumental rationality; the second is the sphere of value rationality. Psychologically the separation of these two spheres of social life is experienced as alienation and anomie at the same time. In the sphere of material reproduction the lack of self-determination and the repression of affectivity is experienced as alienation; in the privatized sphere of one's personal relationships, symbolizations, and recreations, the lack of guiding value standards, established modes of interpretation, and institutionalized rituals of interaction is experienced as anomie. While some people identify more with the sphere of instrumental rationality and others try to organize their lives in a more privately creative and self-determined way, for most of us the dichotomy goes right through our own role-budget and results in a split of our personalities between public and private role identities.

Public institutions try to mediate between these two spheres. The state not only tries to counter the irregularities of the eco-

18. J. Habermas, *Legitimationsprobleme*.

sphere of instrumental rationality (alienation)

corporate activities

sphere of political conflicts — welfare institu- tions

quest for participation

everyday life experiences

sphere of value rationality (anomie)

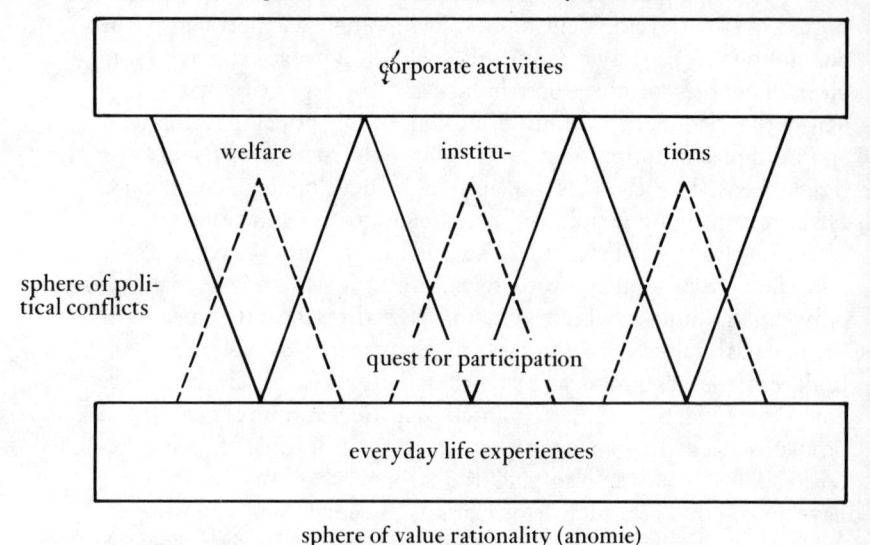

Figure 3-1. Values and Society.

nomic market but also attempts to secure mass loyalty by institutionalizing the welfare system as broadly as possible: health, education, control, and correction of deviants, material security for the young and the old, mandatory insurance system, and so forth. Much of the political struggles and issues of today can be explained by a structural antagonism between these two tasks of the state in capitalism: the political system continuously faces the problem of finding a compromise between the growth and profit orientation of the corporate economy and the quantitative and qualitative material needs of the population.

To what extent the state tends to satisfy the latter depends on the degree to which discontent can be effectively organized and articulated. This is where the differential history of working-class movements and other forms of organized protest in different countries is a determining factor. However, once a certain level of institutionalization of welfare systems has been reached a peculiar dialectic begins to work: it seems that people tend more and more to *claim the satisfaction of their material needs as civil rights,* that is, as a constitutionally guaranteed (and legally specified) status. Thus, the nature of political conflict changes: social classes and status groups are no longer trying to "take over the system," to attain directly the power of the state, but instead push for institutionalization and legalization of the statuses for which they aspire. On the psychological level this corresponds with the spread of an oral demand attitude toward all public and semipublic institutions—a projection of the insecurity felt on the level of private human relations (to some extent due to necessarily deficient socialization procedures) to the level of public administration.

Yet there is another side to this dialectic: since the administrations, which are identified as status- and security-providing agencies, are also experienced as alienating because of the indiscriminate formal rationality of their bureaucracies, a need for more autonomy and self-determination arises which is expressed in the quest for participation. Here, then, is the other side of political conflicts today: the quest for the institutionalization of the aspired-for status leads to the quest for participation in the *process* of institutionalization. Formerly the limits of the public articulation of needs and of political action were identical with the class barriers—a situation which has made political economy the key for explaining the political structure. Today, the "horizontal discrepancies" (Claus Offe) between different status groups and aggregates of roles have an increasing importance in political conflicts, and even class relations are more and more often expressed in terms of qualitative changes and participatory goals. This situation can no longer be explained without the help of categories from social psychology and the sociology of culture.

History is not an autonomous process of evolution but the result of the struggles of people looking for stability of their symbolic and emotional reality as well as the security of the satisfaction of their material needs. Future prospects depend as much on how people define their needs and problems and how they experience the functions and dysfunctions of economic and bureaucratic management as on the system's problems themselves. In fact, while J. Habermas at least insists on the existence and possible extension of people's participation at the cognitive level of communication and discourse, the prophets of the "technotronic age" seem to reduce human beings to the status of elements of systems. And even Habermas's theory of the evolution of communicative competence does not take into account the physical and emotional dimensions of human experience and human action.

Issues and Prospects

It is, then, not easy to come to a conclusion about what the next steps in the development of Western societies will be. We can, however, make an attempt to describe the main issues of our present situation as well as to point out some contemporary cultural developments which will, in all probability, have a considerable impact on the formation of our near future.

It may indeed be said that the main political issue of industrial societies today is that of fraternity. In regard to the growing gap between the professional world of corporate activities and the private worlds of everyday activities, this issue becomes translated into the *conflict between bureaucratic administration and personal participation*. It is by no means clear that bureaucratic and technological management will win in this conflict simply because it seems that instrumental rationality is the best way to handle problems with some promise of positive results. The first objection to this view has been dealt with extensively by the literature on technocratic influences on government politics. It is that all too frequently scientific-technological solutions have produced quite unexpected and not always welcome results (if they were not downright counter-effective), and in addition have employed dubious value standards, as in the case of scientific advice in the Vietnam War. In other words instrumental rationality can be dysfunctional due to sheer one-dimensionality of what is quantifiable and computerizable. Where this is clouded by a smokescreen of scientistic jargon, science and technology indeed become an ideology, as J. Habermas has argued.

Secondly, solutions worked out by crisis management of centralized power agencies may and will be frequently rejected by people subject to such decisions, either because they simply feel that the solutions offered are not the most practical ones or because they feel estranged by their lack of participation in them and by being forced to undergo further repression of emotional needs. Such rejections can take very different forms which are hard to predict. They may vary from private retreatism to public rebellion, from sabotage to corruption to civil disorder, from passive resistance within the institutions to active revolution outside the institutions. No special political insight is necessary for such rejections to develop—though political consciousness usually helps to further more active forms of resistance.

Structurally the conflict of bureaucracy versus participation takes place mainly in three problem areas. First, wherever the *uncontrolled, seemingly "natural" development of science, technology, and economy* threatens comparatively stable natural and symbolic environments of people and their subjectively experienced quality of life, they will tend to react with organized resistance and, to some extent, with the demand for participation in the planning process. As yet such resistance has mainly occurred in the form of single-issue movements against polluting industries and the like. The future may well see an extension of such resistance to the area of legal penetrations of private life (witnessed in the movements for the legalization of abortion and pornography) and also more active forms of counter-penetration of institutions. Also, the question of limiting research and development in certain fields of science will probably gain momentum. The idea that what can be made should be made, the very image of man as essentially *homo faber*, has lost much of the popularity it has enjoyed over the past one hundred and fifty years.

The second problem area of potential conflict is the *standard of efficiency in job performance*. Here, it must first be noted that the Protestant Ethic today works mainly as an ideology masking interests in profit and intensive exploitation of labor. In fact, those theories which tend to hold the counter-culture responsible for a general decline in standards of efficiency have a certain paranoic flavor: radical changes in life styles can well be combined with a high working morale, *provided* the individuals involved retain some feeling of meaningfulness and participation in the work organization. Thus many of today's struggles of the working class are focused on qualitative changes in the work situation rather than on a higher share in the surplus. In the middle classes the mechanization and bureaucratization of much white-collar and even professional work (and education) has changed the traditional value orientation toward work and has urged many resisters to withdraw to marginal economic statuses.

The issues in this problem area are twofold: on the one hand, a whole new organization of work is at stake; on the other hand, the distribution of work (including such questions as part-time jobs with the same level of fringe benefits as full-time jobs, and vocational reeducation programs) will have to be restructured. The reason for the latter is that the quest for more meaningful work will push for further automation of monotonous work; this, however, together with the tendency of corporations to export jobs to cheaper labor markets in the Third World, creates more unemployment. Both problems—the organization and the distribution of work—are, of course, severe challenges to the capitalist system which it will have difficulties to meet. Hence it seems to be a safe prediction that struggles over these issues will continue and probably increase for a long time to come.

A third problem area in which the conflict of bureaucracy versus participation crystallizes is the question of *centralization as opposed to decentralization of decision-making processes*. This problem has not yet been dealt with sufficiently by sociologists; indeed, few have even recognized the problem. The issue here cannot be considered in terms of the sociology of formal organizations with its "staff" and "line" models. The problem is rather which problem areas are best handled by large bureaucratic organizations and which would be better handled by small, possibly informal, groups on a local level. At present a peculiarly paradoxical situation has emerged: bureaucracies are penetrating our formerly autonomous life spheres to an ever increasing degree, yet the centers of power seem to be unable to deal with the growing dysfunctional side effects of technology and bureaucracy. As Henry Lebfevre sees it: "Ce qui s'annonce c'est une crise de la reproduction des rapports de production, au premier plan la défaillance des centres et des centralités."[19] In this situation the demand for local and group autonomy will probably grow. While in the areas of the economy, trade, traffic system, pollution control, social security, and to some extent communication systems and urban planning, probably *more* centralization is needed; there are also many important areas where the power to make decisions should be as diversified as possible. Not only cultural activities, the media, and problems of urban environment but also care for the young and old, the sick and deviant, that is, the areas of socialization and rehabilitation, as well as presumably the whole system of education could be qualitatively better organized by decentralized agencies with a high degree of self-determination and voluntary participation. In America this issue is more apparent because it is not so long since

19. Henri Lebfevre, *La survie du capitalisme* (Paris: Éditions Anthropos, 1973), p. 163.

local communities were the centers of power and because a strong tradition of voluntary associations is still very much alive. In Europe and especially in France and Germany, the tradition tends to be one of leaving things to state administration. Both traditions, however, are equally important once each is related to those problem areas to which it best applies. In any event it is clear that questions of centralization versus decentralization will get more attention in the future as the ineffectuality of some centralized bureaucracies as well as the quest for participation become more visible.

Turning now to such cultural movements and scientific-technological developments as can be observed today, some tendencies may be pointed out which will, in my opinion, strongly influence the nature of the cultural crisis in the future. I begin with three changes in cultural attitudes which will presumably develop their full impact only in the coming years.

First, there is a *growing tendency to state claims on the nature of one's own body and the nature of the environment in political terms*. During recent years, in sharp contrast to the increasing international monopolization of power, the political importance of *regionalism* has increased all over the world. And it has been more and more difficult for the power centers to control these movements. Furthermore, and in some cases related to the regionalism, there is the emergence of what has been called the *new ethnicity*. Racial and ethnic groups, sometimes overlapping with religious groups, have developed a new feeling of identity, sometimes leading to political separatism, more often however merely adding to the cultural diversity of life styles and symbolic traditions. Yet, these additions are not gained without conflict: ethnic groups have to fight for a status in and a share of the industrial cultural market.

Most important, there is the *Women's Liberation Movement*. No movement has better survived the general decline of the radicalism of the sixties; the feminist movement is more popular than ever and is now (in America) gradually spreading into the working class. The movement is particularly strong and successful in Scandinavia and the United States where it has succeeded in making the cause of equal chance for women in the labor market a government policy and in changing sexual attitudes to the extent that the ability to sexually satisfy women has become the second most important property of the ideal male for both sexes.[20] In spite of re-

---

20. See D. Yankelovich, *The New Morality*, p. 39.

sistances and backlashes, it is likely that this development will carry over to other countries. On the other hand, the vanguard of the movement in the middle classes in certain metropolitan areas seems to have reached an impasse. There appears to be a growing awareness that complete integration of women into the labor market only serves to put women under the same pressures as those which the bread-winning husbands have always borne. In fact, the ideal of the "symmetrical family,"[21] where both husband and wife equally share all job, household, and child care obligations, can only be fully realized under the condition of a radical change of our relations of production. In addition, an equal share of work inside and outside the home by both partners in a marriage would require that public agencies take care of the children. And this, it seems to me, will be the wall which will stop the present momentum of the feminist movement. But if, after many battles, it should eventually lose some of its present vitality, it will surely be revived in the future to continue its course on another plane. The emancipation of women is not a new development; it has a long history of which the recent wave of feminist radicalism is only one phase, and there is no reason to assume that this history will soon come to an end.

It is, of course, difficult to anticipate the next stage of the women's movement. However, seen in connection with the other changes discussed here, the *most likely* course it will take is to further radicalize the claim of sole control over the female body and to emphasize the sole right to define femininity. This means that after some amount of professional equality has been attained, women may begin to claim their procreative functions not only negatively, as in the case for the legalization of abortion, but also positively in terms of motherhood. In view of the increasing insecurity and anomie of marriage relationships, it seems in fact almost inevitable that women will reemphasize motherhood and control over the socialization of their children. This may lead to political conflicts over public education as well as to family conflicts between husbands and wives. It may well be that the future of the family belongs to the mother-child dyad, sanctioned by cultural attitudes *and* social securities, and with a male partner (who may or may not be the father) occasionally participating. If this is too strong an image, it should be mentioned that in some fractions of the young middle classes of those living as communes in metropolitan

21. P. Willmott and M. Young, *The Symmetrical Family* (New York: Pantheon, 1973).

areas, this is already a reality. And as a general tendency it may not be a bad one: if, as E. Erikson maintains, "women, in all of Mankind's existence, have learned to respond to the measure of the developing child, to the measure of the child in the adult, and to the measure of manageable communalities within wider communities,"[22] in our culture this may be very much what is missing. Such an attitude could well constitute the core of a new level of feminist consciousness. The danger will be, of course, that the limiting conditions of the socioeconomic system will produce again a feminist battle against "male chauvinism" instead of a joint effort of both sexes to change these conditions. What E. Erikson claims to be a function of women should really be a concern of men as well.

A second change in cultural attitudes is the increasing tendency toward a *new religiosity*. Since this attitude is connected with a mistrust of institutions and authorities, it finds a variety of expressions outside the established churches and denominations. These established churches are increasingly identified with conservative and, worse, bureaucratic forces. A multitude of pentecostal and Eastern religious movements have sprung into existence. But these dedicated movements will probably remain a reservoir for a minority among the young who seek the kind of leadership usually to be found in the charisma of religious leaders. Such movements are only the tip of the iceberg: nobody can tell today how many people are considerably affected by more or less intensive individual religious experiences. Nevertheless, the popularity of religious products on the cultural market may serve as an indication. The enormous extent to which the population makes use of astrological and other occult services is probably no more than a superficial symptom of their alienation. The real change which can be observed is rather toward a spiritualization of nature which begins with a new concern with one's own body. Again the growing popularity of various types of yoga is only an indication. Many different religious ideas and experiences are flowering today. Psychedelic drugs are an indicator of this as is meditation, new forms of popular music, a new awareness of the aesthetic beauty of nature, and a new preoccupation with the problem of death and dying.

What the synthesis of all these trends could be is impossible to say. One common denominator seems to be, however, that many of these experiences, if they can be called religious at all, are mys-

22. E. Erikson, *Life History and the Historical Moment* (New York: Norton, 1975), pp. 123-24.

tical in character. And the problem with mysticism is that it resists institutionalization because of the highly individual character of the experience. Yet, this individualization of religion may exactly be the form most religiosity takes in the future, not in the sense of religion as a private affair but as an acceptable form of an intense personal experience which may or may not be shared with a few others.

That such a development would not leave the established churches untouched need not be pointed out in detail. The process of erosion of theological authority is clearly visible all over the world and is another aspect of the growing hostility toward large bureaucratic and hierarchically structured organizations. This process cannot be stopped by those who try to make the churches more mundane than their clientele really wants in order to preserve its attractiveness. Whether it can be stopped by more sober conservatives, who want to preserve the church as the exclusive institution for the experience of the transcendental, is equally doubtful. The churches are tied to the world of business and politics and this connection is an easy and legitimate prey to the criticism of instrumental rationality. Hence, the form of traditional religion most likely to survive is the small nonhierarchical denomination which is based on the equal participation of believers.

A third change in cultural attitudes should briefly be mentioned: *the loss of historical consciousness*. Seen from a larger historical perspective, this does not seem to be unusual. In fact, during most of mankind's history neither the idea of an evolutionary progress, or at least process, was known nor was the notion that man could be the master of his own historical fate. These ideas have gradually emerged in the theological and philosophical development of the Western world. This development reached its peak during the nineteenth century in the belief in progress. It has given way now to an increasingly skeptical mood toward the future and a growing disinterest in the past, except as a sourcebook for very modern mythologies and imageries. These tendencies have been characteristic of much of the intellectual vanguard during this century, but they have now caught on with the larger population. In addition, the strong emphasis on the present as against the past and the future is new today. This is characteristic of the new religiosity as much as of the preoccupation with nature. The intense experience of the present is more highly evaluated than are memories and guilts from the past and plans and sorrows for the future. This mood takes on many forms and expressions, sometimes irresponsible, but more often as a pleasurable liberation from preoccupations which are considered to be side-tracking from the real issue: to be alive here and now, to enjoy it, and to take care of whatever is of immediate concern. This is a dimension of modern intellectual life, too, which still has to be traced through philosophy and art, from structuralism to the yin-yang imagery. But it is also a dimension which is of increasing importance outside intellectual fashion. Since most people have achieved a comparatively satisfactory material standard of life which they claim as their natural right, they now become intensely concerned with their present, meaning the maintenance and enjoyment of their status. But it also means the feasibility of an exploration of sensual and spiritual dimensions of life which they formerly had no time and knowledge to experience.

It seems to me that the combined effect of these changes in cultural attitudes will be that people will find much more compensation for the loss of the doubtful benefits of more material wealth for private consumption than the misanthropic theories of the necessity for more authoritarian control would have it. The concern with the present, the exploration of a new religious consciousness, and the new experiences of one's physical identity will all eventually contribute to the satisfaction of needs as yet unsatisfied. The counter-culture is of importance because some of its adherents have already tried radically to readjust their life styles to the new values. As Judson Jerome writes in one of the few good studies on the communal movement, the "basic economic discovery of the new culture is not of means to increase property, but to reassess needs. I call it the revolution of alternative rewards: the point is not to do without, but to learn to delight in making do. . . . Renunciation is not much involved in the voluntary poverty of the new culture, because few of its adherents think of themselves as giving up anything. Rather they are moving gladly toward gratifications incalculable in the cash nexus . . . [because they feel] the most pinching poverty is of acceptance, recognition, love, respect, status."[23] Of course, I do not think that such radical life styles will prevail generally even in the middle classes. But attitudes which as yet are stated explicitly only in the counter-culture will penetrate large sections of the population in modified terms and will to a certain extent serve as a compensation for the private limits of growth

23. J. Jerome, *Families of Eden*.

and also function as an incentive for qualitative changes in the sphere of work.

This conclusion is further corroborated by a brief look at certain recent scientific and technological developments which may gain a strong influence on cultural life in the immediate future. Three such developments should be mentioned: recent trends in the biological sciences, in communication technology, and in mind research. In *biology* something like a revolutionary development is taking place. Genetic engineering with all its potential horrors and benefits has come into immediate reach and begins to pose unprecedented moral and political questions. Should genetic research be continued at all? Can it be controlled and, maybe, partially stopped? Who will decide, and according to what ethical standards, on the use of banks for artificial insemination; on the possibility of changing genetic structures in human beings, as for instance in case of inherited illness; on the possibility of raising a fetus in an artificial laboratory uterus; and how can the abuse of such possibilities be checked?[24] The heated debates over the issue of legalizing abortion and actual changes of behavior caused by the availability of birth control pills give us an idea about the future moral conflicts and moral changes which the results of genetic research will cause.

Most likely the radical factions of the feminist movement of the next generation will hotly reject the idea of being biologically engineered and administered, and instead will claim again the autonomy over their body, now including entirely new possibilities. In this field our relationship to nature will become a political problem of unprecedented urgency. And again the basic political issue will be one of the quest for participation and individual or communal autonomy as against the necessities of bureaucratic administration and control.

In regard to *communication systems* we can expect a technological development which will open up more and more the possibility of two-way communication arrangements within the mass media. Cable television may be just a first step in this direction, but it already provides the technical feasibility of a system in which all households are linked directly to the services available within the community—banks, supermarkets, catering services, centers of cultural activities, and so forth. Meetings could be held via television sets; cultural programs could be communally self-created and

---

24. A. Etzioni, *The Genetic Fix* (New York: Macmillan, 1973).

brought to every household. The news and advertisements of the daily newspaper would be superfluous because they could be stored in the local computer and repeatedly broadcast on the television screen at home. No doubt such a system would be financially difficult to realize today. However, the costs may decrease with further technical development and, more important, communities will begin to consider carefully before spending millions for a new town hall, a new cultural center, or new highways if such a system becomes a serious alternative. The use of computers is part of communication technology, and this is where the issue of public use and community control versus administrative use and centralized control becomes pertinent again. In America political debates on availability of access to cable television production facilities have already begun. The possibility of computer systems providing total information on the biography of every citizen and hence the potential for fantastic political control has begun to be recognized by the public at large. Some countries, West Germany for instance, have already begun to prepare legislation for such a state-controlled information system.

Finally, there is the emergence of *mind research* as a field of study which may eventually integrate such diverse approaches as brain physiology, drug research, extrasensory perception, psychoanalysis as the study of the unconscious, biofeedback, acupuncture, computer theory, and biological research on the communication systems of animals and even plants. Mind research is likely to become one of the most exciting fields of scientific endeavor, not only because it radically challenges traditional scientific paradigms, but also because of its potential for pragmatic use. In some cases, such as psychoanalysis, acupuncture, and psychedelic drugs, practical application actually precedes scientific understanding. Today nobody can say where mind research is going to lead us and whether, indeed, it will become an integrated field of study at all. Nevertheless, the social consequences are already beginning to show: there is an increasing general interest in the study of the capacities of our mind, as is shown by the immense popularity of literature related to this issue, and a minority already takes part in this exploration, especially by use of psychedelic drugs. If this is seen together with the easy acceptance and general use of psychologically effective legal drugs which were originally developed for the therapy of mental patients, we can come to the conclusion that the inducement not only of alternate states of consciousness but more generally the alteration and deliberate control over one's sensory capacities and deficiencies will eventually become an accepted strategy in the conduct of our everyday life. All this may, of course, serve as yet another compensation for the lack of material growth as well as of political autonomy, thus helping to produce mass loyalty to the prevailing system of instrumental rationality. Yet, in this area even more than in the others mentioned, we should be aware of the possibility of entirely unexpected consequences. In any case here, too, behind individual attitudes and choices we find the political issue of personal participation versus administrative control.

Given this variety of actual and potential changes within our culture, the present crisis may eventually be overcome by the emergence of a new culture which once again would serve the functions of legitimation of power, formation of identities, and interpretations of the natural boundaries of human life. There is, however, one crucial precondition if this is to happen, namely that the political system be reorganized so that much more personal and communal control is granted. It is my contention that there are many problem areas in modern society where bureaucratic rationality and scientific expertise are misapplied and which are best left to the people who are most affected by them. This is particularly true of the health and educational services which could not be discussed in more detail here, but it also holds for regional planning, the mass media, and most research work. As I have argued throughout, it is simply not true that the pressing problems of the industrialized world today cannot be solved except by giving the centralized economic and political administrations more authority than they already possess. The example of the ineffectuality of the bureaucracies in state socialist societies should serve as a warning here. But even if decentralization and increased direct participation should develop their own dysfunctional tendencies, this still seems to be the only road open to fill the legitimacy gap and to overcome the motivational crisis. To put it in sociological terms, what helps to decrease alienation in the public sphere also helps to decrease anomie in the private sphere.

One result of more participation, of course, will be more conflict, especially conflict over the institution of effective rights of material well-being. But conflict is not dysfunctional—and in this case it may well help to bring about more equality of life chances than bureaucratic capitalism has been able to realize. The most important political goal of highly industrialized societies is not to achieve complete equality but rather to reach some reasonable balance between liberty, equality, *and* fraternity. This balance is today most threatened by Leviathan. His modern spirit, instrumental rationality, must somehow be consoled with the affective needs of human beings.

We cannot wait for this to happen but will have to fight for it. In order to participate actively in the ensuing conflicts, we first have to restructure our political consciousness. The traditional distinctions between left and right and among conservatism, liberalism, and radicalism will be meaningless in the landscape of the new political-cultural conflicts and for the new coalitions they demand. The old definitions no longer point out who is the friend and who is the enemy. What we need is a new political terminology. All praxis is based on concepts and notions—when we begin to understand social reality we have begun to reconstruct it.

4

Serge
Moscivici

*The
Reenchantment
of the World*

*"Life has no time
  to wait for rigorousness."*

Paul Valéry

The year 2000 has begun. A century is preparing to leave the world stage. And, as always, a breath of fear arises. Men are adding up the present and attempting to decipher the songs of the future; a new start is their fondest wish. As the due date approaches, the social machine races; in all parts of the world the accountants of society are beginning to count down toward the grace period we have been granted before the machine goes away or stops. Under these circumstances, how can we fail to ask: On what are we living out the end? What beginning do we hope for?

In times past we were sure of our answers: an end to violence and domination, to poverty and scarcity, to exploitation and ignorance. The route was laid out to lead us there: revolution by progress as in the American example or progress by revolution as in the Soviet example. We had every possibility of safely rounding the cape of the year 2000. Figures and theories well in mind, we were heading directly into an era of social harmony, mastery of nature, and freedom in human relationships. History no longer had to be made but simply applied. If these were simply words, then we must bow to their power, for they moved mountains and masses, exalted or crushed millions of men. Everything that was done, thought, or overturned recently was legitimized by words.

In recent years these answers have aged rapidly. Of course answers grow old like everything else, and when they do, we are in a position to return to their roots, to the questions that evoked them. Why this incertitude? Why have we become so alien to a history which even yesterday seemed familiar? Why this disappointment in the wake of progress and revolution? Why has revolt been transformed into disillusionment at the very moment we were reaching our goals after so much sacrifice? It is impossible to escape it. A great disappointment—the coat of arms of the *fin de siècle*—reverberates in everything that happens. It is impossible to ignore the crumbling of the entire economic, social, and cultural face of the world. At this confused moment between twilight and night, most analyses, words, and actions carry with them the trace and echo of this collapse. But we are creatures who cannot bear to see our hopes drying up; the gravest catastrophes cannot for a single day take from us the obligation or the will to live. Things being unable to go on as before, something must happen. What will it be?

Will it be the end of progress? All evidence points to the conclusion that the more we trust progress to reduce inequalities and produce prosperity, the more it rolls along spreading penury and deepening the differences among classes, nations, and civilizations. Will it be a new revolution? The preceding one stopped short as soon as revolutionaries began restoring what they were to abolish—the privileges of the ruling class, state-imposed discipline, the division of manual and intellectual efforts—and abolishing what they were to restore—collective decision-making, liberty, community. Must we then find another legitimacy for our history and society? As the expression "superpower" states so boldly, the previous one has become naked force. And there is a more precise threat looming above the dim figures of future possibilities, but it is one which is difficult to express. We aspire to an immediately livable world, one which is closer, more accessible, and more welcoming, and we should like not to take the long detour through a history which we are convinced will not even lead us there.

We thought we had an answer, and here we are confronting problems which we must face directly without an escape clause. The second millennium is here. We have a quarter-century in which to liquidate a vast and weighty heritage. Becoming aware of this urgent task removes many hesitations and facilitates the discovery of solutions we can propose. But reality of course reserves the right to surprise us and to have the last word.

"*Sous les scellés, qui donc tient
la nature?*"

L'Internationale

From one end to the other of this era of decision, one question, truly ours and truly new, contains all the others: the question of nature. I have explained elsewhere—perhaps prematurely and surely at an inopportune time—why this question is seminal and why it is ours. One of the reasons, the most obvious, is the disenchantment of the world. As this is the endpoint of a long and painful process, it deserves to be considered. When at last humankind was freed from a thousand superstitions, they began to believe that everything they do—work, science (knowledge), thought—exists or should exist by them and for them. They placed themselves at the origin of everything in their world and in their history. This belief gave a meaning to life, making the universe tangible and habitable; it made the light of reason desirable and linked the future to the present and the past. Against this rather idealized backdrop came the movement whose passwords are still these: purify work, science, and thought of every human element; strip the world of everything that suggest the capacities and actions of men; endow history with stages and laws independent of human desires and intentions. The ultimate aim was, of course, to attain a more objective knowledge, efficient production, and progressive economy.

The formula is well known: all modernization is gained by replacing man. With the exception of a few senseless and sterile revolts, nothing theoretical or real can oppose its application. And the more it is rooted out, the more we lose sight of its traces—so that the social, scientific, and industrial machine becomes even more efficient. After the death of God, it is the end of mankind. The analogy between the secularization leading to the former and the rationalization leading to the latter is not fortuitous. But the parallelism is not yet understood.

The consequences are these: when individual and collective man is no longer the foundation of everything, when he senses no human meaning in his production or in his relation to other men and their work, however modest, when he is ashamed of his origins, of his own nature, and of nature itself, when so-called technical and economic conditions have condemned him to obsolescence, then he lives in a society and a culture which disenchant him and feed on his disenchantment. Contemporary culture and society are like that, not because events have made them inhuman and abstract, but because they make and reflect this kind of image of the world. Because we are human, we cannot recognize ourselves in such a reflection. From then on we lose our center, roots, and vision justifying present and future efforts, the very *raison d'être* of all communities. Cut off from the past and flung toward an impenetrable future, our community can henceforth live only from one day to the next.

Now we must understand why these consequences bear upon the question of nature.[1] The answer emerges from three tendencies which determine the content of these consequences. First, the tend-

---

1. The idea of the disenchantment of the world expresses certain visible aspects of the bureaucratic and capitalist system. Max Weber of course has related it principally to the social question.

Beyond the Crisis

ency to *universalize history*, giving it one direction and one law: the conquest and mastery of nature. In the last century, under the banner of progress, men seriously undertook to realize this singleness of direction. Everything singular and divergent was eliminated from our societies in favor of certain systems: the city replaced the country, industry replaced agriculture, society replaced communities, and positivistic thought dominated natural thought. Under the banner of growth, men in other societies today still execute this task of replacement. Their leaders encourage their people to abandon their forms of life, their multifarious and inefficient means of production and organization, and to adopt more uniform and efficient ones—that is, ours. They enjoin their people to leave nature for history and to contribute to the continuation of *our* history instead of trampling out their own.

As we contemplate the endless devastated history of these peoples, we have perhaps failed to notice that modernity is not at stake in the games of growth and progress; it is *identity* which is at stake. It guarantees us that all human collectivities are converging upon the same history and that all histories converge upon the same human collectivity. Why? There is a single obligation that forces men to unite their energies, abdicate their liberties and their own particular experiences, and put their individuality, past, and way of life into the blender. This is the obligation to submit to a common law, that of combating and controlling animate and inanimate forces alike. History is nothing more than a succession of man's imperfect attempts to win a definitive victory in the war against nature. The distance between societies as measured in relative degrees of superiority or inferiority is simply a translation of their stage in this war. Work, knowledge, and acculturation have a common aim: where nature was, let history come.

Some thinkers proclaim that history and nature are opposite and incompatible—there is no dialectic in nature, nor shrewdness of reason. People with a history lead a hard life compared to those without—*natural* people. Both groups know what they do. But the fact is clear: from one stage of evolution to another, the stature of history grows in grandeur and sovereignty. Its determinations seem universal; its decrees, without appeal. It is in the name of historical law and no longer natural law that men seek to reach superior levels in the social and cultural sphere—we no longer say "tradition has it . . ." or "nature intends . . ." but rather "history wills that. . . ." And in the same breath we celebrate the abasement of nature and the utopian time when nature, having become the immaterial material of every society, will be nothing more than a conquered necessity.

There is also the tendency *to split society*. The separation induced by rules and the organizations of production, habitat, and knowledge between our civil society and our personal society is glaringly evident. Civil society tries to expand to the detriment of personal society, cutting off our relationships as citizens, workers, and intellectuals from those we have as young or old, men or women, members of a family unit or a circle of friends, so that the latter become mere shadows of the former. Without respite it opposes the daily details of our lives—productivity, money, competition, docility—to our daily life—meetings, desires, conversations, the need to eat or sleep—as if opposing a necessary silence to superfluous chatter or time earned to time wasted. In private rhythms initiative, wandering, civil society sees only steam bursting from beneath the cover of a cooking pot, because civil society is precisely that, a lid on a pot.

In reaction to this, personal society shrinks into itself. It becomes a place of refuge and reconciliation with ourselves and others, a place where we dream—and is not a dream a desire made real? At the same time, we are isolated, dispersed, and chained to a reality which takes pride in imposing an unrealized desire on most of us. Thus, we are drawn into the Brownian movement of the *parallel life*. Secretive and clever, ironic and impotent, it is diffused, invisible, in the air of civil society. This is, to be sure, banal. Nevertheless, at supersonic speeds from West to East and North to South, the parallel life has entirely rent the social fabric, and the tugging and pulling thus created place a strain on the social body and feed its hypertension. Furthermore, this rending accentuates the process of division within civil society itself. Watertight bulkheads separate individuals and groups, sealing them into compartments that outlast generations of men. By its symbols, hegemony, and the sanction it imposes on questioning, divisiveness has become, from the perspective of power, knowledge, and work, the most important force for order and discrimination.

Let us consider a long historical period. From the point of view of property, we see a succession of class-structured societies. Evolution in this perspective moves from slavery to feudalism, from feudalism to capitalism, from capitalism to socialism. From another angle we can see a series of marked divisions: between the sexes and the generations in the prehistoric and cynegetic world, between city and country in the old agricultural world, between manual and intellectual work in the modern mechanical world. Each time, heads and bodies are separated. The operation which is repeated thousands of times divides them more and more as if by fission until nothing is left but atoms of heads and atoms of bodies. By superimposing on class-structured societies the traits of caste-structured societies, these divisions split them once again.

We finally come to these *hierostructures* which hold concentrated in their own hands all material and spiritual means (under the current bureaucratic and technocratic form) and pose as the guardians of history, growth, and so forth. On all sides these hierostructures impose vast organizations, unified plans, and an essentially technical mode of resolving human problems. Using any means possible, scientific as well as technical, the hierostructures deck themselves in mystery, block free access to knowledge and power, and keep for themselves the privileges of those domains. The list of interdicts, discriminations, rituals, and codes grows with prodigious speed under our very eyes. Methods of selection and cooptation multiply in each carefully limited sphere, and the *numerus clausus* becomes a general principle of social relations. They warn against a mixture of competences and label as illicit any ambition to achieve totality and direct cooperation among people. The concepts of collective property and private property do not affect the substance of hierostructures: they change hands but not natures. Should the regime of classes disappear somewhere, one will discover the regime of castes beneath the surface with its rigid structures based on segregation and domination and justified not by property but by division. It simply replaces the old adage "to each according to what he has" with "to each according to what he *can*."

This is also clear in the binary nature of social functioning. Who manages our businesses? Answer: capital and the technostructure. What is the power unit of the economy? Answer: there are two—profit and organization. What is the nature of the generalized contemporary wage-earning group? It has a double nature: on the one hand, it is the force of work with its purchase and sale prices; on the other hand, it is the possession of economic, administrative, and cultural apparatus. Every proletarian may well be a wage-earner, but this does not necessarily make every wage-earner a proletarian. This obvious statement would eliminate considerable confusion in the definition and composition of social classes if it were taken into account. I grant that this is quite simplified. However, as unpleasant as it may be to admit, it is difficult to describe correctly the current evolution of society if we do not consider this reality, *our* reality: that of two societies in one. Like two geometric curves each having its own equation, our two societies cut across each other at one or several points and sometimes have a common tangent or derivative. But despite all this, their intrinsic shape inevitably draws them along two separate paths.[2]

Preserving these splits in all their vigor means continually scouting out "untamed" energies, "uncontrolled" impluses, and "irrational" needs—that is, scouting out inner, organic nature. To this end is created a tight network of institutions which pursue their quarry of spontaneity in activity, thought, speech, or private rhythms in work and life. There is also a wooden language, including slogans, commercial formulas, statistical terms from the world of management, and acronyms (research frontiers, G.N.P., 4 percent growth rate), which serves as a way of expressing one's daily relationships to oneself, one's intimates, and one's surroundings. For this reason these words do not unite us but rather maintain us in an enormous vacuum. (Is it so surprising, given these conditions, that linguistics, the science of language which subordinates the spoken word, occupies a privileged place in the hierarchy of our sciences as in the universe of our discourse?)

Designed to adapt us to the labyrinth of social compartments, the conditioning of gestures, reflexes, and thoughts—behavior control— makes us accept them both. Both make us accept the repression of impulses, affects, and sensory responses, because they are represented to us as the threat of animality directed against humanity or that of biological man against a civilized collectivity. Thus is derived the idea that controls and interdicts create man, as a function creates an organ, as well as the idea that man exists by obeying that which prevents him from existing, that he is in society at the price of renouncing his nature. Renouncing is too weak—at the price of extirpating his nature from himself like some primitive urge which is best forgotten as soon as possible.

Finally, there is the tendency to *make archaic* the natural, as this

---

2. Because of this duality, the socialization of means of production changes only one aspect of the social structure: the elimination of wage-earning classes would change the other. That would not put an end to the mercantile nature of the work force, but it would shake the foundations of the hierostructure, since the wage-earning classes (in addition to their functional advantage) represent the modern form of its holdings, of the surplus it extracts from social work.

Beyond the Crisis 139

is the condition of passage from a past state of penury to the future of abundance. Scientific and technical progress guarantees the passage by the discovery of unlimited new resources that can be substituted for the limited resources of former times. From these discoveries comes the irresistible urge of science and technology to accelerate obsolescence and push for the abandonment of abilities, ways of thinking, bonds with the land, tools, and habits, with men who have lived out their time. I mention only obvious examples. They have as corollaries the constant expulsion of people from their work, understanding, and world, of which the result is really the uprooting of people from work, knowledge, and the world. At every stage of this abandonment certain things still subsist—a tree, a landscape, an artwork, a way of living or thinking. They are tolerated as necessary evils, as impermanent traces left by the reign of nature and destined to oblivion in a little while.

The more progress gains momentum and distance increases, the more it seems, to us inhabitants of the first world, to move backward toward a third world. The golden rule is that everything old is natural, and everything natural is old, and is thereby condemned to accelerate its aging process until it reaches the fatal point of disappearance. A pathetic aura surrounds any existence devoted to an object, a bond, a trade, or even a science, because we know in advance that the object or the science will become outmoded and added to the garbage heap of the age without even enough respite for one to finish the task undertaken. The zealous application of this rule reveals a firm conviction that everything which is destroyed will be replaced, that resources of energy and materials are inexhaustible, and that human physiology and psychology are infinitely malleable and flexible. Thus, anything can be imprinted upon them, and everything can be erased. Ultimately, then, progress has simply enlarged upon one of the great neolithic discoveries—domestication—and by pushing this to its most completed form has consecrated its most widespread variant: the domestication of man by man.

I willingly limit myself to the present, having no desire to draw up a balance sheet of all the tendencies that aim at conquering external nature in history, at compressing internal nature in society, or at pushing one or the other into the past. By what standard shall we measure them? They seem destined to run their course. On the black page of history, on the *tabula rasa* of humankind, and on the deserted land of nature, their course was inscribed and programmed;

the dates were virtually fixed. We will know later at what point the machine fell sick, at what moment the one-time human and nonhuman objects rebelled. As if by a kind of fatal reversal, everything we have touched since then has changed into its opposite.

The more exacerbated the struggle against nature becomes, the more we celebrate the inimitable works of research and industry—and the more this struggle turns against us, because it saps our very nature, ruining such irreplaceable masterpieces as a species, a material, a tree, or an animal. As science advances faster and faster, the abyss widens which separates it from other knowledge; as scientific alphabets increase in number, so do the number of scientific illiterates and, indeed, of illiterates in general. The more light is shed, the more knowledge dispels the mysteries of the universe and instruments make distant objects visible, so much do most people feel the shadows of their ignorance deepen, the mysteries of their tangible universe multiply, near objects become invisible. The more progress claims to bring abundance and narrow the gap between the living standards of nations, the more we realize that progress is busy maintaining rarity and producing differences. Statistics prove this incontestably.

Yes, we realize it, because industry and the economy stop when there is a plethora, when needs are satisfied and resources trivialized, and because they pick up again when penury appears, when needs demand to be satisfied, and when resources are reserved to a class of individuals or nations. To assure their continued functioning, they have to destroy what exists and promote what does not exist yet or hardly at all. Progress devalues what is abundant and values what is rare: that is its law. This law transforms progress from a modernizing and liberating force into a means of pillaging the world, a way of organizing wretchedness and fomenting strife among classes and nations.

Progress rarefies previously plentiful natural resources—air, water, minerals—and produces fruit that does not nourish us, wheat that cannot be made into bread and bread that does not satisfy. It creates distances: What do the American and the Peruvian workers still have in common when everything practical separates them and only a concept unites them? We used to believe that we were about to master the secret of life and matter, but by destroying cities and countrysides we prove our inability to master ourselves and inhabit our own planet.

Little by little the world is being turned upside down. The results obtained from any endeavor are usually the opposite from what we sought, and limits appear in the very places from which they were to vanish—limits on resources and men and limits to our tinkering with things, organic and inorganic. An eclipse has covered modern society; its horizon is darkened, and its shadows are more visible than its light. By dint of burrowing as if it were not there, we have reached the bedrock of nature. And we ask: "Is it true that nature is not unlimited?" "Is there really a human nature?"

Both these questions endure and pose a challenge. None of the sciences—economics (the science of scarcity), psychology (the science of behavior control and repression of instincts), or sociology (the science of the disenchantment of the world)—predicted this turn of events. Only popular wisdom knew that nature put out by the front door will return through the back. Many people are persuaded that the world turned upside down is a passing phenomenon, that it will soon right itself so that we will not have to store away all our notions about history, society, or nature. We have seen the tendencies by which this propensity for the disenchantment of the world has raised the question of nature; you understand clearly that we cannot evade the question, because it is not in the least a passing one.

"If you say that is utopian, I shall ask you to tell me precisely why."

B. Brecht

It is a curious thing that the question of reenchantment is so simple. Everyone understands it at once. And it is no less curious that it arouses such immediate resistance. No one understands its weight in the evolution of human affairs.

Take as examples the recent movements of youths, women, ecologies, ethnic groups, communities, and even arts. They have been described separately: in terms of generational conflict, sexual liberation, and quests for identity; and as marginal or leftist. The movements themselves have accepted these categories so graciously placed at their disposal. Which of them could have recognized that their motives might be different from the ones ascribed to them? Could they realize that, by taking up ready-made theories and language, they muddled their own exigencies and became something other than what they declared themselves to be? Like all vital movements, they have been turned into a kind of vaccine by institutions and mentors of all kinds, and so they are incapable of creating authentic forms of expression. Great masses of young people, women, and militants have risen up swelling with hope only to fall again like badly leavened bread. Their collapse and their salvage (as if democratic and socialist movements had not already had the same experience) were interpreted as signs of their transience and their lack of real value. Much was made of Oedipal drama between man and woman, parent and child, of the graven laws of ethology which require respect for the hierarchy of power and sexes, and the dissolution of the bourgeoisie which masks one set of conflicts with another, and of other bromides taken down from the same shelf.

I shall discuss neither the premises nor the conclusions adduced in the framework of concepts invented by the requirements of a cause. Is the tree on which they grow so old that it produces only blasted fruits? Even as new kinds of social and cultural currents are clearly emerging, these arguments shed no light on real events. Their authors have cast their ideas in worn-out molds and will not lay them aside. Instead of hypertheses shown by such explanations, I prefer a simple and direct hypothesis. Every movement appears at the precise instant that a breach is opened, that there is an extreme need for that movement. The breach made by the nature question inspired these movements *together*. Judging them from their context and their aims, they are naturalistic.

In an initial phase they burst out like a sharp retort to the predominant lines of force in society. Changes follow changes, but nothing is changed; progress progresses and growth grows, but their cancers stifle ordinary life. Deep disorders gnaw at individuals and groups as they become fragmented and destroy themselves; only nostrums and simples are provided for the pain. These are the procedures we denounce. To put an end to them, this *reactive* or poetic naturalism makes an appeal to the idealized materials of the past. With tireless ardor it brings back to life the buried dreams of the harmony of lyre and bow, the scent of flowers, the warmth of the sun, the beauty of landscapes and earthly creatures.

Beyond hostile indifference, it celebrates shared love; beyond all calculations of the possible, it affirms its intention to attain the impossible; beyond submission to utility, to rules, it proclaims the sovereignty of spontaneity and superfluousness.

Stimulated by its appeal, communities have begun to appear. Breaking with the exacerbated individualism of industry and capital, attempting to link up with older and other forms of life, they have tried to regenerate the values of vanquished cultures. They represent neither the categorical *no* nor a flabby anarchy, but rather they are a reflecting surface in which the thousand faces of our society and our history see themselves as they really are: old. Everyone has heard the cry that accompanies this movement: return to nature! Nothing justified the panic inspired by a current whose explosive charge can be condensed into three words. Or perhaps the panic is justifiable. It is, after all, a measure of their power to reactivate energies that had been domesticated and to evoke in man the notion of a people, in society the notion of community, and in nature the presence of life.

Social and intellectual bodies (of adults, I might add) owed it to themselves to react; they canceled the party and sent to bed the children who had asked for the moon. Such bodies are made in such fashion that they most often pardon murderers but rarely dreamers and sleepwalkers. But the breach remained open. Armies of journalists and specialists (in what? No matter!) grown gray in harness, brought up in the seraglio, were momentarily disoriented by the unfolding of renewed ideas that touched so many hearts and minds. But they closed ranks and plunged in, carrying briefcases and reports instead of flowers and songs. Camped out in lecture halls, offices, and other technocratic nests, communing in their clubs and research teams, they substituted information theory for poetry. It served them well as they concocted their fat reports—and even better as they made careers in some shiny new "-logy" or "-nomy" in the Department of Nature or the Quality of Life.

Even the political machines, aware of where the wind and the ballots were blowing, added a bit of green to their flags, a sprig of ecology to their platforms, and to their staffs a detachment of experts in the art of tastefully arranging the ruins of the "ecosphere." This *ecological* and *technical* form is the second phase of naturalism. In its groups of specialists, by its proposals, it cautiously advances its pawns on the road to reform. The essential goal in its view is to correct the excesses of our current relationship to nature (or to the ecosystem, if you prefer), to grow in equilibrium, and to equilibrate growth. This position inevitably recalls the era, the mentality, and the function of social-democracy in the evolution of the socialist movement. I shall not, however, go on about this, because no comparison is as good as a reason. We cannot hold it against this second phase to have poured a bit of cold water on the enthusiasm of naturalism—or was it rather a case of throwing out the baby with the bath water? And what can we say about the mountains of paper that brought forth a few hollow formulas? Except to admit in all fairness that they also produced some knowledge, a few useful instruments, and some practical experiments.

Here we can put a finger on the limits of this naturalism. Just as the fox is not charged with keeping order in the chicken coop, so technocrats and administrators even of goodwill cannot saw off the branch they perch on in order to commit themselves to a radical solution of the nature question. I take my hypothesis a bit further and predict that today's social, cultural, and political currents, having reached the zenith of their movement and worn out from occupying center stage for so long, have exhausted their historical trajectory and will decline. Furthermore, capital, overdeveloped technology, and the hierostructure have created conditions of life so intolerable that we must sketch out a third phase of the movement.

This is the mature phase—that of an *active* naturalism which takes problems of nature at their root, is political, and is historical in the true perspective of problems of nature. At the pace our century is taking, this must be accomplished soon. Let us note that, given the evolution of capitalist and socialist societies, East and West will tackle the problems together. It is indeed highly probable that the first impulses will come from socialist societies. In them the elimination of the masters of capital makes even more incompatible and intolerable the characteristics of parallel life, the logic of man's domestication by man, and the wooden language where combinations of signs replace sentences, where clichés pass for thought—in short, every expression of death and abstraction rather than life and concreteness.

Collective property, a working class in power, and a party with an iron hand are, of course, trump cards. The rest—everything that concerns youth, women, ethnic groups, and the uprooting of individuals and groups—may have changed contexts but has not altered its nature; that is a handicap. This "rest" is like a hyphen between social systems which simultaneously provokes dissent among groups that might reorganize the movement, and strongly represses them. Nothing is more explosive than the pressurized contents of an empty and tightly sealed container.

I have no illusions. Most theories exclude this hypothesis. I should still like to know how they can be sure that a landslide is not about to happen at the heart of the reality they ignore, a landslide that would ruin the body of triumphant knowledge they point to so proudly. Most interests and biases also exclude renewal of the naturalist movement and plan. I should like to be shown one single basic problem—and the nature problem is fundamental—which stops being posed and re-posed before its solution is outlined. But these exclusions are not the issue: reality will decide. The essential point is that we have at our disposal a new horizon, one that covers every aspect of human life: the reenchantment of the world. It embraces a different universe, and these are the four points of its compass.

Struggle for Nature

The struggle for nature is the battle in which many men won their spurs through a better perception of the close link between the natural and the social spheres. Like many things in our time, actions and ideas received the baptism by fire of concrete experience in this struggle. The ones that survived the test were definitively forged by it.

Among those ideas is a very simple one: men produce themselves, and they in turn produce their natural environment. Men's intervention in the evolution of physical and biological phenomena is normal, as is that of other species. The problem arises from proceeding as if one intervened from outside, rather than within, the natural cycle. Current modes of intervention are harmful, not because their accelerated rhythms engender imbalances but because acceleration and imbalance have been deliberately chosen. They have been presented as the permanent and positive goal of intervention. The deadlock comes from this fact, and technology will not get us out of it. It is rather up to us to get technology out of its dead end. What has been attempted to this end? To induce an "involution": to replace "hard," "modern," "artificial" techniques with "soft," "traditional," "natural" ones, and to stop with that. The limits of such an undertaking were predictable from the outset, as were the results: instead of rescuing nature, we have created an enclave for it.

On the contrary, it is important that we encourage an evolution. Current techniques are *mecanomorphic*. They attempt to substitute men's strength and talent for all other kinds, and every technical discovery has as its purpose an extension of the material milieu into the human milieu. Almost all machines have been conceived of as representatives in our midst of an external power (mechanical, electrical, or nuclear). Another common characteristic is that they seek to alter maximally the structure and play of material forces, thus to *artificialize* them. I add that they work—or that we make them work—according to a principle of physics: *maximize* one or two parameters (time, speed) without paying attention to the total system to which they belong. This is the very essence of productivity: maximize the use of one or two properties or resources to the breaking point. Waste results from this. In fact the quantity of energy and materials actually utilized represents only a small percentage of the quantity brought into play and consumed (not to mention the human energy involved). But we cannot evade the significance of this in the perspective of the man-nature relationship. It is the distortion of exchanges between the human world and the material world. It posits nature as a reservoir of animal and vegetal matter and men as operators who, through agriculture, industry, and research, exploit it as best they can (or as badly). Thus a relationship of externality and mastery between conquering men and conquerable nature is established.

The kind of technique we wish to promote is *biomorphic*. As part and counterpart of the human organism, it expresses the organism in the surrounding environment. It does not perceive the environment as a source of limits and instruments, but instead is associated with the techniques of the body as well as its milieu and substance. Its task is not to eliminate but to amplify them. And there is more. In the years to come, we will have to reinvest value in agriculture. Given the scarcity of cereals and proteins that threatens the globe and the destructions perpetrated on the terrestrial environment, the production of foodstuffs and related environmental questions will once again assume great importance.[3] We have tended to locate our principal source of wealth in the

---

3. The time has come for a more rigorous evaluation of the current tendency to industrialize and chemicalize agriculture. A part of the economic and technical data I have seen makes me believe that we should agrarianize and biologize industry in order to avoid catastrophe.

abundance of the earth's substratum. But it is in fact in the fertility of the soil itself. Creating techniques in this domain and with this goal in mind would allow for a radical reorientation. The techniques would be based primarily on biótic cycles and would generally modify the structure and the interplay of material strengths as little as possible. They would be recycling techniques, and therefore they would be naturalized. The important threshold to cross is in conceiving of them as having biological models. This would *optimize* the components of the whole, including the human component. Simple viability, the capacity for reproduction and regeneration under optimal conditions, is the decisive criterion in choosing one or another method or technique.

This orientation casts new light on the relationship between man and nature. Men are considered as one natural force among others, and nature is the normal milieu in which knowledge and resources are active and self-restoring. Their clear interest is in letting other forces and other beings reconstitute and regenerate themselves. They have a responsibility in this regard: having lived for millions of years in a vegetal and animal world, they must now sustain animal and vegetal life in what has become a human world. Their authentic function is neither to conquer, safeguard, or protect (as this would still be external, a kind of attenuated conquest), but *to create*. Only this function, properly understood, can change the meaning of work and of technique. This alone gives birth to the truest human relationships: creators in nature, creators of their nature.

Nature is part of our history; the transformations of nature and history go hand in hand. This is the second idea. It has the effect of underlying the double impossibility of a return to a prior state and an automatic evolution toward a future state. There can be no preestablished harmony between us and the universe around us, no privilege of a true nature that has vanished, and no forecast of a transparent nature in the future toward which we could plunge head first without knowing its outlines. We cannot go back on what we have gained by reducing pollution with every means available, by limiting the scope of destruction, and by allowing vegetal and animal life to survive. However, paying attention to all these means brings with it the risk of our forgetting the end or of our substituting the means for the end. That end is to abolish the means and thus to eliminate every kind of pollution. This implies an end to the bifurcation of nature into one that is close, tangible, and sensible and one that is distant, abstract, and alien to the first. Breaking the long chain of habits and behavior which have sliced up reality invites us to imagine a new science and a new art. Instead of perfecting a schism, we must remake a unity.

Remaking a unity necessitates abandoning laissez-faire principles and refusing to submit to an evolution outside and above ourselves. Otherwise we will eventually have to confront nature in a universal condition established once and for all. Nature is a dimension of history, a combination of men and material forces, and we have endowed it with a history which is the outcome of the successive combinations of everything that exists without us and receives another existence with us. But we scarcely know the beginning of that history, and we do not at all know the end of it. *Nature* is always historical. Only its present is accessible to us. And this leads us to pose for the first time the problem of defining the state of nature which is best and most appropriate to our objective situation, as we previously had to do for the state of society.

It is understood that science and technology cannot provide this definition. Human groups must develop for themselves a plan for nature just as they develop a plan for society with all the effort required at the levels of thought, relationships, and practices. Today on the eve of the twenty-first century, we can begin consciously to formulate the human history of nature, as in the eighteenth century men began consciously to write a human history of society. The battle against pollution does not go far enough; a return to nature is a powerful illusion. What we must have is very precisely a return *into* nature.

These two ideas put forward a single obvious fact: it is not the individual but the collectivity which forges the links in a relationship to nature. Society is at one and the same time a part of nature and one of its creations. It has been claimed that these bonds reflect only the weakness of human capabilities and the scarcity of resources and that the elimination of the one and the other would also mean the elimination of any bond. Progress toward mastery or plenty would bring us closer to a natureless society, just as regression flings us back upon a state of nature without society.[4]

Reality lies elsewhere. So long as we go on thinking, doing, inventing—and how could we do otherwise?—we create resources,

4. I wonder if this logic does not represent the perspective of a strongly anti-rural city dweller. (Nature? It's for yokels!) But the joint destruction of city and country now makes this inconsistent.

while simultaneously existing resources become obsolete or are transformed into something else. Scarcity is the key to that, as neither art, technology, nor science eliminates it. On the contrary, they engender it and keep it moving from one domain to another. The possibility of abolishing scarcity and with it our ties to nature is a chimera. Practical and theoretical conclusions drawn from it have no solid bases. Of course human society is fated to disappear; it has even provided itself with very refined means of self-destruction. But before this event occurs, everything invites us to make note of the possibility that society is multiplying its links with nature, that it is less than ever able to do without it. The break with the past and the profound transformation of social relationships are nothing but touchups if they exclude these bonds from consideration. They are real only if they open onto relationships with nature and onto a new nature.

As we go further, we reach the conclusion that the moment has come to take society in hand and live it as the form fleshed out by our efforts to reproduce or to invent the organic and psychic characteristics of men and their environment. We cannot go on living it as the place where we band together to barricade ourselves against nature. We call for a society which is pro nature and thus freed from its greatest fear. These ideas can be discussed, but nothing can diminish the impact of the problems they pose: to create nature, return into nature, and join together for nature.

Make Roots for Men

We must join together for nature, to be sure, and we must do it above all for the people who live in it and for everything that favors life. In our euphoric moments, we forget that life is a rare phenomenon in the universe and that the calling of each species is to reproduce it. Figures provide a breakdown of the cost of our forgetfulness: waste of irreplaceable resources and species more brutally destroyed by industrialization, urbanization, and conspicuous consumption than they would have been by a new Ice Age. The figures condemn without appeal our present way of reproducing people and things, and they dictate the necessity of revolutionizing it. I remind you of the most urgent reasons:

- The swamping of the environment by a rising tide of population and urbanization
- The constant overturning of means of production, which is always accompanied by underdevelopment of means of reproduction

Experience has shown that by rationalizing and socializing the productive side of society we do not necessarily transform its reproductive side. On the contrary, by carrying their productive forces to their extreme limit, new societies have merely exacerbated the tendencies set in motion by former societies: the separation of people, the brutal dissolution of urban and rural milieux, and the pollution of the environment. This recalls the myth of Ur: invited to live a new life, the souls of the dead always choose one identical to their former life. They hope to see more clearly into their passions, whereas it is their passions that blind them. In the same way, classes and people who hope for a new society run the risk of creating always the same one. They think they are remaking it more rationally and more productively, but it is precisely this rationalism and productivity which cut them off from any innovative possibility. And thus they are lost like the souls in the myth.

One word evokes and sums up this reproductive mode which so urgently needs reform: deterritorializing. It means, as we know, continually gathering up human groups, dissociating them from a particular milieu, product, way of knowing, or life style in order to associate them with others that are the same at all latitudes and longitudes. Nothing in space, everything in time: the criterion of age or modernity is crucial in the choice of objects to be reproduced or not. Everything in technology, nothing in human beings: the criterion of efficiency is decisive in designating what reproduces and what is forbidden to reproduce.

The methods for this are well known. Divide and subdivide tasks and functions, repeating from generation to generation and place to place, in a shrunken and fragmented form, things that formerly existed as wholes. Thus the great separations are accentuated (city-country, worker-peasant, man-woman, Occident-Orient), individuals and truncated groups are displaced and kept apart. Mobility uproots them less from their modes of existence than from their *raison d'être;* they are not at home anywhere. For those who have not yet been separated or displaced, it is only a matter of time before the next division. They camp out in the pres-

Beyond the Crisis 151

ent and in obscurity as if they were already in the past, in the grave.

Giantizing, in its turn, is well expressed by three words: bigger, faster, identically. These are the three ingredients of the magic recipe for making three modern economies: the economy of scale, the economy of time, and the economy of effort. What does it matter if waste men pile up along with waste materials like side effects? The essential thing is to multiply by reproducing and to reproduce by multiplying the level of scales and performances.

I am not attached to either economics, scales, or performances; they contain no marvelous mysteries. But giantism is a response to another obsession, that of reducing the autonomy of nations and of social and cultural units, and of shrinking the citizen's control over his city, the individual's control over his work and life, the collectivity's control over its own power. A disproportion results whenever one thing grows at the same time that a related thing dwindles. There is a disproportion between suprascience and the researchers it hangs over and integrates into a central program of research and thought. There is a disproportion in worldwide communication when the eyes and ears of men can be reached from a distance of 10,000 miles, while the same eyes and ears are blind and deaf to communications from someone ten years away. Yet another disproportion exists between the growth of means of production and the diminution of means of existence. The first socializes the worker in every person, while the second desocializes the human being in every worker. In the overblown volume of social and cultural space, every person and worker represents a monad that is smaller and smaller, less and less visible, more and more neglected.

Finally, normalizing comes down to reproducing by one method and in one form something formerly produced many ways; it means adopting a model that anyone can make, anywhere. That has happened and continues to happen in agriculture, animal husbandry, and art under the auspices of industry with its plant factories, animal factories, and masterpiece factories. It is happening in cities and towns under the sign of a megalopolis hemmed around by suburbs that are living and sleeping factories and for the needs of the South, North, and East under the sign of Americanized needs (the Cocacolazation of needs) with its food, drink, fashion, and love factories.

To be a child of the times, individuals and groups alike must forget their own logic and learn a logic of imitation. It enjoins everyone to copy styles of relationships, behavior, technology, and organization which are hegemonic because they are modern, and modern because they are hegemonic. It enjoins people to follow the avant-garde in order to reflect it and to classify themselves in relation to the reflected image. (From this come questions like: When will Russia catch up with America? And Japan with Russia? And France with Japan? . . . Are you still in the third world or have you already been promoted to the first? Are you pre- or post-industrial? Are you underdeveloped? Developed? Overdeveloped?) One can claim that such classifications are dictated by progress (the loan-name of everything aspiring to domination on our entire planet), but they are in fact instruments of the Jacobin unity of the world,[5] which will be realized when technical, intellectual and political organizations are the same everywhere on earth. This creates a deep disturbance of the kind one feels when foundations are shaken. We begin to renounce our past, our singularity, and we kill what we love; we see ourselves exclusively with the faces of others; we let our mental and physical territory be nibbled away until nothing is left. Dividing, giantizing, normalizing, and deterritorializing are all the same thing.

Reproduction in these modes has no doubt had certain advantages. But neither fear of the future nor nostalgia for the past makes us believe that it has no further advantages: it is rather the lesson of the present. When a machine becomes too complicated and expensive, its fragility indicates that it is time to invent a simpler and more economical one. There have undoubtedly been urgent reasons for affirming the primacy of production over the reproduction of life. But the nearness of a day of reckoning makes us believe that it is now time to uphold reproduction of life against its mere production. For a long while, we systematically destroyed the wealth of the subsoil and the sites of the soil itself, organic and inorganic matter. Production for production's sake was the key to everything. If we are a bit more concerned with the ravages of nature today, it is not because we have changed keys and put production in its proper place. It is simply that as they become irreparable, these ravages create conditions which put production in its place.

For a long while, those who bear the burden of production and

---

5. Naturalistic movements have given close attention to the problems of imperialism and class exploitation in the perspective appropriate to them. As I have spoken of this elsewhere, I will not elaborate on it here.

Beyond the Crisis 153

feel its consequences in their flesh have been told: "Wait twenty (or a hundred) years, until the productive machinery is perfected. The poor will vanish thanks to progress, and the rich thanks to revolution. Then you will be where we are now, you will be our successors." Most of the audience for this speech now understands its fallacious character. They know that waiting is not the best method. Since this route is clearly the wrong one, it is necessary to turn around and strike out resolutely in the opposite direction. We are condemned to earth. It is our mooring. Cut off from it, no person, no group, no culture takes root solidly or attains full growth. Moving from the need to reconstitute units of life and units of production which reproduce and complete each other, units anchored in their own spaces and rhythms, the nascent mode of reproduction aims at *reterritorializing*. There is one method of attaining that goal: cross-fertilization, proportioning, or rooting.

Horizontal cross-fertilization of what has been separated on the vertical axis constitutes the first step in the generation of such units: this can be accomplished by regrouping occupations, kinds of knowledge, and means of production destined to be renewed. This tendency exists already in the sciences and in technology, where the hybridization of autonomous domains fertilizes those that exist and permits the discovery of new ones. If it were generalized, it would make contact among activities, practices, and distinct occupations conceived in other times with different rhythms and, by combining them, would reintegrate them into the cycle of collective creativity. The passage from "ancient" to "modern" thus becomes an expression of regeneration and recognition.

Proportioning responds to an imperative: do not change the scale of anything which has not also changed in relationship or structure. Large or small have no inherent virtue. But to enlarge and multiply something without creating new beings and new relationships is like feeding a cancer in the physical and social body. Our cities, industries, and collectivities, by their self-destruction, justify this imperative. Nature increases her numbers by creating new beings—species, elements, galaxies—and regulates her dimensions according to their creation. Our reproduction should follow the same principle. It would begin by acting upon effects, establishing the limits of dimensions compatible with evolving physical and social relationships and limits of productions able to grow without destroying these relationships.

Then it would act on the cause of disproportions: artificial productivity. Abolishing productivity as a choice criterion of the techniques and aims of our businesses, our exchanges, our distribution of time and space, have become both possible and desirable. Why cut down the seconds of a man who works while taking away from millions of others the possibility of entering the work circuit? How to set aside profit and wages in a revolutionized society, while at the same time increasing the discontinuity and the uniformity of gestures, needs, and relationships? What good is talk of cooperation and equality when the race for high yield continually casts individuals and nations back into competition and inequality?

Only when productivity is abolished will we see the death of frantic competition; of the waste of people, energies, and materials; of the grip the industrial model has on the personal and social domains; and of the increasing hostility toward the idea and the reality of work. Our deepest aspirations are toward equity, democracy, and the direction of affairs by those whose concerns they are. But no general plan can realize these aspirations unless it makes a frontal attack on the very foundations of the pyramids of the modern world: factories, cities, research centers, and states. Immense key sectors of our societies (take research, arts, service professions, even construction) function without the good of productivity. Thousands of societies have known how to benefit from their surroundings and let human resources flourish.[6] They let workers know what they are doing and organize themselves to do it, fixing their own rhythms and their own norms for the yield from a tool or a trade. They have not uselessly humiliated those who work, nor elevated performance to the place of God and Moloch in their existence. Why do we not do as much by abolishing productivity and naturalizing reproduction? Is this regression or a simple palliative? Neither. It is simply an attempt to abandon current problems in favor of higher problems—those of the relative viability of resources, milieux, and technical facilities given the necessities of the duration and the survival of populations that are stifling, countries that are in death agony, and civilizations that are destroying themselves by their own hand.

By rooting we mean remaking a form of life and production, a relationship to men and nature starting from their own bases and spirits. Some solid facts show us how improbable it is, in the fore-

---

6. Recent studies have shown that the productivity of so-called primitive techniques was very high, and that its level could not have been surpassed, given the circumstances. Furthermore, the societies that had developed them lived in a state of relative abundance.

seeable future, that the urban industrial "model" can be universally implanted. The facts also indicate that collectivities, reinstated in their own history, could adopt the model that best corresponds to their aspirations, traditions, and the land they inhabit. This would mean freeing them from the obsession of the single model and reversing the tendency to take every initiative and every inherited singularity as the expression of retardation, deviance, or confused understanding. They could then follow the logic of creation: start with the self, take inspiration from others, and finally reach an appropriate form and an original characteristic.

To tell the truth, technology and the sciences are in no way linked by necessity to a determined way of life or a relationship to nature: the factory and the superlaboratory are not indispensable to them. They flourish quite as well in the field or in the workshop with the discovery of new concepts and objects. It is sufficient to suggest tasks and ends to them, to modify the conditions under which they operate in order to make them adopt a different course. Is underdevelopment anything other than the inability of a nation to follow its own path because it is barred in the name of universal conformity? To the denial of life we must respond with an affirmation of the will to live. In any case a change of direction is already perceptible: instead of going toward the universal norm, most nations and vital currents are heading toward particularized form, which alone will allow them to participate in the universal concert. The great struggle is no longer between ancient and modern. *Progress* is no longer the problem. The struggle is now between the singular and the plural, between imitative and creative development. The problem is that of the *rebirth* of everything that was being forced to choose between being unborn and disappearing. After the windstorms, droughts, and frost that the human race has just experienced,[7] we seek to fulfill our obligations to life for a

---

7. Planning for reproduction is a secondary aspect of our current problems. Theoretically it palliates the disadvantages of laissez-faire and market economics, substituting order for disorder. Practically speaking, it ultimately reinforces the tendencies below the surface of laissez-faire and the market to produce real waste instead of abolishing it. When crises begin to appear, it is believed that calculations were wrong and that planning should be reinforced with perfected tools. It is a rare conclusion indeed that planning is being asked for what it cannot do. Planning is a therapy for disorder and dysfunction, but it is not a principle of order and smooth functioning, which is precisely what reterritorialization is. In addition, it would be advisable to stop playing all music on the keyboard of rationality and irrationality. Like the scientific revolution, the change in modes of production is accompanied by a revolution of rationality.

new birth and flowering. And to this end it has begun to cross-pollinate its philosophy and practical knowledge; to proportion its volumes, speeds, and efforts; and to give roots to its development.

Reoccupy Societies

Societies are moving away from us like expanding galaxies. They have required great sacrifices, stirred up vast hopes, promised justice and liberty, and promulgated wonderfully phrased and duly calculated programs. To the modern ear attuned to the song of history, this is all that was perfectly composed, clear, and harmonious. Then the ledgers were opened: crises, concentration camps, increasing distance between the ideal state and the real one. Popular progress has still not taken place—When will the conquered really overcome?—and heavy national and international hierostructures, the accomplices of so many inequalities and oppressions, almost make us regret the frank inequity and repression they claim to suppress. We certainly did not seek those results. But does this mean that no one is responsible for them? And can we go on living as though there were nothing wrong?

No one believes in the possibility of an ideal society. If it is absurd to compare an ideal past or future society to a real and present one, it is still reasonable to compare the ideal of a society to its reality—just as scientists confront theories with facts. And it is facts which judge theories, not the opposite. We know now that our ideals, if they were not thrown overboard in the first squall, have been put to a difficult test. Can we wonder at the indifference or ironic lack of feeling shown by youth, women, workers, and other groups that have been dislodged from their society? From these circumstances are born total negation and anarchic violence. But negation and violence cannot touch the causes. The very matrix must be attacked, the place where reports of distancing and dispossession are inscribed: the hierarchy.

Wherever hierarchy reigns it sorts out individuals and groups: men and women, directors and agents, experts and know-nothings, developed and underdeveloped peoples, classes and countries with gray matter and classes and countries without. Those on top live like porcupines to protect themselves against those on the bottom; they hide behind the hedges of money, power, and knowledge.

They announce openly that nothing could function without the social division of functions, which are, of course, immutable. Individuals may change but never the ladder of ranks, the permanence of rights, or the list of privileges.

There is also the widespread habit of speaking "in the name" of another—people, class, or nation—without their having the right to speak for themselves. This exorbitant privilege stems from the hierarchy's claim to representing within society the superior claims of something outside and above it—history, God, growth, or science. These things supposedly produce a society, so it is under their auspices that a society should reproduce itself. The upper echelons of the hierarchy pose as exclusive intercessors with these higher powers and as their permanent incarnation. As they did not hoist themselves up to the places they occupy under the impulse of private interest, but were borne there by the interest of history, God, science, or whatever, they are not the repressive and oppressive masters. Objective necessity has simply made them the overseers of an order which they must guarantee.

That is not all, as we know. To concretize the hierarchy, its organizers have the right to initiate and to decide; the organized have been allotted the right to follow and to accept. They are not stripped of power and knowledge, but they can accede to it only in the wake of those who govern them and on the condition that they stay in the shadow of the organizers. The threat is always that they might step out of line, make a gesture, or think a thought which would upset the deliberate divisions between leaders and followers, and precipitate spontaneous chaos. This assumes that people left to their own devices live in anarchy. And this conclusion is periodically "proved" when panic, crisis, and instability attack the collectivity and are explained as the results of a confusion of ranks or a blockage of institutions. Just as one captures a bird by seizing first the tip of a claw, so men are captured by the tip of their fear of disorder.

Thereupon, instead of altering plans, elements, or structures, people begin to reorganize them, believing that the best method is one that establishes a center—the brain of the hierarchy—multiplies the intermediate echelons, and proceeds on the principle that the better the parts are organized, the better the whole will function. It also appears necessary to increase the number of people who exist exclusively to give work to others; their productive and creative underyield is compensated by an overrun of direction and domi-

heterarchies. Thus everyone is alert, takes parts, is affected in turn, and can verify that the foundations of his world have really been changed.

Untame Life

The question is not is there a human nature, but rather, how can one not exist? Miners undoubtedly suffer less in extracting coal from the depths of the earth than we do as we try to extirpate our prejudices about human nature from the tortuous entrails of culture. Our era has subjected human nature to every kind of test. Of course it is flexible and historical, not fixed as some people continue to imagine it. (One would really have to be blind to envisage a humanity cut off from its nature.) Denied, left on the seller's hands, this nature is avenging itself; it is bursting out like steam from the valves in a machine. The explosion is in proportion to the enormous decline of energy due to the separation of civil society and personal society. Like a lack of air or movement, this separation weighs on all aspects of existence; prohibitions and discriminations are the material of every discourse. Even those who pretend to laugh about it while discussing it privately submit to it for lack of another way out. How much energy we waste, bearing the unbearable!

Untaming life first means liberating the energies compressed by the splitting of society and reuniting what had been separated by aerating the space taken by interdicts. Can we say that everything becomes possible, that everything is happening or can happen? That is not the issue: our societies are piling up prohibitions without explaining why there must be one life which is openly manifested, and another, the life of the body and desires, which is shameful and hidden; why they ration out to men and women their sexuality, feelings, and language; why they preserve the norms of authority, the family, and censored communication, throwing the others gaily overboard in the name of change and progress.

Before that part of humanity for which the smallest question is taboo, the part of humanity that raises even one question on this subject looks like the vestige of a savage past. Then societies become enraged and set in motion the machinery of law, schooling, or business. "That's the way things are," they tell us. But we must try to understand "how things are," to act and live in agreement with them. That is what aerates their space and allows us to breathe, by leaving men to their groping impulses, interest in the events of the immediate world, and wonderment at ordinariness; by emancipating woman from domestic authority, youth from tutelary authority, the servant from possessive authority; by liberating needs, speech, and bodies; by going beyond interdicts (of sex, knowledge, nature); by restoring the bonds between man and woman, ignorant and wise, natural and human. We insist upon it: these diverse facets are one. None has more or less importance than the others, and only historical circumstances determine their content and the way they take shape together. The essential thing is for men and women to exalt their curiosity, intelligence, and sensitivity as their own nature inspires them to do.

Then we must shake up discriminations. They enclose every group in a tunnel whose orientation and degree of darkness are determined by the map of social divisions. The tunnel frequents only itself, judging others to be foreigners or even nonexistent. There are feminine and masculine tunnels, as well as tunnels of young and old, black and white, management and labor, urban and rural. They are aligned, superimposed upon each other, and separate, according to the maxim: "Raise man above man." But how can we enclose life in these labyrinths? Do these tunnels satisfy real and permanent needs; do they stick like second skin to human nature? Concerning human relations—With whom do I produce, eat, live, think, and make love?—present discriminations are no longer tolerable criteria of coexistence among individuals, groups, or cultures. Their shadow need not cover every aspect of social life. People ask only to know each other, share their experiences, and be together. Or to say it differently, they ask to be free of fear: fear of nature, people, and power. It is time to end the mutual confiscation of men, the fragmentation of the individual and social body, and the dissociation of political, economic, and intellectual functions.

It is time to attempt once again to found a collectivity with an appetite for living, in its time and place, on something other than prohibitions and discriminations; on *alliances*, notably, in which we are rediscovering solid qualities for the re-creation of common wealth, organizations, and knowledge. Their sole condition would be to respect the maxim of allies—not to raise man above man. Is such a notion more able to encourage people, touch hearts, and determine societies today than it was yesterday? Or is it too much to ask of men, heart, and societies that have become so cautious on this subject? The fact that this maxim resounds and is heard, that it is periodically reaffirmed, that I can inscribe it among the promises for the future, bears witness to its force and its necessity.

Untaming life also means breaking from the roundabout path. As we follow it we acquire the habit of putting off until tomorrow the delight that could be ours today. We tolerate present unhappiness because a future happiness is dangled before our eyes; we whitewash today's means with the ends that are to come; we deflect every close feeling and action toward a distant reality and faraway people. To deflect is to set something up against its own nature. How? Wealth is deflected by being stored up; concrete work, by being made abstract; science, by being changed into power; reality, by being symbolized; and sexuality, by being sublimated. Everything becomes its opposite. The human and nonhuman world slowly empties itself of passion and enthusiasm; it grows cold. And the sought-after effect is achieved: we live as if we were living an absence. If the road is difficult and the sacrifices seem too great, if present existence is scoffed at, if man must let himself be "programmed" like a vulgar machine, then there is no alternative: necessity takes over. Everything will be paid back later with interest—both the time we have lost and the life we have not lived. But while we wait, death continues to eat into life.

Nothing would exist without detours: the mind is a detour of the body; man is that of animals; society is that of communities; history is that of our origins—so they say at the domestic extreme. The untamed extreme short-circuits, detours, and reembarks on the return road. It turns problems inside out and sets out in the open the goals that had been ignored by common consent.

For the individual the goal is the body. We live in our bodies without feeling their vitality. We do not know how to manage this unique and personal treasure. The pretexts of decency, the prestige of the mind, the imperatives of thought, and the ruses of productivity (of which sports are one, with their obsession for records) conspire to make the body an object of thought, a scarecrow suitable only for shutting up in the closet of private life. Its health and its silence are all we care about—forgetting it, in short. Every excess points to its remedy.

We must liberate ourselves through our bodies, welcoming as

perfection their possession and expression. We must openly register in public life its obstinacies, rebellions, and impulses as they were registered for thousands of years. We must listen to its pleasure as a song of life and dread its apathy as a threat of death. And we must be liberated through our bodies, letting them become flesh in us again in our fancy. It is necessary to multiply sensations, experiences, and occasions for enjoying them and to connect thoughts to feelings, and the desire for understanding to the desire for action. Once the first flip is given, there is no need for constant surveillance. The body watches over itself quite well as long as it is not frustrated by the violence of a civilization drunk with its dreams of mastery and possession.

For the collectivity the goal is ethnicity. Demanding recognition of ethnicity as some are doing means affirming that no one form of association has the monopoly on collective life, reducing all others to the level of partial or sub-collectivities. Then it means stating clearly that despite revolutionary transformations of all kinds, whole segments of social and cultural life continue subsisting and perpetuating themselves in their own space and time. And it means revealing the general principle of historical metempsychosis. According to this principle, when the death of a culture or a people is announced, we must wonder who wrote the obituary and how the culture of the people will rise from its dust and be reincarnated. In short ethnicity expresses the tendency to redefine the nature and proportions of the collectivity. A crisis force and a creative force trace its contours. The crisis force bores into nations whose godparents are capital and industry, who were brought up in the spirit of an implosive imperialism that sweeps urban and rural masses alike into the market, the factory, the city, and the state. It exterminates the languages, the cultures, and the habitats of these masses so as to leave only one language, one culture, one habitat; it confiscates for the benefit of one ethnic group the revolutions of all other classes, categories, or ethnic groups. Until now these state-controlled nations have more or less kept up administration and public services. Patriotic identity has replaced ethnic identity.

At what stage are they now? Explosive imperialism has been momentarily damned up and has flowed into anonymous economic forms. Drawn by the logic of division, nations have conceded their wealth to multinational groups, the logic of giantism has deflected them toward the supranational, and the logic of normalization has weakened their identity with uninational sloganeering (in a word, "life style" as a universal concept). Their own vast size has accelerated their disintegration and caused them to collapse. There is a loss of quality in public services, a decline in institutions, and decay in the systems of political representation. Yielding to the dizzying perspective of supraorganization, these nations have gathered the threads of political, cultural, and social life into the hands of bureaucratic hierostructures which then weave a net of decisions and anonymous and automated relationships on which no one has a firm grip. And the ruling classes devour themselves. Under pressure from events, they respond punctually with reforms—regionalism here, linguistic concessions there—designed to stave off the inevitable, or they respond with maneuvers intended to hasten the advent of some notion—a single society, for example. From reform to reform, from one escape forward to another, they always keep problems and the future under lock and key without producing anything new or necessary.

The creative force of ethnicity demonstrates the will to be reborn rather than to die by its own hand. In this world which is perhaps harder on people than any other has ever been, a world where genocide and ethnocide are raging, where overpopulation shrinks individuals and groups, where linear, competitive societies battle each other ferociously, we see, rising up like islands, repudiated collectivities. Emerging from the ocean of nations, they lay claim to a past and a future (their own). They demand their territory, their culture, their language. They denounce the territories, cultures, and languages that have realized their claims to universality first by dominating, then by destroying authentic singularities instead of assimilating them. The future belongs to communities[9] that have knocked out inner partitions and free themselves from the obsession with over-organization and giantism, uniformity and minimums. These communities are nonparochial ethnicities, integrated into the universe that is theirs. They accept initiatives coming from the periphery, because they represent rebellions at the limitations of private property—communitarian property has a solid meaning and a solid history, rebellions against the seduction of prefabricated social and economic models, naturally open to exchange and borrowing. "Circular" societies, these communities have no meaning unless they move through the past, renewing it and themselves, unless they assimilate in new ways the potential of the milieu that has been created while they were ban-

---

9. They are curious socialists indeed who are so strongly opposed to the creation and the existence of communities, to the restoring of those "communes" in the name of which revolutions were fought.

ished from reality and history. At this price we can speak of new ethnic communities.

Let us summarize the present situation. On the one hand, there is a sociogony which has as its horizon the dissolving of state-controlled nations into a planetary society. Reason wills it, uniform progression of productive forces pushes it, and men lean toward it. On the other hand, there is an anthropogony which, by the subversion of state-dominated nations, would concretize itself in a planet of societies. I must confess that after considerable reluctance to draw a firm conclusion, I find the second alternative preferable. Nothing forbids it. Evidence shows that identical forces of production can be reconciled with the existence of diverse and autonomous societies. And vice versa, one society can develop on the basis of very diverse productive forces. This solution is supported by reason, taking into account the needs of people who wish to reoccupy their social space and time. In this case it is clear that the new ethnicities are engrafted on the naturalist movement. Not only does every movement expand when it identifies itself with a unit of this type—the bourgeois movement with the imperialist nation, the worker movement with the anti-imperialist nation—but this movement[10] is the only one to identify itself with the quest for an alliance with nature, with reunion of the interrupted community. It is the only one to welcome a more profound prior humanity which turns the present around and which returns in the present.

Twice now, in the year 1000 and in the year 2000, we have heard the same voice crying: "Eden now," "happiness now." Twice the priests—of the Christian religion then and of science today—have been seized with holy fury when they heard these words. For they spoke clearly of the desire to transform the spirit of a history which, like the moon, always shows us the same face, that of final solutions. For these giving value to the present means compromising the ideals of the future, while giving value to the future means compromising the reality of the present. The present is always sacrificed: justice, liberty, every inner surge is put off until that uncertain day when God will come on earth, when science will at last take the controls, when growth will be continu-

---

10. Numerous themes of the naturalist movement can be integrated into the perspective of a planetary society, but at that point they begin to sound a sinister totalitarian melody which is so alien to the movement's origin and spirit that the movement would be well advised to give up hope for that approach.

ous, and so forth. And these words spoke not only of desire but of resolution: begin now to plant Eden, to change life, to know happiness. For the present is the measure of past and future, and the best guarantor of what is becoming.

That is what returning to the present means. It is returning to roots that send up new sap into sluggish individuals and communities, into bloodless groups and cultures. It transfuses routinized historical relationships which force everyone to live his future like someone else's past (the underdeveloped is the past of the developed; the poor is the past of the rich), and oblige man to reproduce a second-hand becoming rather than inventing a brand new one for himself. It also means coming back to a history which, for some time, has moved in a direction opposite to the one it claims to take, and which henceforth is understood and made by groups without a history (youth, women, excluded peoples). It means recommencing history itself and the history of those who have had no history.

For centuries men have proclaimed this clear truth: we are right to make and unmake the course of things, rather than let them or ourselves grow old, to reinvent and revitalize them for every generation. But it is not enough to know or say this. To want it, as one wants to live, is the decisive thing. And we seem to want it now in the midst of flabbiness and disenchantment. In this way life is growing untamed; it is switching men onto another track, making them the causes and the authors of their own immediate destiny and making them possessors within themselves of a wealth that cannot be eroded: the certainty of being firmly planted in the soil of nature, of their nature.

"Man is not as old as the world, he bears only his own future."

Paul Edward

The reenchantment of the world: twice we have touched this horizon of our time, and we have been burned. We were not clearly aware of what is taking shape out there. It is not simply a new way of understanding and acting for which we were unprepared, but an exceptional historical event, a surveyor's rod for thinking and doing that will last a long time. In the political, scientific, and philosophical orders, everything is moving toward that marker; everything begins to be marked by it. It is certain that the sculptured horsemen which protect habits and all that are standing ready. But are they a real obstacle?

In a time when we have accomplished things that were believed impossible, why should we be incredulous at the thought that this horizon can be ours and for a long time? Most of the managed, domesticated, and excluded elements of our societies have every interest in it. Is its extremism frightening? Disproportion somehow reassures the condescending. Against its powerful and obvious reality, they set worn-down phrases: historical necessity, economic growth, the imperatives of industrial society, scientific reason, and others. Reenchanting the world, however, is not without growth and necessity, nor without imperatives, which is evident when we look at history, economics, industry, and nature at a deeper level. This is necessarily true in the degree that it touches more exceptional human regions than the ones in which we currently move, regions where we reinject into individual and collective life a thought and a history more ancient and less well known than those which previously occupied us. This is a beneficent regeneration of thought, a beneficent regeneration of history.

Far from being the expression of a rear-guard, far from giving the floor to the abandoned merchandise of history, reenchanting the world represents the will to experience avant-systems and crystallize the movement of great awakening which is snatching us from dogmatic sleep. It is setting fire to the only available energy that stands out in the grayness of our time and trails its shining wake across the modern world.

Its aim is not the cult but the practice of nature. Its method is not to remedy the ills of existence but to produce new modes of existence. Its lever is not the body or daily life, but politics entering with it into the body and into daily life from which it will not soon emerge. In its horizon and tomorrow in ourselves, we will at last know that fighting for nature in our nature, rooting men, reoccupying society, making societies of living beings, untaming life—these are all one and the same thing. Tomorrow we will reenter earth's atmosphere, this green planet that the astronauts have glimpsed in space, the *only* planet, for we have no other.

5

Richard
Sennett

*Destructive
Gemeinschaft*

It is a psychological truism that people experience crises which reinforce the warring elements of their personalities, rather than break up these elements or give one side a victory over the other. Every therapist will have spent hours with clients who are in the grip of emotions which cannot be reconciled. There is a struggle in which the force of the emotions acquires a more powerful hold over the client, the longer he or she attempts to effect a reconciliation. The very origins of the word "crisis" in Greek link the phenomenon to suffering, to the passive undergoing of and submission to pain, rather than catharsis.

But the truism that crises are agents of reinforcement is alone an inadequate formula, either abstractly or therapeutically, for how people experience reinforcement through a confrontation of warring elements in themselves depends as much on the cultures in which their personalities have developed as it does on interior conflicts in individual experience. All cultures have collective rituals or collective rules which define the understanding people within that culture will have of what "a crisis" itself is. In this essay I want to describe changes in the definition of crisis which have occurred in bourgeois society from the middle of the nineteenth century to the present time. There has, in fact, occurred a great change in the environment of crisis experience over the course of this hundred-year period. The result of this change is a present-day situation I shall call "destructive gemeinschaft." Its chief feature is that it seems to be an environment of liberation from the repressions of nineteenth-century bourgeois society, but in fact is not. New forms of reinforcement of psychic distress have replaced the restrictiveness of former times. This destructive gemeinschaft has arisen from two historical shifts: first, a transmutation of nineteenth-century eroticism into modern sexuality and second, a transmutation of nineteenth-century terms of privacy into twentieth-century terms of intimacy.

Gemeinschaft, in the sense of the sociologist Ferdinand Tönnies gave it, meant full and open emotional relations with others. In opposing it to gesellschaft, he meant to create a historical, rather than a purely analytic, contrast. Gemeinschaft relations obtained in the precapitalist, preurbanized world of the *ancien régime;* gesellschaft relations, in which people dealt with each other partially and in terms of shared functions, he used to characterize the emotional transactions which prevail in the modern world. Gemeinschaft has been redefined as an idea since Tönnies's time: full disclosure of one's feelings to others has come to identify a moral condition—of authenticity and good faith, rather than a social condition dependent for its maintenance upon personalistic, hierarchic ties. The celebration of gemeinschaft relations today is captured in the ordinary English translation of the word—community. When people are open with each other and expose their feelings to each other, they create a moral-social group, a community. What has occurred with casting this twentieth-century use of gemeinschaft into technical psychological terminology is the celebration of inter-subjectivity as a moral condition.

What I want to show is that this celebration of inter-subjectivity is in fact inter-personally destructive: that is, gemeinschaft relations under the conditions of advanced industrial society are mutually destructive to those who want to be open to each other. My intent is to explain in psychological terms Adorno's critique in philosophy of the cult of authenticity and Lionel Trilling's critique of this same phenomenon in terms of literary culture. In ordinary bourgeois life, gemeinschaft is experienced so that crises of inter-subjectivity arise which cannot be solved within the moral framework of inter-subjective relations themselves.

Eroticism Transformed into Sexuality

When we think of our great-grandparents' experiences of physical love, we are most likely to think about inhibitions and repressions. Victorian bourgeois prudery was so extreme it occasionally acquired an almost surrealist quality: a common practice, for instance, was to cover the legs of grand pianos with leggings, because a bare leg as such was thought "provocative." This prudery lay at the root of a number of psychopathologies especially acute at the time, not only hysterias but also what the Victorians called "complaints," which among women were manifested by such symptoms as uncontrollable vomiting at the sight of menstrual blood and among men by such symptoms as acute attacks of anxiety after the discovery of an ejaculation occurring during sleep.

Certainly, no one today would hope for a continuance or a return of these repressive disorders. Yet it is important to discover the rationale behind the sexual repression and even to comprehend a certain dignity among bourgeois Victorian men and women in these puritanical struggles with themselves, holding on to the repressiveness the Puritans of the seventeenth century had practiced in sexual matters. Within this logic there was a code of eroticism which ruled nineteenth-century bourgeois consciousness, an eroticism composed of three factors.

The first and foremost factor of this erotic code was based on the belief that states of feeling and signs of character show involuntarily. What is deeply felt or deeply rooted is beyond the will to shape or hide, but rather appears unbidden and at moments of vulnerability to betray the person so moved. The involuntary expression of emotion received its greatest theoretical elaboration in Charles Darwin's *The Expression of Emotion in Animals and Man*. Darwin connected the involuntary betrayal of emotion to the necessities of biology which ruled the composition of the human organism. But the same idea had more popular expressions, as in the practice of phrenology and Bertillon measurement: the shape of the skull, hand, or foot supposedly revealed the presence of certain characterological traits which a criminal, defective, or salacious person could not disguise. Similarly, neither could more transitory states of feeling be disguised. Depression was supposed to reveal itself by involuntary tension in the cheeks; an episode of masturbation, by the sudden growth of a spot of hair on the palms.

The involuntary expression of character, furthermore, involved a particular system of cognition. Character traits were to be read through details of appearance. The Bertillon measures of criminality concern millimeters of difference between the cranial shape of the criminal and the law-abider. Little details of facial appearance or gesture were taken as signs of a totality of feeling for the more transitory emotional states. And it was the very miniaturization of these involuntary clues of personality that made personality itself so difficult to control; one might control most of one's behavior, and still some little thing would give one away.

Under such conditions anxiety about sexual matters formed part of a larger belief that the expression of all feeling was beyond the will to shape. The only defenses were either to shield oneself as completely as possible; to neutralize one's appearance, as the Victorians did through their clothing; or to attempt to repress feeling itself. After all, if once a transitory emotion is felt, it will be manifest through miniaturized clues to others, security comes only through an attempt to stop feeling in the first place. Concealment and denial, then, are logical consequences of believing in the *immanence* of personality, the necessary presence of inner emotions in appearances made to others, once the emotions are strongly felt by the person himself.

The second factor of the Victorian erotic code was the belief that personality states could be read through miniature clues, "fetishized" appearances themselves. I use this term more in a Marxian than a Freudian sense to indicate how trivia of appearance could be believed to be signs of a whole human being. This fetishism is the doctrine of immanent disclosure of personality viewed from an opposite perspective; if the self speaks through minutiae of appearance, then every appearance must be a guide to some characterological state. Thus it becomes logical to cover the legs of a piano with skirts, because a leg exposed is the sign of lewdness. This fetishism of appearances was especially strong in the clothing of the Victorian era. For example, a gentleman wearing a drab black broadcloth coat could be distinguished from an ordinary bourgeois wearing almost the same garment, because the buttons on the gentleman's sleeve actually buttoned or unbuttoned. In sex as in class, this fetishism applied, although it was directed more to the dress of women. The differences between the dress of "loose" women and proper ladies who appeared in *Le Moniteur de la Mode* lay in minor distinctions in the use of color for shawls and hoods, or the length of gloves. Each of these articles of clothing, then, bespeaks a particular mentality, and the minute differences between objects speak of vast differences in feeling between those who wear them.

In the section of the first volume of *Capital* where Marx takes up the subject of fetishized objects, he states that modern capitalism uses this phenomenon of employing objects as class indicators to avoid productive relations, so that the inequities of production, which might be visible if goods were conceived of simply in terms of use, are obscured. Instead, Marx further states, these objects seem to contain mysterious and enticing psychological qualities. Missing in his analysis, however, is a consideration of the psychological consequences of becoming mystified, of believing in minutiae of manmade things as personality omens. The Victorian bourgeois was trying to make logical sense of its daily experience on the basis of an illusion. The result of that effort was a contradictory, tense attempt to read others for signs of their private lives while at the same time one attempted to shield oneself from being read by anyone. This double process of searching and shielding did not permit a simple state of equilibrium or balance between public and private, for the signs of private emotion were continually erupting beyond one's power to control. Nevertheless, an effort to accomplish contradictory ends on this irrational base was made, and even though the sexual dimension may appall us, the enterprise as a whole had a dignity in its very painfulness and seriousness.

The third factor came as a consequence of the first two: sexual relations in the Victorian world had of necessity to be social relations. Today, having an affair with another person does not call into question his or her capacities as a husband or wife or as a parent. For the Victorian bourgeoisie, those connections had to be made. If every act and feeling counts in terms of defining the whole person, then emotional experience in one domain carries unavoidable implications about the character of the person acting in another. Thus evolves the logic that a violation of morality in one sphere means a moral violation in every other: an adulteress cannot be a loving mother; she has betrayed her children in taking a lover, and so on.

I wish to call attention not so much to the brutality of result as to the premise which produced it. The immanence of character in appearances meant for the Victorian that experience of one sort had to be weighed against its relation to and effect upon experiences seemingly quite dissociated. For all the desire to flee the world at large and hide in privatized, isolated places, the acts of the private sphere were still measured in relation to more public acts. This is how a system of social relations was produced.

The Victorians' more social view of their sexuality compared with our contemporary society's can be shown in contrasting the Victorian term "seduction" with the more modern term "affair." A "seduction" meant to our great-grandfathers breaking down the barriers of moral and social order which one person caused in another. "Seduction" connoted a concrete, double act of violation, of the other person and of society simultaneously. An "affair" is something more amorphous; it stands for a sexual relation between two people, but it is a blank term. "Affair" is a word without a specific imagery which can be shared socially in speech.

People who spoke a language of involuntary expression of feelings and fetishized objects, each of which contained clues to the personality of its wearer or owner and who conceived of their sexual relations as social necessarily inhabited an erotic world. The Victorian culture was a sensual world, overwhelmingly and uncontrollably so, and its logic was to set up attempts at repression and self-discipline which were in fact of the most destructive sort. This eroticized world was the capitalist bourgeoisie in its first epoch of domination in Western society. What has occurred in the present century is that, hoping to escape from Victorian repressiveness, we have overturned the semiotics of that world in such a way that we have substituted a new slavery for the old. We have desocialized physical love, turning eroticism into the more isolated and inward terms of sexuality. This change from eroticism to sexuality reveals how the processes of destructive gemeinschaft have come to take form in everyday experience.

I may give the impression that the terms of personality in the nineteenth century can be totally divorced from the meanings ascribed to sexual and other personal relations today, but I do not intend that divorce. Rather, the principles of nineteenth-century bourgeois culture have developed to such an extreme point today that a sharp qualitative difference has arisen between past and present. In a very real sense, we remain under the spell of that past culture even as, through a process of taking its principles to an extreme, we have sought to escape its repressive effects. The desocializing of physical love, which has taken place in the present century, is a result of extending to the extreme the principle of personality immanent in appearances. The extreme version of personality discernible, causally at work, in all kinds of human experiences is that the world soon seems to appear only a mirror of the self. Meanings in the world become psychomorphic; the sense of meaningful and *also* impersonal life disappears.

It is a truism that Americans and American culture tend more to such a psychomorphic view of society, one in which questions of class, race, and history are all abolished in favor of explanations which turn on the character and motivation of participants in society. But American society in this view represents a kind of ultimate example of a point of view which is taking hold in Western Europe in the present century as well. Think, for instance, of the foundations on which particular leaders in England, France, and West Germany are spoken of as "legitimate" or "credible." These judgments are based not so much on the leader's ideological purity or coherence as on his ability to appeal personally and thus command the votes of those who do not share his ideological interests. The leader legitimates himself as fit to rule in the eyes of the public not by his public position but in terms of his personal appeal. Or think of the increasing tendency of people in the upper working classes and the new *classes moyennes* to view their positions in society as a result of exercising or failing to exercise their personal abilities. This taking of personal responsibility for one's class makes an emotional appeal even as members of these classes may understand in the abstract that their positions result from blind slotting in the class structure.

To view one's experience in the world as a consequence or a mirror of one's personality structure and to measure such questions as political legitimacy in terms of personality both have a specific psychological dimension. It is narcissism. By this is not meant love of self, but rather the tendency to measure the world as a mirror of self. When the principle of immanent personality is extended to such an extreme that all appearances in society come to matter only as manifestations of personality and personal feelings, we are talking about narcissism mobilized as a cultural condition, as a code of meaning.

Let me pin this down more specifically. The psychological disorders which psychotherapists treated most often eighty years ago were hysterias; these hysterias were the raw "data" upon which psychoanalysis was built. But today, hysteria is a relatively rare complaint, as are the derivative hysterical phobias and compulsion repetitions. Instead what appears most commonly in clinics for treatment are "character disorders." The patient feels empty, dead, or dissociated from the people around him but has no objectified neurotic signs, such as an hysteria or a phobia. These "character disorders" are usually related in treatment to narcissistic deformations; one has this feeling of deadness, of an inability to feel or to relate to other people, because one has begun to conceive of that outside world as a peculiar mirror of self. It exists to fulfill the self; there are no "human objects" or object relations with a reality all their own. The peculiarity, and the destructiveness, of this narcissistic vision is that the more the environment of the human being is judged in terms of its congruence with or subservience to self-needs, the less fulfilling it becomes. Expectations of the outside grow enormous, the outside becomes a sea in which the self floats without differentiation. For the very reason that expectation of fulfillment becomes at once so vast and amorphous, the possibilities of fulfillment are diminished. Because there are no boundaries between self and other, experiences lose their form; they never seem to have an end or a definition of completion. Concrete experiences with other people, therefore, never seem "enough." And because gratification from this oceanic, boundaryless outside never seems enough, the self feels empty and dead. The obvious content of a character disorder is "I am not feeling"; the hidden narcissistic content is "the world is failing me, and so I am not feeling."

The reason that a shift in clinical data has occurred from Freud's generation to the present day is that the society in which therapists work has changed. Today's society has mobilized the forces of narcissism that are potential in all human beings by intensifying the culture of personality immanent in social relations to such a point that those relations now appear only as mirrors of self. The result of this mobilization is to desocialize such personal experiences as sexuality or parentage by erasing the very notion of society itself—"society" means that different domains of experience are judged in terms of one another, but are not equated as emanating from the same source, and "society" also means that external, believable constraints operate upon the self, having a reality of their own.

Let me give an example of how this mobilization of narcissism operates in one of the popular ideologies of sexual liberation. A book like Germaine Greer's *The Female Eunuch* starts with a clear and incontestable picture of the domination of men over women in jobs, education, homelife, and so forth. She states that this is because a social "system" operates in society: men are not tyrants; modern life simply makes them play that role. Well and good. The contention is then made that a woman has to rebel against this system by being able to do anything a man does; she "deserves" whatever men have. Gradually, as the book unfolds, the idea recedes that a system of social relations created female oppression in the first place. A woman who gets what she "deserves" in the system plays an oppressor's role so that she has simply changed positions with men in a game of musical chairs. Would the system itself be changed by women entering into the positions of dominance? Such a question is put aside as the author argues that women should try to get "total gratification" and that they deserve whatever they want. Thus, in the course of making an argument for the equality of the sexes, Greer winds up denying the very social realities which created the problem in the first place. Total gratification of the self becomes the alternative to systematic discrimination against females. In the course of the book, the world, at first seen as concretely unjust, becomes a mirror or resource for the self. This is the process of narcissism at work in an ideology of liberation, defeating the goals of that ideology by gradually blotting out the reality which caused the problem. It must also be said that this conversion of the desire for liberation into the desire for personal liberation well serves to maintain the system as a whole; the social network of inequalities is not altered, although the sex of a few of the players may be changed.

The use of the term "narcissism" may mislead in that it suggests a culture becoming childish as the mirroring of self in social relations takes an ever stronger hold on people's consciousness. What is truly perverse about narcissistic projections is that they are seldom self-evident, nor do they represent simple demands for pleasure. For example, if a person from the petit bourgeoisie attempts to explain to himself why he has failed to rise to a higher status in society and arrives at the conclusion that some personal failing of his is the cause, he is mirroring the self onto the world, despite all his abstract knowledge that social organization makes it difficult to be mobile the farther down the social ladder one is. This is as much a narcissistic formulation as is the credo that liberation from a subdominant role ought to end up with free gratification of the self through the "resources" of society.

Elsewhere I have argued that there is a correlation between the increasing bureaucratization of modern capitalism and the mobilization of narcissism in society.[*] Large-scale bureaucratic structures function on a system of promised rewards based on the supposed talent, personal affability, and moral character of the employee at work. Reward thus becomes tied to the exercise of personal ability, and failure to gain reward—in fact a systematic necessity since large bureaucracies are sharp pyramids—is increasingly interpreted by those in the lower middle positions as a failure on their own parts to be rewardable, by virtue of their personalities. This explanation complements, rather than underlies, the explanation based on processes of collective consciousness given above: both for functional reasons and as a consequence of the intensified belief in personality immanently disclosed in social relations, narcissism has come to be mobilized.

[*] Richard Sennett and Jonathan Cobb, *The Hidden Injuries of Class* (New York, 1972).

Therefore, it has become possible to believe, as the Victorian bourgeoisie could not, in a "protean self." The American psychiatrist Robert J. Lifton defines a "protean self" as a belief that one's personality is always undergoing fundamental changes, or is capable of doing so. There is no core of "innate" human nature or fixed social conditions that defines it. It is a self so totally immanent in the world that it is a creature of immediate appearances and sensations. This selfhood puts an immense premium on "direct" experiences with other people; it detests reserve or masks behind which other people are felt to lurk, because in being distant they seem to be inauthentic, not taking the immediate moment of human contact as an absolute. Lifton is highly ambivalent about this protean self: he sees it as a pure analytic construct to be valuable, because the vision of an infinitely malleable human nature gets away from the whole problem of ahistorical, innate personality factors. But as a cultural phenomenon, he somewhat fears this protean man. In dedicating oneself so thoroughly to a sensate, direct life of experience, one cannot make long-term commitments, and resistance to immediate moments which are malign or unjust becomes difficult. A protean man may live a rich immediate life, but only at the cost of accommodation to his environment. Differently put, only a sense of something constant in the self produces the will to resist what ought to be resisted in the immediate life-world.

Belief in a protean self follows logically from the erasure of boundaries around the self. If the world of impersonal necessity is erased and reality becomes a matter of feeling, changes in feeling—impression and sensation—seem to be fundamental changes in character. The self is thus fetishized, as objects were a century ago. This totally phenomenological view of the self has had one of its most dramatic expressions in the commune movements of North America and Western Europe during the last decade. These communes were founded not so much on the conviction that new forms of group life would be valuable or pleasureable experiences in and of themselves for their members, as on more millenarian beliefs that they could serve as "examples" of how the larger society ought to reform itself. That millenarian belief is really the conviction that changes in one's immediate life space are so important—that changes in the quality of feelings between people who become intimate are of such value—that they somehow become emblems of what the whole of society ought to be like, which is really to say that there is no imagination of society as something different from intimate transactions. That changes in immediate feeling are political in character and that these changes have any consequence beyond the boundaries of immediate experience becomes possible to believe only if one believes that the whole of society is made up of creatures whose real being consists of immediate feelings; that is, that society is composed of protean selves waiting for a "model" of changes in feeling to guide the transformation of the whole.

In the realm of sexuality, this belief in a protean self suggests to people that "who" they are depends on who their lovers are and how much they experience in love. Lamartine could write as a poetic conceit in the last century that "who I am depends on whom I love today," but that conceit has been transformed in this century into an all-too-common everyday conviction. Sexuality thus becomes burdened with tasks of self-definition and self-summary which are inappropriate to the physical act of making love with another person. There are now many studies of the anxiety with which people approach the matter of sexual selection of a partner, and there is some evidence that this anxiety has replaced the rather different anxieties of two generations ago about the subsequent experience the partners might have. If the act is freed of repressive checks, the selection of partners seems to carry a different kind of, and perhaps more onerous, burden—choosing someone to sleep with becomes a reflexive act; it tells who you are. Thus, in the Van Burgh researches, there appears a consistent worry about whether "this person is right for me" over such formulations as "is he or she attractive" or "do I like him or her." Once the self becomes a protean phenomenon, the reality of the other person is erased as an "other"; he or she becomes another "resource" of inner development, and loving the other person for his or her differences recedes before a desire to find in another person a definition for oneself.

The belief in protean selfhood produces in its turn a peculiar code of interpersonal interaction. This code treats intimate interchanges as a market of self-revelations. You interact with others according to how much you tell them about yourself; the more "intimate" you become, the more confessions you have made. When the partners run out of self-revelations, the relation all too often comes to an end; there is nothing more to say, and each takes the other for granted. Making human contact by marketing confessions results in boredom, rather rapidly realized. Psychologists will have had direct experience of this notion of human contact as self-revelation in their training experiences with beginning diagnostic interviewers. The tyro interviewer is convinced that to treat another human being with respect, he must match whatever is revealed to him by some personal experience of a similar sort of his own. This shows he "understands," he "sympathizes." The vision of human interaction as a card game—in which the players match card of identity for card—rules more widely in the culture. It appears in such situations as encounter groups, T groups, and the like. It has become one of the main modes of interaction through which married people experience short-term extramarital affairs, which are initiated by that classic complaint, "My spouse doesn't understand me." The market exchange of confession has logic in a society ruled by the fear that one has no self until one tells another person about it; this is the protean man's dilemma.

In therapeutic work with people who harbor a protean sense of themselves, this consciousness poses an extraordinary problem. On the one hand, the therapist and the client operate on the joint assumption that actual changes in personality will occur in therapy; on the other hand, these changes can realistically occur only when the client has abandoned the belief that he must exchange his old, bad, damaged self for an entirely new model. At a social level the same problem holds. Collective change cannot occur so long as the fantasy exists that collective life can instantly change its essence, substituting a "new" model for the old. And this is why it is no accident that Western bourgeois radicals of the last decade could so easily arrive at a notion of changes in immediate personal relations as "models" of what should happen to the whole society. That fantasy in no way challenges the structures of domination; it simply sets an asocial alternative against these structures, so life goes on much as before and people dream of a different selfhood.

Let me now summarize the differences in culture which stand behind the nineteenth-century idea of eroticism and the modern idea of sexuality. The repressive eroticism of the nineteenth-century bourgeoisie was the product of three belief structures. The first and most important was that individual personality was immanent in appearances in the public world. The second was that every appearance, every object of use in making an appearance, had by consequence a personalistic meaning so that appearances became fetishized. The third was that for all the desire to retreat from social relations and make securely private the realm of feeling, these intimate emotions like sex remained exposed and judged in societal terms. The belief structure of the modern bourgeoisie is also composed of three parts. The first is the intensification of the idea of immanent personality to such a point that the world becomes a narcissistic mirror of the self. The second is that the self becomes a protean phenomenon. The third is that this immanent, protean self interacts with others and creates the conviction of its own existence by engaging in market transactions of self-revelation. In part the semiotics of twentieth-century personality are only the consequences of the nineteenth-century terms, taken to an extreme; in part also, these modern terms of personality coincide with the increasing bureaucratization of industrial society, for the elaboration of bureaucracy, impersonal as it initially seems, in fact powerfully personalizes the experience of those who live out their adult lives under its terms.

What then are the consequences for the experience of crisis in modern life of these new terms of personality? To answer that question we have to start with the assumption that confrontations as such are unavoidable between human beings, that no matter how tyrannically pure or fraternally utopian the social settings in which they move, differences between people are still going to involve painful encounters, an occasional sense of betrayal, a more usual sense of anger, when these differences are expressed. So that the question really is, What difference do these modern terms of personality make in the unavoidable fact of crises in interpersonal relations?

The difference they make is that today people experience these unavoidable clashes as contests for personal legitimation. The appearance of an unbridgeable difference in another human being becomes a challenge to the worth of one's own self. An unavoidable difference challenges the basic modality of seeing the self mirrored in the world; the processes of mirroring, processes of projection, sharing of similarity, and the like, are shattered. The persons involved are faced with a problem which will not signify according to the terms of immanence, protean self-definition, and market exchange of confidences, which dominate the culture. The experience of interpersonal crises then escalates to a higher question of which person, which side of the difference, should legitimately exist at all.

Let me give a concrete example of the escalation of painful human differences into a crisis of personal legitimacy. Some years ago I interviewed a working-class young adult living in Boston who was recently married. He and his wife were having sexual problems which centered on his disgust of oral-genital sex and her repeated desire for it. As this conflict went on, gradually the issue changed for him from disgust at the act to disgust at his wife as a person who would wish to engage in it. She in turn moved from a sympathy for his reluctance to a feeling that there was something basically weak about him. Each time they made love, whether they engaged in oral-genital sex or not, they began to think of the sexual encounter as a testing of the other person's worth. After a few months, this testing moved out of the bedroom. All sorts of petty signs and behavior were picked up as signals about one or another being "revolting" or a "coward." Their interchanges thus came to be matters of pinning immense characterological labels on each other via smaller and smaller details. At the same time, they both became disturbed that they could no longer talk freely to each other, and what they came back to again and again was the fact of this difference in one part of their sexual tastes indicating some vast chasm which made *any* talk difficult, because all talk seemed burdened with the unbridgeable gap symbolized through the disgust-coward difference in bed. After ten months a separation occurred, and in the period of separation each spoke of their new aloneness as a chance to be at last really a new kind of person, as though the fact of encountering a difference ten months earlier had prohibited each one from being "authentic" in the presence of the other.

There are two ways to generalize crisis experience of this sort into collective forms. One is simply to write it large; those who talk about the supposedly high rates of divorce now or the equally misleading crisis of the family do so. These images assume that interpersonal crises directly translate into institutional instability, an assumption which later in this essay I shall challenge. The other way to generalize the formation of interpersonal crises as crises of legitimacy is to recognize that there is a continuity in the process of creating meaning from a small to a societal scale. On this ground the modern environment of crises converts conflicts of group, ethnic, or class interest into conflicts in group identity.

Just as individuals framing a conflict in terms of legitimacy are struggling over who they are rather than specifically what they want, modern collective units in conflict gradually come to substitute for questions of power, entitlement, and flexibility of action more abstruse, amorphous, and asocial assertions of the moral legitimacy of the group. It has an identity, a collective self, and therefore it deserves to be fed and its demands met. Because the members of the group feel close, feel as one, their claims upon the society are legitimate, no matter what the substance of the claims or the means of their realization. As an extreme example of this, I would cite ethnic-terrorist groups. The fact of having discovered a common self legitimates the means of terror to preserve that end; this is equally true at the opposite end of the political spectrum in Falangist or other modern Fascist groups. If one moves from these political extremes to more ordinary forms of collective conflict, the same process is at work. The locality asserts the integrity of its demands against a central planning organization not on the grounds that the actual practices of the central bureaucracy are unjust per se, but rather on the grounds that the solidarity of the locality will be destroyed. It is no accident that local politics conducted on this basis of identity-as-legitimacy so often self-destructs. While the locality fights the outside world for threatening its solidarity, within itself it conducts continual tests of who really belongs and who really expresses the sense and the interests of the collective whole. These tests inevitably lead to fragmentation, intramural struggles over who is an authentic and therefore legitimate member of the group, and so on. Powerlessness is the result of collective action formed out of attempts to define a collective identity, a collective self.

When a crisis escalates to the question of legitimacy of self, a destructive gemeinschaft is created. Openness to others in the hope of sharing feelings is the modern meaning of gemeinschaft. It operates on the principle that selfhood can be generated through mutual confession and revelation, and under the illusion that experiences of power, inequity, or domination all have a meaning subsumed in psychological categories. The destructive quality of this gemeinschaft when tested by external or internal conflicts is that questions of unity of impulse become more important than discussion or defense of common interests. If there is not unity of impulse, and given the construction of the human being it is a rare event, then the struggle is in terms of whose impulses are real and legitimate. Thus the community of the marriage or affair becomes a meeting ground for the testing of personalities, rather than an institution with interests of its own; larger communities self-destruct on the same lines. There is withdrawal from others with whom one cannot share. No matter what the scale of modern gemeinschaft, the logic of sharing feelings is that the self is made powerless when feelings cannot be shared. This is why there exists the conviction, now so prevalent among those who come into treatment, that one's real problems are those of the arousal of feeling in the presence of others. Overtly, in individual cases this problem is framed as a matter of self-failure; covertly, in collective as well as individual desires for gemeinschaft relations with others, there is an accusation against the world for not mirroring back to one the finished resources for completing an identity.

In speaking of the psychological semiotics which make of human differences crises in legitimation, I am entering on a domain Jürgen Habermas takes up in much different terms in his *Legitimationsprobleme das Spätkapitalismus* (The Problems of Legitimation in Late Capitalism) where he presents a critique of the vision of a better society, one in which interactive processes of communication are free of the problems of societal domination. He advances a theory of cognition (*erkenntnisleitenden*) in which, ideally, distortion-free communication between people is possible. The legitimation problems of modern society are taken by contrast as relevant only to questions of domination and control. I think this view is psychologically naïve. Precisely, the problem of modern culture lies in its assumption that human beings must somehow get away from the issue of domination in order to be communicative and open. To dream of a world in which psychological processes of open communication, processes which are taken to be moral goods, are free from social questions, is to dream of a collective escape from social relations themselves. The preference for psychological canons of openness over the social problematics of power is precisely the dynamic of destructive gemeinschaft. Habermas's work is not so much a critique of the problem of legitimation now faced by the culture as the very embodiment of this problem.

Having outlined the historical processes which have created destructive gemeinschaft relations in modern society, let me turn to the region in which this destructive gemeinschaft operates most powerfully: the family.

Privacy Transformed into Intimacy

Today the phrase "the private family" seems to connote a single idea, but until the eighteenth century, privacy was not associated with family or intimate life, but rather with secrecy and governmental privilege. There have been numerous attempts to explain the confluence of privacy and family life in the modern period, the most notable and direct being that of Engels. Because of the sterility of human relations in the productive system of capitalism, Engels argued, people displaced their desires for full emotional relations to a single sphere, the home, and tried to make this sphere privileged—that is, exempt from the empty interactions of office or factory. Engels's idea of privatization supplements the process Tönnies saw in the larger society, of a movement from gemeinschaft to gesellschaft relations where the family becomes a miniature gemeinschaft in a largely alien world.

The term "privatization" has become a cliché today among those who study and write about the family and has taken on two overtones which obscure its meaning. All too often in writings on the private family or its technical form, the isolated nuclear family, it is assumed that privatization can accomplish its own goals, that people who desire to create little hidden regions of open emotional expression in society can actually do so. This is the assumption of the historian Phillippe Aries and those of his school when they talk about the family withdrawing from the world in modern times. Missing in this approach is the sense that what has the power to divide work from family has the power to divide the family itself. If we accept this latter view, as I think we must, then the experience of privatization of the family in the nineteenth century appears as an attempt to make the family a warm, full, emotional unit, but it is an attempt which constantly fails, precisely because the alien world organizes life within the house as much as without it.

Secondly, the cliché "privatization" misleads by suggesting a static condition—privatized life—which results from the dynamic processes of society. What happens once the family then becomes "privatized"? In a curious way, those who use the word cannot answer the question. After all, this process of privatization has been at work for two hundred years, and yet its students use fixed emotional states to describe it: "isolation," "emotional over-involvement with kin," and the like. Surely the families of *Emma Bovary*, *Buddenbrooks*, and *Herzog*, all overtly privatized, are not the same.

It is important, therefore, to construct a picture of changes in the experience of private family life. The changes in the culture of personality between the nineteenth and twentieth centuries outlined above can be used, at least to provide some indication of the profound shifts in family which have occurred within the last four generations and the effects of these shifts in experience of crisis within the family setting.

Let us return for a moment to Engels's view of the pressures creating privatization in the nineteenth century. These are all pressures of displacement; the flow of pressure is in one direction from a work experience more and more empty to a house attempting to provide a forum for the full range of emotional relationships, including those which properly belong and have been displaced from the public world of production. Let us then ask what would set up a contrary pressure so that the family fails in its efforts to provide a refuge, fails to become securely privatized. Critical in setting up this contrary motion were the very semiotics of personality which had crystallized by the 1860s and early 1870s.

In the childrearing manuals which appeared in the 1860s in both France and England, a common, almost monotonous theme appears. For children to grow up with stable characters, they must experience orderly appearances in the family circle; not only must the child, whether boy or girl, act consistently through good "habits" and "beneficent rules" but the parents must observe good habits and rules themselves in respect to their children; above all, they must observe these rules *consistently*. This advice about family dynamics was given because of a fear among the Victorian bourgeoisie that if appearances were not routinized in the home, if spontaneity were not suppressed, then personality would never crystallize or the child would not grow emotionally strong. This fear comes out of an equation whose elements we have already uncovered. Personality inheres in appearances, and for personality itself to acquire a form, appearances must be rigidly formed and disciplined.

This code of child-parental behavior is an instance of the way in which the codes of personality prevalent in the last century pushed family relations, in spite of the desire family members had to withdraw from the terrors of the world into a relaxed warm zone, back into the contradictory impulses of order and immanence which ruled the public world. Between husbands and wives, the same pressure for stabilization of behavior occurred. Love between man and woman in the family was measured precisely by the ability of the partners to conform without deviation to the rules of what love should be. Just as that adherence to a construct of propriety was the necessity for survival in factory or office, it became necessary at home. But the realms of work and home were not therefore identical. In the home changed appearances would threaten the partners' sense that they knew who each other was as a person; a repressive, rigid routine became the means of certifying that the marriage itself was real—just as the child was thought to grow in a healthy way only if he experienced others in terms he could "trust." For the Victorians "trust" meant trust to be the same.

Thus, when we talk about the "privatization" of the family experience in the nineteenth century, we are on the one hand talking about a belief that the family ought to be removed from the tremors of the outer world and be a moral sphere higher than that outer world, and on the other hand, we are talking about a code of human interaction derived from a belief in immanent personality which thrust the family back out into the very anxieties about order and immanent meaning which ruled public life. *Both* the desire to retreat and the reconstruction of the outer society are elements of privatization; the first would soon have exhausted itself as a desire had not the second so insistently thrust family dynamics back into the public contradiction so that the family's mission of withdrawal always seemed yet to be achieved.

For families of the present generation, privatization on these terms has ceased to exist. Half the equation of pressure has changed. The pressure dividing family experience in people's minds from the experience of work and adult social life does continue. In fact, there is some evidence that in the last forty years the gap has grown wider between the actions which middle-class adults believe make them good parents and the actions which they construe as making them powerful or at least powerful enough to survive in the world. However, because the terms of personality have so altered in this century, the other set of contrary pressures does not obtain. There is no longer a world alien to the self to which the self refers. For example, for the sake of preserving a marriage as a social contract, people today are not willing to make great sacrifices of their immediate feelings and perceptions about the other partner in the marriage. Again we come upon the conundrum that liberation from repression has come to be couched in terms of a liberation from the social dimension itself with rules, restraints, and a logic alien to the logic of human sensibility. What has happened, then, is that the forces creating an ideology of familial withdrawal from the world have persisted, but the contrary force has weakened which nonetheless would refer consciousness of the marital bond back to being judged in terms of other kinds of human bonds.

Given the picture of so many nineteenth-century people imprisoned in loveless, respectable marriages, the breaking of such an equation of pressure may well seem all to the good. The problem is that this change in the terms of privatization has not liberated individuals within the family but, paradoxically, has made the family bond of even greater importance and even more destructive force. When family relations are perceived to be withdrawals from the world and also to have no reference back to nonpsychological conditions, the family group itself is magnified. The family comes to seem, in fact, the terrain on which all emotions are displayed; emotions which are not familial have no reality because the world outside is only instrumental. The more people believe in family relations as a purely psychological matter, the less they can believe that valuable psychological experience ever can exist without reference ultimately to the family. The constraint of convention over sensibility is today being broken down in the family, but in turn the reality of sensibility outside the family is also breaking down.

When people rebel against a bad marriage, it is not usually to go live alone in the world but rather for the sake of, or in the hope of, finding a newer, more emotionally satisfying mate. When children express anger at their parents, it is not usually because the parents were parents but rather because they were "inadequate" parents. Because the breaking of the old equation has led to an increasing belief in family relations as a complete universe of psychological relations, the historic change has to be thought of as a movement from the family as an unsuccessfully private institution in the nineteenth-century bourgeois experience to the family as an illusionary psychological category in twentieth-century bourgeois experience.

In this movement from privacy to intimacy, the family has become the domain in which the processes of destructive gemeinschaft are played out. The family defines the territory of a community of feeling. In order to criticize it as such, I want to be as clear as I can about what it means to perceive a family at once socially withdrawn and emotionally complete. It is important to do so because there is so much loose talk about the family as "in crisis" at the present time, talk of crisis which in fact only serves to reinforce the family as a model of psychological experience in the minds of those who perceive the family falling apart.

What is the rationale of conceiving the family to be socially withdrawn and emotionally complete? The rationale is that of the narcissistic mirror. If the family is withdrawn from crass contingency and morally "better," then what appears in this particular psychic network has a reality and a purity unsullied by alien contingencies, masks of necessity, and the like. Once freed from the world, the family appears as a disclosure of pure psychological experience. This is then mirrored out beyond the family nexus, and emotional transactions in the world are judged in terms of categories which are familial in their form.

Let me give some concrete examples of this. Patterns of friendship among adults at work today follow a course unlike those of four generations back. The more a friendship between adults at work grows, the more attempts are made to integrate the adults into the respective family circles and form friendships between families. American middle-class workers open the gates to the home rather readily to their friends, French bourgeoisie rather reluctantly, but the path of friendship is the same. One of my students has done a comparative study of friendships between middle-class adults in London and Paris in the 1870s, as these are portrayed in the pulp fiction of the time, and he found something entirely different from this modern pattern. Among males a friend became someone with whom you could escape from the rigors of the family; a friend was someone to take out rather than invite in. Among females, friendship also involved progressive dissociation from family relations; a friend was someone who could become a confidante for grievances against both children and spouse. Because women were incarcerated in the house, female friendships appeared familial, but in fact friends in the house meant a chance to rail against the tyrannies of the home. A century ago, then, friendship was for both sexes a matter of escape from familism; today it is a matter of progressive induction into familism.

Another example is something quite out of the ordinary, and seemingly opposed to the mores of the bourgeois family: the hippie commune. In a study of 1960s-style communes, Rosabeth Moss Kantor found them to be insistently concerned with reliving old family issues and relationships so as to create a higher kind of family. These communes were not formed around work per se, but around shared experiences of survival labor tied to the building of a collective family. She found, indeed, that there was a great problem created for people living in communes when psychological rights were asserted against the collective whole; that is, rights to multiple dimensions of psychological experience outside the commune which could not be absorbed into the higher family or at least made consonant with the commune's values. For example, if you were sleeping with someone not part of the commune, why is it you didn't ask him or her to come live in the commune? The refusal to familize these relations was taken as a betrayal.

The most profound indicator of this new family imagery comes from the realm of ideology. Today, the concept of psychological emancipation which dominates the culture involves liberation of the self rather than liberation from the self. In ordinary speech and desire we use such terms as being able to express one's feelings or feeling free to do so. Habermas's model of open communication has its vulgar counterpart in the belief that social institutions are bad as soon as they get in the way of human expression. One example of that vulgar belief is Greer's *Female Eunuch;* another is the marital break-up outlined in this essay, a case in which both partners came to interpret a sexual conflict as a problem of being able to express themselves rather than interact with each other.

Liberation of one's feelings along these lines is basically a familistic ideal. Liberation from one's feelings is a nonfamilistic ideal. The first refers to the possibility of experience in which anything one wants and any sensation one has can be received by others; that is, liberation of one's feelings supposes an accepting environment, one in which interest in whatever one does feel will be shown by others and appreciated by them simply because one does have a feeling. This environment can only be that of the child displaying himself to an audience of parents. Liberation from one's feelings refers to the possibility of experience which is impersonal and in which the person observes a convention, plays a role, or participates in a form. Its classic locus is the city; its classic name is cosmopolitanism.

But the contrast cuts further. The display of newly discovered feelings to a fully accepting environment (usually of parents rather than peers) is usually a post-Oedipal phenomenon; that is, it follows upon the child's first consistent declarations of his own independence. The display of play behavior, in which the child participates in a social form with impersonal conventions, is usually a pre-Oedipal experience; it follows upon the child's discovery that he can engage in games. Conservative critics of the modern culture of a "boundaryless self" usually base their attacks on the notion that this culture is regressive and childish. The real problem is exactly the reverse. The terms of modern bourgeois notions of personality are not regressive *enough;* these notions do not permit the adult to call upon the most fundamental and earliest born of the social impulses, the impulse to play. Play is pleasure in the observance of a form, a convention not dependent on individualized, momentary impulse. The reproach one ought to make to the notion of liberation of the self is that these energies of play remain dormant as the adult celebrates a freedom later apparent in his cycle of maturation, one in which the spontaneous discovery of spontaneous impulses in himself will be received and accepted by others. An ideal of regression only to a post-Oedipal family relation insures that only the most fragile and withdrawn moment of family history becomes enshrined as a cultural ideal.

The distinction between liberation of the self and liberation from the self has a last dimension. The first is a wholly secular belief. In a society harboring any notion of transcendence of the self, it is impossible. Such a society need not be overly religious or have a ritualized creed. The notion that humanity ought to struggle to be liberated from the boundaries of psychological impulse is possible in any culture which perceives the self to be a little cabinet of horrors. In such a society, the goals of social life will be the suppression of these impulses of petty desire, greed, and envy for the sake of a sociable existence passed in the company of other people. A vision of society in these terms informed as much of Rousseau's idealism as it did Freud's forbodings. When we speak of a society given over to liberation of the self, we are speaking of a society refusing to take into account the high probability that human beings are capable of destructive feelings which should at least be hidden from the sight of others. This is why a society like ours celebrating the sheer existence of human feeling cannot in the end be called "privatized," for there is no vision of the social necessity of keeping certain impulses a secret from others, harboring them only in private. Instead, we consider this very necessity for disguise to be only a further proof of the authoritarian injustices of present social arrangements; we are prone to convert discretion and tact into signs of domination. For this reason I cannot see how the word "liberation" itself denotes a state of progress in the present time from a century past. A hundred years ago, personality was socialized only by ideas of repression; today it is not socialized at all. Surely these are opposite and equal evils.

Let me now conclude with a discussion of the impact of this familized intimacy on the experience of crises within the family itself. The family as an intimate terrain, a world of its own, a measure of psychic reality, has magnified certain necessary crises which must occur in all kinship systems to such a point that the issues in the crisis become unresolvable, and yet the hold of family life on those caught in these crises is strengthened. The process of destructive gemeinschaft was described at the end of the previous section as a contest for personal legitimacy which arises when psychic conflicts become manifest. On the family terrain, desocialized and a seemingly complete psychological system, conflicts for personal legitimacy with other family members become life-and-death struggles for dominance, struggles based on who has the superior, better, or more complete set of feelings.

One of the necessary traumas of family life in which this dynamic rules is the shift from one adult generation to the next. In societies where feudal status is transmitted or in circumstances where adequate amounts of property pass from one generation to the next, intergenerational change in the family is tied to the acquisition of power in the world. When a society contains a bourgeois class occupying for the most part bureaucratic positions which cannot be passed on by inheritance, the correlation between generational change and worldly position breaks down. Or at least it breaks down in a direct way; children from the bourgeois families have a better chance of occupying bourgeois positions than children from lower-class positions, but this is not the same situation as one in which the sheer death of a parent is the means by which the younger generation acquires its power in the world.

Under the circumstances of bureaucratic life, how is a change of generations experienced? We can say it is more purely an emotional matter, but this alone does not take us very far. There are few known societies in which the eclipse of one generation by another is a neutral, smooth, nontraumatic process; feelings of betrayal, loss, and triumph are always involved. The real question is how these traumas are organized. In modern society, the trauma of intergenerational succession is framed in terms of the replacement of an emotionally inferior generation in the family by a new generation with psychological dominance over the past. I think Simone de Beauvoir is right in her intuitive perception that the aged are abandoned for reasons far beyond the fact that they have become productively useless. They are abandoned because they have become psychologically useless to the next generation. This psychic closure to the generation dying out is in its turn a declaration on the part of those younger that no further psychic transactions with the aged are in the interests of the younger; psychological authority is claimed in the act of surviving. This is why therapists who work with families where three generations occupy the same house find again and again that the aged are tolerated only so long as they behave submissively and why, according to one set of evidence, even the rates of senility are higher in these three-generation households than for the aged who are simply abandoned to live alone.

In a culture where family relations are psychological absolutes, the struggle for legitimation of the self sets up a struggle for psychological dominance over others. It is a zero-sum game in which you cannot feel legitimate in, of, and for yourself unless you delegitimate someone else in the family. Just as this process leads to a tyranny over the aged, it sets up a profound problem in the relations between adults and their children and among the children themselves.

For a parent to assert a behavior rule under these conditions, the rule itself becomes not a code to be obeyed or rejected in terms of its own value, but rather a symbol of whether the parent is legitimate in his or her own eyes. The child's submission becomes only a means by which the parent reassures him or herself of his worth as a person. Thus, in place of the nineteenth-century fear that the child will do himself harm if he or she does not rigidly adhere to a rule, what one encounters among parents today is a fear that there must be something wrong with themselves if the children do not obey. This fear ought logically to make parents far more disciplinarian than their great-grandparents, but the process works at a deeper level. The parent applies his or her own sense of psychological reality—that one has real feelings when one can express them freely—to the child so that in dimension family relations become what the psychologist Robert Holt has aptly called "adultomorphic." At the same time, the parent is faced with the child's needs for rules to survive in a world the child cannot yet manage on his or her own. The parent feels he must assert rules for the sake of the child but fears he is violating the child by ruling him. However, in having the child subsequently respond to these rules, the parent confirms his or her own sense of worth. The fact of what the rules are objectively thus gets lost easily in a much subtler but stronger process of asserting the self, guilt over that assertion, and triumph over the child in which the child is only a means to the parent's need for legitimation. If such a process is tangled up, the results are unfortunately all too clear, for these are precisely the means by which a confused sense of object relations is instilled into a growing human being; that is, the means by which a narcissistic character disorder is created. And these character disorders form the dominant class of treatment problems which separate the present time from Freud's generation and its psychic discontents.

Built into the very idea of sibling rivalry is the sense of a zero-sum game; children who compete with each other for parental approval quite naturally believe that attention or rewards given to one child must diminish the rewards given to another. But under cultural conditions in which everyone in the family operates in terms of a zero-sum game, sibling rivalry takes on a peculiar form. The sibs must maximize the differences between themselves in order to have a turf on which they can attract any notice, for they are competing not only with each other but also with their parents. One of the most striking of these patterns of differentiation revolves around the issue of competency and ability. If one child begins to show himself able, another attempts to attract attention via differentiation through systematic failure. The same principle of maximizing differences will be applied to psychological competences, so that one sib reacts to another's emotional strength by accentuating his or her own fear, weakness, or passivity.

Certainly sibling rivalry in which failure becomes a means of attention-getting knows no boundaries of time and place. It is a question of how much the specific historical culture reinforces the pattern and on what grounds. What is special about the tendencies to reinforce sibling failure in the modern family is precisely that both male and female sibs are exposed to this principle of differentiation. In societies where girls are taken as ineluctably different from boys, some of the tasks of difference are already established for the sibs without them having to create differentiation through intellectual or psychic failure. The more modern society equalizes its promises, at least of sexual equality, the more the sibling rivalry through failure is spread to all the sibs in the family. It is one of the reasons why the research of Horner and others turns up a pattern among young women of wanting to fail at being independent; if they are independent they will crowd their male sibs' territory and so lose parental love. The answer to such a dilemma is obviously not to restrict again the freedom of women but to change the modern patterns of family life which work against this freedom.

The chances that such crises of family life will transform the family itself seem slim to me. Rather, the reverse seems likely: the kind of crisis experience on this intimate terrain reinforces the dominance of the family as a total field of personal relations at the same time they make members of the modern family suffer. The reason these family relations reinforce is that the premises of personality are not challenged in the family group; rather, the persons in the family appear to be failing to have adequate personalities. It becomes possible, as the communards of the 1960s did, to dream of a higher family in which no one suffers; it becomes possible to think of building more "meaningful" human relationships by being less competitive, more open, and so forth, but these also are forms of reinforcing the idea of gemeinschaft, which states that significant human experience is intimate and moves on a terrain where people want to know each other's inner feelings. As long as warm intimate relations are given such moral priority, familism will continue, no matter how frequently people divorce and remarry, no matter how unusual their sexual practices, no matter how many affairs they conduct in search of someone who "understands" them. And as long as this intimate familism prevails, destructive competitions for personal legitimacy will rule. I haven't much hope, therefore, that people can use their intimate experiences as a model for rebuilding society, but rather I think that a new kind of gesellschaft will have to be built in order to change the destructiveness of intimate relations.

6

Norman Birnbaum

On the Possibility of a New Politics in the West

Exploitation, hunger, and terror are the fates of most of humanity. The pervasive disorder of world politics threatens a quick march to catastrophe: it is not reassuring that our best defense against that is the uncertain condominium of the superpowers. It does not guarantee peace, and it certainly guarantees trouble for those peoples and regions who seek control of their own histories. Both the state socialist and liberal capitalist societies have claimed that they had the means to autonomy for their own populations: economic growth. The performances of both economic systems have been lamentable. The Soviet or Polish citizen on a queue at a food store may be pardoned doubts as to the intrinsic superiority of a mode of production which produces so poorly. The unemployed American or French worker, meanwhile, can be permitted a certain skepticism about the recent conversion to "qualitative growth" of their own elites. The proudest legacy of the liberal capitalist societies has been, precisely, the efficacy of liberalism: it generated a politics in which the claims of citizenship could be asserted against the forces of the market. We now hear that the constriction of the market makes imperative a redefinition of citizenship: in the name of (an entirely hypothetical) common good, we are supposed to renounce our search for a larger practice of equity. The social innovations of the future, we are told, will have to reflect and deepen the disciplines of renunciation. A putative politics of renunciation, indeed, may require the sacrifice of present and potential freedoms: Athens will have to become Sparta. By comparison with the rest of the world, however, we shall remain Greeks: they stay barbarians.

The argument, obviously, appeals to several interests, sometimes contradictory ones. Those who view full employment and labor militancy with regret for their own weakened market position are surely not averse to promulgations of a new and enduring condition of scarcity. That not entirely small fraction of educated opinion which objects, on principle, to anyone enjoying anything has welcomed the discovery of new and immediate limits to growth. In general, the idea of an end to (or a drastic curtailment of) prosperity suits those for whom a thoroughly rationalized secular despair is the only valid contemporary article of faith. What, however, of the sobered proponents of a tempered optimism—the surviving heirs of the Enlightenment? Those of us who persist in the belief that a humanity moved by love and strengthened by knowledge can make a humane community, a true polis, can claim neither scriptural nor scientific warrants for our belief. If historical extrapolation exhausted social thought, we should indeed join another party—or seek the consolation of fragments of mysticism imported from other cultures which have turned to other ways of confronting themselves.

Contemporary history, however, is open to several readings. With one I propose to sketch, it presents possibilities which would allow us to construct a realm of freedom. Engels once wrote of a leap from the realm of necessity to the realm of freedom, but his distinguished senior colleague Marx put it differently. The realm of freedom, he declared, would coexist with a realm of necessity. Looking back on the disappointing history of socialism, we can conclude that freedom may consist of a superior organization of necessity. Superiority would be characterized by moral and spiritual dimensions, rather than technical ones alone. The new politics open to us would require a degree of cultural creativity impossible to enact by decree. We require new ideas of community, new conceptions of human sensibility and human nature itself, different uses of technique. Impossible to invent simply because we need them, these goods may lie about us in inchoate form, mistaken for the epiphenomena of contemporaneity, for *bricolage* on the margins of our history. Suppose, however, that an examination of our present situation allows us to identify discontinuities in constraint, *lacunae* in systems of control, resistances to consent and consensus?

This essay is an inquiry into the possibilities of modernizing the tradition of Western socialism, modernizing it by actualizing it, in circumstances far different from those envisaged by the socialists of the nineteenth century. Its method is a scrutiny of the will to change apparent in different sectors of the society (put in another language, the identification of the elements of a new historical bloc). That scrutiny entails, in turn, the confrontation of the interests of concrete groups—both active and as yet unarticulated—with their political capacities. Political capacities include the ability to distinguish substantial from ephemeral problems, to recognize ideologies for what they are (which is to say, to identify their perpetrators), to express new demands, to invent techniques of collective action. It is easy enough to describe political capacities when they are fully developed, appreciably harder to do so when groups in need of autonomy confront situations which could (but may not) induce them to begin their own education.

The notion of politics as education is indeed a legacy of the Enlightenment: must it also imply trivializing discussion, avoiding the hard struggle for power, and transferring social conflict to the realm of the spirit? Not necessarily: the formulation, after all, envisaged politics as education, not education as politics. A political education rests on the analysis of the struggle for power rather than a flight from it. This essay's focus on a socialist solution will indeed insist that the socialist tradition requires critical revision or transformation—particularly in the sphere of the political implications of culture. A rigid demarcation between a base constituted by a system of production and a superstructure organized by a system of beliefs is untenable (and was not adhered to by Marx and Engels). The importance of conflict in culture does not vitiate the importance of the struggle for the control of the system of production: it does enlarge the dimensions of that struggle.

It is entirely possible, of course, that the future belongs to no version of the socialist tradition. Quite apart from the danger of a thermonuclear holocaust, one of two lines of development for the Western societies may prevail. The first would be a continuation of the present society, subjected to external and internal modifications which would not greatly affect its substance. A continued reliance on the market would combine with the maintenance of a pronounced hierarchy in power, property, and culture. The socialist movement would have much to say about the administration of that hierarchy, and something to say about its modification in somewhat more humane, even egalitarian, directions. The Democratic party in the United States would constitute a reformist majority, approximating the Social Democratic parties of northern Europe—parties which, in turn, domesticated Communist parties in southern Europe would begin to resemble. Socialism, in this historical progression, would function as a politically plausible mode of administering capitalism. Put in a rather more generous way, a socialist presence in capitalism would facilitate the reconciliation of the market with the claims of citizenship.

Many, whatever their abstract preferences, would settle for this as a concrete historical development. It would appear to guarantee a large measure of political stability, more than a modicum of democracy and humanity, and a chance to develop our heritage of culture—even to enlarge its social basis by heavier investment in education. There are two difficulties with the postulation of this line of development. The first is that it has already stopped. External shortages of resources, internal failures in the management of the business cycle, profound popular discontents, and systematic doubt on the part of elites combine to erode belief that our society's conflicts can be contained in this way. The second difficulty issues from the first. Even if we retain the relatively protected historical space required by these assumptions about the immediate future, we shall have to experience much more conflict (some of it very brutal) than is implied by so schematic and serene a picture as that which has socialism as a benign presence in a capitalism which hardly dares utter its own name. Think, simply, of the toil and blood needed to wring the least reforms from early capitalism. Think, too, of the large decline in living standards which has resulted from the present economic crisis: reformist gains seem peculiarly fragile when productivity declines. The defense of previous gains, the extension of control over the market, will require considerable political mobilization and cultural conviction: a series of frontal assaults on concentrated economic power. It is self-deluding to suppose that this will occur without severe and continuing rents in the social fabric.

The possibility of the eruption of conflict uncontainable by our political system obliges us to think of a second, and far more regressive, line of development. The new Sparta might become just that, a society so bent on efficacy that it would curtail political freedom. The verbal form is deceptive: societies in reality do nothing; human beings in concrete historical circumstances do everything. We can conceive of a bargain struck between classes, between elites and a tired populace—as well as a classically authoritarian solution imposed by a party using the state to stabilize property relationships and enforce a cultural discipline. Fascisms have economic and cultural components (the former seeking to destroy working-class socialism, the latter to liquidate cultural modernism), while politically hostile to the democratic and liberal traditions in any of their forms. Fascisms are also historically specific, and the situation of the Western societies finds them in conflict (or the danger of conflict) with other blocs. Fascism or something like it may be as necessary for conflict management as for mobilization to win in that sort of external conflict. Evoking the possibility of fascism dramatizes analysis: all that would be required is a slow constriction of political autonomy for the segments of society, a pervasive inhibition on experiment, an increasingly explicit centralization of decision (or a purposeful attribution of competence to the peripheries by the center). A new authoritarianism might not quite resemble the forms to which we have become accustomed, and it might be more and not less effective on that account. Surely, the pseudo-liberal and anti-Communist consensus which dominated American politics from 1945 to 1965 was extremely effective at very low cost: not only did it permit the mobilization of resources for the Cold War, but it greatly hindered social criticism and possible political experiment. The current preoccupation, or obsession, with "radicals" in the German Federal Republic is strikingly similar to aspects of the American situation of a generation ago. If, in the United States in the late winter of 1975-76, the situation appears more open, it is not least because the right has decided on a concrete sociopolitical program with a certain ideological appeal: an attack on public "bureaucracy," which is to say, an attempt to cut the costs of the public sector. The resultant social situation, with its emphasis on individual and familial competition in a market, might seem not to require ideologies of authority and discipline. What, however, of those groups in the population disadvantaged by the market? The return of economic power to the market may, in the end, require a strengthening of the repressive authority of the state: European conservatives like Powell, Poniatowski, and Strauss are more systematic in their thought than their North American counterparts.

In short, there is every reason to fear the development of an authoritarian politics in the Western societies. It already exists in practice as well as program. Its full development is blocked, by democratic convictions in large public groups and amongst elites—and by the combativeness of a socialist movement which knows that the struggle for democracy is indispensable to the struggle for socialism. For the moment our fear of a new authoritarianism may be tempered by the realization that what it promises (the containment and diminution of conflict) is precisely what it is least likely to accomplish. Its regressiveness consists of its tendency to repress rather than resolve the social and cultural conflicts of the industrial democracies. The technocratic managers of liberal capitalism, at least, seek legitimation on the basis of their competence in conflict management: they do not promise to make conflicts go away. The technocrats' diminished legitimacy, of late, results from their obvious inability to go beyond conflict management—an inability rendered more obvious by the decrease in the social product over the distribution of which the technocrats have presided.

A perfectly reasonable objection, at this point, suggests itself.

Let it be granted that the new authoritarians (who, in any event, are not entirely devoid of technocratic rationalizations and technocratic support) are bound to fail. Their attempt to exercise power may prove exceedingly expensive for those likely to come under their rule: all will pay heavily, and some may succumb. Even then, if not too many persons go to prison, the realization of values we cherish, the extension of liberty and fraternity, cultural experiment, and social innovation are likely to be stopped for decades, if not longer. It would seem to follow that our attention ought to be fixed on modes of averting regression, leaving the vision of a better future to be developed at some subsequent date, when history favors us with better opportunities to resuscitate ideas of progress.

The objection is reasonable, but not entirely so. It is quite true that history in itself generates no values: there are plenty of occasions upon which it is necessary to act from the conviction that the alternatives offered by history are unacceptable, even abominable. However, the search for a defensive analysis can degenerate, quickly, into an ideology in which pretension does not quite conceal a quintessential vulgarity—in which thought claims to encompass the movement of society but registers only the anxieties of those worried about what they could lose. It becomes intellectuals little to assert that they alone speak for the conscience of humanity—above all, in an epoch in which so many have found tongues. This set of essays is an attempt to delineate contemporary possibilities—that is, to affirm the possibility of choice. It is easy enough to write an eschatology, harder to make a secular analysis. The value of the socialist tradition, however attenuated, is that it accepted the logic of the secularization of history, but did not confound blasphemy with profanity. A contemporary analysis in that tradition is faithful to it when it scrutinizes society to ask what choices are in fact contained (if concealed) in the flux of events—that is, we ask what new structures of community are possible. The eternal prospect of regression can be taken for granted.

Societies are not emanations of cultures. Were we to suppose that they were, we would have substituted the mechanical production of value for the mechanical production of constraint—and have come no closer to understanding. Societies are the result of long processes of historical accumulation, in which constraints and values perpetually struggle toward an equilibrium never attained. There are good reasons, for instance, to interpret Marxism as the

gence in these societies of the claims of national culture and tradition, the pressures exerted by society on the state. Iberia, Greece, and southern Italy are societies with historical rhythms quite different from those of Western or Central Europe, but the political and cultural influence of the more northern societies has drawn them into their historical orbit. The recent evolution of both Catholicism and the Communist variant of socialism in Italy and Spain attests to something other than a uniform process of modernization: it expresses the effect of national distinctiveness in a changed socioeconomic situation.

To what extent, then, can we explore the possibility of a new politics in a historical totality as broad as Western Europe and North America? If history is concrete, must not the historical specificity of each society in the area require separate treatment? Evoking southern Europe has brought up the problem of the periphery. Mentioning Central Europe evokes another zone of influence—not without effect on the societies at our center of attention. Relationships with the Communist superpowers and with the Third and Fourth Worlds set the West in a world system in which it can clearly claim only a relative autonomy. These are, indeed, difficulties—but not insurmountable ones. In a world of over-determination, relative autonomy is already much.

The phrase, relative autonomy, has attached to it an important specification. Western society as a whole is relatively autonomous in the world system, which is to say, it is the subject and not the object of domination over much of the world. Within Western society, however, domination is exercised by elites anxious to maintain internal as well as external power. In this volume we do not join the discussion (once, apparently, timeless but now winding down) as to whether power in contemporary society is economic or political. Late capitalism, in all its national forms—even in the United States, where all society resembles nothing so much as a gigantic market—has extinguished the distinction between economic and political spheres. It is easy enough, of course, to distinguish a firm from a ministry, a trade union from a political party, private from state property. It is impossible, however, to delimit privileged spheres of action in which economy and polity confront one another, or can be distinguished (as in the nineteenth century) from society. The elites have to maintain control in all spheres—or none. The spheres interact, indeed interpenetrate, to make up one system. The ease and the frequency with which rulers and their immediate servitors move from posts of command in the economy to the state and on to the cultural apparatus (and back again) have given rise to a proposition which stands as a contemporary article of (socioanalytic) faith. We are ruled neither by capitalists who own concentrated property nor by bureaucrats in permanent occupation of the state apparatus. We have, instead, to submit to (or struggle against) technocratic governors. They control, nay constitute, centers of power identifiable exactly as their function: coordinating points of decision, weighing stations for conflicting interests, gigantic books for the computation of social accounts. For those installed in these centers, of course, what counts is not so much the precision (much less the justness) with which they exercise these functions but the maintenance of their monopoly of decision. To what extent, however, is this article of faith sustainable? And what does whatever truth value it has—in the event, no small amount—tell us of the future of politics in the West?

When Marx referred to Hobbes as the father of us all, he apparently meant two things. The first was Hobbes's relentless analytical method, his thorough decomposition of phenomena into their essential elements. The second was Hobbes's reconstruction of the polity (indeed, of the totality of social relations) with the Leviathan as the concrete embodiment of what had been a transcendent principle—the mortal God. In the search for structures of effective and legitimate power, social thought since Hobbes has indeed pursued secular incarnations of transcendence. The depiction of technocratic elites as the very mortal Gods of modern society seems to be a reduction *ad absurdum* of the process of secularization, recapitulating many of the previous images of social thought. The technocratic elites, incapable of deriving an additive will of all, generate their own version of the general will. Newtonians, in Saint-Simon's figure, they are also masters of a Benthamite calculus. An executive committee for the *bourgeoisie* (the very term sounds almost pleasantly antiquarian), they have also expropriated the means of administration. The uncertainty with which we observe and categorize the technocrats may point to their transitional historical role. They are on top, but we can hardly say of what or for how long. Worse yet, apart from its gross features, their *modus operandi* is obscured—because we do not quite know how to apprehend, or more precisely, reconstruct the series of social relationships from which they have emerged. The very notion of a vertical social structure may be at fault: suppose the technocrats are not at the top but rather pursuing a moving and elusive historical center? Our article of faith is valuable as a point of beginning for a skeptical inquiry.

We may begin by asking what is the technocrats' essential resource. In a classical depiction of capitalism, domination was a consequence of possession of the means of production. Technocrats administer a society which may be conceived as a vastly expanded system of production; it would appear simplest to portray them as those who manage on behalf of large concentrations of capital. A number of objections attach to this depiction of the technocrats' essential resource as access to the power of capital. The power of capital, in the first place, is not restricted to the system of production—and when we conceive of society as a vastly expanded production system, we encounter the production of culture, of consent, in short of processes impossible to conceptualize as goods or services. There is a more telling objection: the power of capital is very large and extensive. For a century, to be sure, it has been opposed. In the most advanced capitalist societies, we also find the most advanced institutional limits on the autonomy of concentrated capital. True even of the United States, this is perfectly evident in other Western societies with stronger trade-union movements and powerful socialist parties. Technocratic power, however, is not diminished where capital's freedom of political movement is restricted—on the contrary, it is even larger.

It would follow that the essential technocratic resource (to refer to it as power is to describe, of course, what has to be explained—the predominance of the technocrats) is a mediating capacity. But for whom and by what standards of choice is this mediation conducted? In a society characterized by structural conflict, conceptions of the public interest must have an invented quality, an artificial one in the pejorative sense of the term. Ideologically, the technocrats do invent notions of the public interest conveniently consonant with their own power. In a situation of recurrent conflicts, each with a different content, pragmatic solutions based on the assessment of social costs much appeal to everyone as the most rational way for society to get on with its tasks. So runs the technocratic argument, which of course hypostatizes just what it ostensibly is defending, technocratic competence.

History is no planned process and even less a logical one. Do we confront in technocratic domination a usurpation of power, the emergence and consolidation of a quite accidentally developed elite? The very phraseology bespeaks our bondage to linear and schematic models of historical development. Technocratic domination is, to borrow psychoanalytic terminology, a compromise formation. It has arisen in a situation in which the market, having destroyed an estate system of social organization, proved incapable of institutionalizing one of its own. In a sequence not as rapid as that envisaged by the Marx and Engels of the *Communist Manifesto*, but fast enough by most historical criteria, capitalism engendered an opposition incapable of devising its own form of society—but impossible to eliminate. Technocratic domination intrudes where society is unable to organize itself about either transcendent or secular principles, where society's awareness of itself is in principle but not in fact accessible to the collectivity. We confront new arcanae—all the more difficult to decode because of an explicit claim to be the code of codes, the only possible language. The rhetoric of systems, of information, of decision is the speech of technocratic communication. It communicates, like all languages, a world view—and one which legitimates the technocrats' positions at the intersections of economy and polity, society and culture, their seizure of the mechanisms of command and control.

Words referring to an accidental elite, the seizure of power, and usurpation require more explanation. Technocratic domination has occurred when two historical forces, alternatively collaborating and colliding, seemed themselves to exhaust political possibility. The first was (and is) the system of production and exchange organized on a market. The second was (and is) the idea of citizenship—which most certainly encompassed liberal as well as socialist opposition to the organization of society on pure market criteria. The extension of the market, the development of large corporations which have so easily crossed (and at times, redrawn) national frontiers, the necessity of integrating science and technology in the production process, the growth of a tertiary labor force—all these processes combined to alter the market. The economy itself required coordination and prevision: think of the very words which describe a knowledge industry, or a cultural industry. A different kind of capitalism, in other terms, produced its own new system of self-regulation.

On this reading we can parody the famous phrase from the English religious conflicts of the seventeenth century: new technocrat is but old capitalist writ large. Substantial numbers of those whom we designate as technocrats work directly for large banks or corporations, seek profit maximization, and not infrequently own shares. Others vend professional and technical services to capital. Objective market position and ideology fuse to render both groups servitors of capital. In his emendation of this formulation, Galbraith argued that the personnel of the "techno-structure" take a political (and not merely economic) view of the organizations for which they work. Their interest, accordingly, is in maintaining—if necessary, by extending—the power of their organizations. They work, then, to a different time scale than that entailed in yearly statements of profit and loss. Indeed, their calculation of profit and loss is not invariably quantitative. Galbraith's views have the merit of calling our attention, once again, to the political dimensions of modern capitalism. These are two: internal (the predominance of the "techno-structure" in the organization of the enterprise) and external (the attempt to control and stabilize the market and the environment of the enterprise, generally). There is, however, another aspect to the argument. Galbraith was not the first to claim that those who served capital by managing it developed special interests of their own, specifically, the reinforcement of their managerial prerogatives. Suppose, however, that the requirements of the modern market—the long-term interests of capital, in brief—are entirely consonant with those prerogatives? The language of the technocrats, in other terms, is not simply a convenient legitimating device for usurped power. It is an indispensable element of communication in a society in which the very notion of capital has become more fluid, the conditions of its increase more complex, the processes of administration and production interconnected.

The central problem lies elsewhere. The United States has been described as a society which functions as a gigantic market. By contrast the neocapitalist economies of western Europe may be described as extensions of the polity. Surely there are differences, of perspective and interest, between technocrats in the sphere of production and those in the sphere of administration—differences not quite eradicated by the fact that in many cases, production is an affair of state. Do the state technocrats, however, respond to political imperatives—or, by monopolizing competence, do they themselves often set the terms of political debate? Moreover, politicians are most successful when they demonstrate an ability to move in a world of hard facts—or the appearance of facts. They have to compose with realities which are presented in the language of technocratic choice. The duality of technocratic power is real enough; it organizes itself about two centers, a system of production, and a system of administration. The last responds to the demands of citizenship, as the first encompasses the market. What we confront, however, is a duality within a system—indeed, a duality which itself constitutes a system. As long as it is necessary (or deemed necessary) to phrase the demands of citizenship in the language of administration, of mediation, there can be no transcendence of technocratic domination. The paradox is that the extension of the powers of the state has incorporated the just claims of citizenship to serve as a higher order of moral and political reference than do the derivatives of the market. Familiarly, one form of domination has replaced another. Worse yet, as we have seen, they interpenetrate—brother enemies, their very conflicts heighten their resemblances. Where, in this system, is the possibility of a redefinition of the terms of discourse, a political process which may open the way to concrete new forms of citizenship?

We have to start with a historical difference. The culture, the polity, and the society of Western Europe are marked by the socialist tradition. A previous analysis depicted the working-class movements of Europe as organizing counter-societies, and their own (extremely bourgeois) versions of counter-cultures. The decline in the homogeneity and integrity of working-class cultures in the European nations, a result of higher levels of education, rising standards of living, and the industrial production of culture, has not been accompanied by a decline in the socialist idea. This, in its fusion with ideas of parliamentary democracy and equality, has instead spread to cultural elites of a very different sort. They have added to it a spiritual critique of the market, new demands for human autonomy and development. Socialism, in its European form, includes far more than the material demands of the working class. The boundaries of that class have changed, its composition has altered—and the quantitative and qualitative definitions of material demands are different. Socialism, in other terms, has become a framework for the elaboration of the ideology of a new political coalition. It often sets the terms of immediate political debate, and despite the technocratic imprisonment of all political thought and practice, it is a potential reservoir of a new politics.

The situation in the United States is, of course, different. The absence of a precapitalist past, the particular form of spiritual domination exercised by Calvinism, a formalized notion of the relationship between individual and community (which allowed extremes of communal servitude disguised as individualism), did not encourage the development of socialism. The ethnic diversity of the population (and the profound division between the races), successive waves of material advance, and the institutionalization of a state regulatory system which facilitated capitalist development made socialist politics difficult. Most important, perhaps, was (and is) the fact that the struggle for political democracy could not be identified with socialism: liberalism and even libertarianism prosper in the United States in other political forms.

The American working class has been and is militant in concrete terms, and has a clear perception of its immediate interests. It shares with an influential intelligentsia and a large salariat (a working class of a new sort, by any sensible definition) a devotion to libertarian ideas, a sense of social and economic justice, a skepticism about those in authority and power. Recurrently, a critique of capitalism has been developed by the intelligentsia. The present American intelligentsia is in an ambiguous position. Beneficiaries of technocratic domination, comfortably installed in a large cultural industry, its members have again developed a qualitative critique of capitalism. (Its unemployed younger members, unable to become schoolteachers or university professors, unemployed lawyers and scientists, may well think that a quantitative critique suffices.) This has begun to merge with the concrete reformism of the left wing of the Democratic party. We may well experience, in the decades ahead, a new American socialism—but much depends on the success of a West European model as yet untried.

The fronts, on both continents, are mixed. It would be convenient to insist on an unequivocal opposition of socialism and technocratic capitalism—but that is far from the case. Some socialists see their chief present task as the control, indeed the occupation of, the technocratic apparatus. They conceive of themselves quite explicitly as technocrats of the left, as exercising competence on behalf of the public. That is, clearly, the case of a large component of the German Social Democratic Party (about four of ten of whose parliamentarians are in fact state officials). Some who oppose technocratic domination are liberals, by no means unsympathetic to a capitalist economy, or at any rate by no means converts to a socialism which they imagine as a variant of bureaucratic servitude. At the apex of capitalism, in the multinational (mainly, of course,

American) firms, in the large national banks and corporations, liberalism has long since disappeared—except as an occasional source of secondary ideological defense against a socialism which might threaten to move beyond the administration of capitalism. Socialism, however, will have to move beyond that—not least because the technocratic management of capitalism is proving so difficult to stabilize. A socialism which takes seriously its own libertarian tradition would have to develop a critique of its own technocratic distortions.

We have to face a problem of relative historical time, as well as of differences of national tradition. The United States is an advanced capitalist society, but underdeveloped in its welfare institutions and its political consciousness. Elites confront a population culturally homogenized, but not totally: Americans have a surprising degree of preconscious or unarticulated resistance to the American forms of capitalism. Moreover, its cultural elites are increasingly disaffected. A putative American socialism might have a chance of combining an attack on capitalism with a search for forms alternative to technocratic governance. The least one can say is that there is no American socialist movement which has recently been corrupted by integration with technocratic power. It is, presumably, the relative homogenization of the population (a derivative of the way in which all society has become a market) which accounts for depictions of the United States as historically more advanced than the Western European societies. The idea lacks not only precision but sense. The socialist component in European culture, and in its state traditions and practice, means that the European societies will never move in an American direction (a direction, moreover, from which the United States has begun to turn). It also means that European socialism has the difficult task of both using and extricating itself from technocratic power. The idea of relative historical time—in an era in which American international corporations and American political and military pressures (some of them covert) are factors in European politics—does have its limits. Our analysis of the West as a historical totality, however, depends upon analytical categories in turn inextricably connected to images of political possibility, of an ideal community.

It is appropriate, then, to consider the ends of politics and in particular socialist politics. Three components make up the socialist tradition. The first is the defense of the material interests of the working class. Defense has to be taken in a large sense, to imply cultivation and extension: the material interests of the working class are the concern of a socialist politics in a larger historical perspective than that entailed by the state of the market for labor at any given time. The notion of the working class, too, has to be taken in a larger way—or if socialism is to make sense in a situation like our own, in which not only manual workers are dependent on the market and in which many of them have in any event become technicians. This first component of the socialist tradition is unthinkable, however, without two additional notions which are part of it. The first, simply, is that of collective action: the interests of the working class are conceived and acted upon not as the arithmetic sum of differentiated individual interest but as a value or standard common to the class. In that way—and this is the second and more general notion—they escape specific material form: they provide (adequately stated) a human standard for regulating economic behavior. We come close to the original Marxist assertion that the interests of the proletariat were identical with those of humanity.

That proposition, however, can be argued in two ways. The first would point to the proletarianization of most of humanity. The second (another way of putting it) would argue that the proletariat's struggle for liberation would create the conditions of a human community. It is the idea of a realized human community that is the second component in socialism, the source of its fraternal dynamic—and also of ambiguities which at times have proved fatal for parts of the socialist movement. The unspecified idea of a higher, or truer, or more authentic community—after all—tells us too little about the specific social forms of a transformed society. Elements of fraternity, equality, and liberty clearly enter into the idea of a realized community. More precisely, its institutions may be judged according to their efficacy in attaining these ends. Yet the ends themselves are stated only in very general terms: is there a more definite way of delimiting them?

The idea of a realized human community implies its consonance with hitherto blocked human capacities: a true human community would provide the opportunity for an authentically human existence, measured by the psychological fulfillment of the personality. The third component of a socialist politics, then, is an idea of development. Marxism drew upon romantic aesthetics, upon early humanism's idea of incarnation, for his idea of the full human personality. That is behind us now, philosophically: we struggle with more complex and darker interpretations of human nature.

It is not surprising, in view of our disappointment with human nature, our secular rediscovery of what most theologians knew all along—that human beings until now in history have been hateful, even murderous—that we should find it difficult to justify a socialist politics on the grounds that it would express a higher humanity. Difficult, perhaps, but (with emendation) not entirely impossible: socialism does rest on the premise that humanity can be freed from material anxiety, from the humiliation of gross oppression, that our benign aspects can be cultivated. In the end, then, is modern socialism to succeed to the psychological theory of conservativism—defending a social order not because it expresses the best in human nature, but because it may diminish expressions of the worst?

Some part of the disarray of those who seek a new politics comes from their conviction that a fundamental human nature at once unchangeable and terrible stands in their way. There have been two recent attempts to solve this problem. Both entail a radical historicization of the idea of human nature. The first position avoids referring, with Marx, to the blockage of a human potential. The emphasis has been put instead on the internalization by humanity of a stage of social development. When a new stage is reached, a new character structure will be possible. The humanity we see before us, less than sublime, may with confidence be expected to transform itself. Marcuse and Reich, if with different arguments, take this position. The second attempt is rather different, since it does not renounce the universalism of socialist aspiration but again postulates it as an end toward which social development tends: an inclusive human identity. The road to that human identity, however, leads us through particular identities (of peoples, classes, generations)—identities often brutally ignored or suppressed by exploiters and oppressors throughout history. What is internalized by humanity is not, then, simply a stage of social development: identity is the characterological expression of a particular experience. Specific segments of humanity can go on from their particularity to join a wider humanity: they can hardly do so if their own integrity is not respected. Erikson's utilization of Freud's late ego psychology in his work on identity is political. In its insistence on the value, the justness of fit, of specific psychic constellations, it has anticipated a recent political development. Classically, socialism reflected an idea of a single humanity, fraternal and united. Newer tendencies in socialism dwell upon the rights of particular groups, upon their drive to authenticate their own existence by assuming responsibility for it. The psychological image of humanity at issue places us on a level of discourse quite different from that of the rhetoric of instinctual liberation. Whether this represents a deepening of the socialist tradition, or a return (in another language) to the old discussions of the national question, we cannot at the moment say.

The idea that the authentication of the existence of groups and categories can be part of a socialist politics surely enlarges the limits of political discussion. It does so, however, in a way that requires us to think hard about the problems before us. Where every issue is political, where every aspect of society and culture is suffused by conflict, where the very question of personal identity (a formulation which itself implies a choice of ends) is political, we may conclude that we are already in a revolutionary situation. That, however, would also presuppose a pervasive delegitimation of the contemporary state, a high degree of awareness of the interconnection of conflict in the separate spheres of existence, a generalized determination to create a new society. Some of our cultural elites are at this point, others at a vaguer state of disaffection. A socialist avant-garde, among activists in the unions and the parties, is clearly ready to assume the leadership of a movement to change society: the experience of the previous decade, in Western Europe, could be interpreted as an apprenticeship in revolution. A single, but very great, difficulty remains: the majority of the population by no means interprets our situation in so decisive, so clearcut, a fashion.

Historically, any number of revolutions have been made by elites guided by a general program and followers motivated by specific discontents. Alternatively, diffuse popular opposition has been manipulated by revolutionary leaderships with precise objectives. It is impossible to imagine a revolutionary process in our societies under either of these sets of conditions. The citizens of modern democracies are, no doubt, not educated enough. They are too educated, however, to be manipulated into revolutionary attitudes. The weight of conventional opinion must necessarily fall on the side of the status quo: its very facticity is an argument—and those who have heard savants demonstrate with syllogistic rigor the impossibility of any change for the better in our condition cannot criticize ordinary men and women for believing that what they see exhausts what is real. The chances of a new politics lie in the visible dissolution of that reality. The construction of a new society, however, demands not only the passive assent but the active participation of an educated citizenry. That alone would guarantee a new politics against some of the fatalities of an old politics—more accurately, since there are no guarantees in history, that alone would give us a chance to construct a society worthy of mature men and women. It is the very process of making that society, a continuous control of governors by the governed, the development of institutions for an alternation in these roles, that can create the conditions of maturity. There is something self-defeating, however, about beginning with the assumption that contemporary populations have to show immediate revolutionary zeal. A revision of the socialist tradition can profitably begin with those concrete popular discontents which are translatable into the language of a new politics.

Negativity is not enough. Most adults who live in the West (and most adolescents as well) distrust the institutions of our society. They do not think that these are capable of meeting their self-proclaimed ends: freedom, prosperity, stability. The currently dominant cultural critique has spread from cultural elites to broader sectors of the population: the values of continuous material accumulation, rigorous separation of work and play, ascent in the social hierarchy are increasingly regarded with skepticism—although neither a coherent alternative value system nor another schema for different social institutions follows, for most persons, from their initial critical impulses. A central component in the pervasive current skepticism is a conviction difficult to describe either as a rigorous sense of justice or as a demand for recognition, although it partakes of both. Fusing the elements of outrage at the organized inequalities of social structure with a desire for the resources which would make possible more autonomy, this temper (it cannot be described as either a conviction or an ideology) accounts for a creeping delegitimation of established elites. What is important about this usually unarticulated complex of beliefs, impulses, and sentiments is its widespread diffusion; it is not confined to the margins of our society. Moreover, its diffuse character makes of it a reservoir for sudden outpourings of anger. Much attention has been given to the ultra-left, to its occasional recourse to guerrilla actions. Protests, resistance, sabotage of all kinds are not the work of the ultra-left alone, and at times have provided a focus of crystallization for groups and movements conventionally identifiable as on the right—or, on a customary political spectrum, not quite classifiable at all.

The problem of the several socialist movements with this negativity is that it by no means requires a socialist ideology, nor a socialist politics, for its expression. European fascism no doubt was a result of the structural crisis of capitalism in its middle period, and mobilized a large anti-socialist front. Nevertheless, European fascism also had a profound anti-bourgeois component. The necessity for a revision of the socialist tradition arises, not least, from the problem of negativity: it may overwhelm conservative and socialist alike, install new gods (or a simulacrum of sacredness), and transform the present crisis into a perpetual oscillation between illusion and repression. A revision of the socialist tradition would, to be sure, involve socialists in their traditional effort to materialize spiritual discontent, and to spiritualize material discontent. Noble paradoxes, however, provide few concrete political projects.

There is an aspect of reality which is, visibly, in dissolution: the capacity of technocratic capitalism to do two things at once—exercise its control and satisfy the exigencies of the populations it dominates. Images of modern society as a machine—delicate, responsive (indeed, omniscient)—fuse in one parody the idea of an invisible hand and a more contemporary fantasy of a supercomputer. In fact, the very scale of technocratic control requires an effective decentralization which the system is unable to generate—since an effective decentralization would, clearly, interrupt communication and command. A regressive decentralization is now in progress (in ideology and in the practice of some of the states of the Federal Union) in the United States. A spurious devolution in fact abolishes or reduces the resources of centralized institutions producing public services—leaving these to be produced by local or regional agencies which cannot afford to do so. The presentation of this program as a qualitative change in politics, as a critical response to "bigness," surely constitutes one of the more effective political frauds of recent years. The phenomenon may alert us to the spurious element in some recent ideologies of decentralization propagated by technocratic thinkers on the twin grounds of efficiency and humaneness: large-scale systems, they argue, work best when decision is entrusted to a plethora of smaller nodes. The argument ignores the fact that there are no uniform systemic properties of systems of domination (apart from colossal banalities on the order of their consisting of those who dominate and those who are dominated). What is at issue is not a large-scale system in general but the attempt by those at the nodal points of this historical society to control the entirety of its surface. The assurance of political stability, the oligopolistic preemption of the economic market, is now not enough: vacuums of consent and deficits of value have evoked a large fabrication of culture.

Technocratic capitalism cannot, perhaps, harmonize its summit and base—but it is still remarkably effective in blocking the emergence of a concrete alternative. A revision of socialism organized about ideas of participatory democracy and self-management faces a terrible initial difficulty. The centralized power of domination apparently can be broken only by the concentration of a counter-power. Further, just when control systems expressed as hierarchies of status and distance are beginning to show marked traces of overload, the cultural critique which would describe a concrete utopia has failed us. The anti-technocratic, anti-hierarchical, anti-developmental beliefs of the counter-culture still define themselves negatively, as an anti-language. We are in spiritual bondage even (or above all) in opposition. The joyful anticipation of an anti-world does not contain any concrete indications of how it can be called into being—except for the varieties of flight from this one. Flight, however, will result in the establishment of counter-communities here and there (none at the centers of production and power). It will leave the rest of the world still speaking the technocratic language of system, control, choice—and one of the choices exercised by technocratic capitalism may well consist of an allocation of resources to counter-communities, as a mode of disarming a potential opposition. (In 1973 at the Institute of Social Science of the Central Committee of the Communist Party of the Soviet Union, I noticed a very large and systematic interest in research on the Western counter-culture.)

Pervasive hostility to technocratic control exercised from remote centers of decision, seizures as a result of which the controllers' power is diminished, the ideology of an anti-world—these do not lead arithmetically to a canon of opposition, much less a project for a new society. Historical experience suggests that such projects are threatened by a double fatality. They may begin by seeking to make a *tabula rasa*, may create new institutions—only to experience a return of the repressed patterns of the past at the first profound moment of stress. They may, however, seek attachment to a supposed historical logic, in the expectation that the further development of a flawed set of institutions will present us with their perfected successors. In these circumstances, there can be no surprise: old flaws beget new ones. How, then, can experiments in participatory democracy effectively oppose both the power of technocratic capitalism and its accompanying defects of hypertrophy?

The inability of the socialist movement to go beyond the prescription of the appropriation of the means of production and exchange to a politics of public control of production is disturbing. State industry in France, Great Britain, and Italy frequently reproduces the bureaucratic remoteness, hierarchical order, and material incentive structure of the capitalist environment. The presence of these state firms in our society does not mean that the transition to socialism is all but accomplished. Compare, however, the empty rhetoric of public discussion in the United States with the more solid European argument about the economy: the fact of appropriation has its advantages. Much of the insistence on the sameness of the social and psychological order of state and capitalist industry is political—the consequence of either a despairing conservatism (nothing can change) or a calculating one (nothing must change). The obvious necessity of developing new modes of appropriation ought not to detract from the indispensability of appropriation. Perhaps, however, the most promising sort of appropriation would result from a conjunction of public requirements and the demands of the industry workers themselves.

These, however, are very different. The public requires new criteria of efficacy in production: the integration of the product (and the process of its production) in an economy regulated by purpose criteria of the public good. The producers need employment and income, the amelioration of their working environment, and may demand a large measure of control of production. Society cannot renounce to socialist enterprise its (the society's) right to determine the larger structure of the economy, and socialist producers can hardly delegate to socialist planners all decisions affecting themselves. Our experience of the capitalist market does not allow us to suppose that a socialist market can harmonize these conflicting interests. It would be utopian to suppose that a new social calculus can be applied to the making of decisions. New ideas of value, new conceptions of cost and wealth, may well develop from the explicit processes of conflict in socialism. They can only do so if the institutions in which these conflicts occur are conceived so as to maximize both the visibility of conflict and the participation in its resolution. Put another way, the institutions projected by a new politics should have a coherent educational function. It is customary to suppose, in socialist theory, that the proper allocation of competence and representation to governing bodies will see us through many of the problems of transition to a new community. (The Common Program of the Union de la Gauche, for instance, envisages public, consumer, and worker representatives on the boards of socialized enterprise. It will no doubt surprise the authors of that Common Program attempting to resolve some of the conflicts between older and newer French models of socialism, between Jacobin *étatisme* and doctrines of self-management not entirely remote from an anarcho-syndicalist past, that a recent public opinion poll showed a majority of Americans ready to consider putting such representatives on the board of capitalist enterprise.) The allocation of competence to representative bodies, the designation of the groups and interests to be represented, presupposes just what has to be generated: a new idea of the public or general interest. The expansion of and alternation in the specific social functions of individuals may be one way of overcoming the fragmentation of the citizen, consumer, person, or worker (a fragmentation which in our own society leaves the task of integration to a culture quite unable to reconcile what reality has split asunder). It would, presumably, enlarge the capacity of individuals to conceive of a general interest—by enlarging, at first, their capacity to experience more specific interests as their own.

We find ourselves with the problem of the division of labor—in a setting of cultural and intellectual complexity not quite anticipated by early socialist theory. Suppose that the current division of labor responds not only to scientific and technical imperatives, but (as Gorz and Marglin have argued) to political ones: to the necessity of maintaining hierarchy in production. The key to the development of new forms of representation, to the transcendence of bureaucratic organization, appears to be cultural: new conceptions of the relationship of knowledge and production, a change in the self-consciousness of the labor force, in the idea of the dimensions of work itself.

Two ideas of socialism confront us (and each other). The first presupposes a social consciousness, or a general interest, and derives from this new institutions. That social consciousness or general interest is found, partly blocked, partly hidden, partly undeveloped, beneath the semblance of values propagated by capitalist society. It remains only for socialists to adumbrate and develop their more general version of social consciousness—and in its name to constitute themselves a governing party, occupying the central institutions of society, giving these (in effect) new ends. The second idea of socialism asks how a new social consciousness can be created: what are the possible institutional conditions for its production? This idea, clearly, is far less linear, more open to experimentation. It brings questions of culture and psychology to the center of attention: the process of value creation becomes political. The first idea entails a notion of redistribution, a perception that something is wrong with society according to an existent code of distribution. We could term it quantitative socialism. The second version of socialism, however tentatively, asks if the language of distribution itself is of any use. We could term it qualitative socialism. It has received enormous impetus, recently, from those questions of autonomy and identity now being discussed as aspects of a new politics.

Some simple formulations are convenient but only for a time. How easy it would be if we could assert that quantitative socialism attests the socialist movement's incorporation of (or in) technocratic domination! How simple if we could claim that qualitative socialism frees political thought of the detritus of both the market and bureaucracy. The rhetorical usage of the distinction ought not to confuse our historical sense. Where large groups in the population do suffer from material deprivation (measured by the capacity of the society to produce), a large place remains for a quantitative socialism. Where a qualitative socialism remains hypothetical, fascinated with questions difficult to concretize, it may so concentrate energies on the development of a new discourse that it diverts them from activity. In this situation the problem of a socialist politics is to move from quantitative to qualitative socialism not in the enclosed space of theoretic discussion but in a program.

Two areas are of particular interest, the production of public goods and services and the production of culture. (The latter phrase, to be sure, eludes a number of questions—but it also has the virtue of raising some, about the interaction between market and spirit, public and private realms.) These are problems which concern the society as a whole, and their solution (or programs for their solution) must entail concrete provisions for political alignments. In other terms, they mobilize general interests across class lines—while touching specific class interests strongly. Finally, they entail acute problems of command and coordination, resolved until now by the development of technocratic power—visible in the production of public goods, more hidden (but increasingly less so) in the sphere of culture.

What is the difference between a public good or service and any other kind? The distinction in fact rests upon the designation by a society of a sphere of public production, sometimes directly, sometimes indirectly, undertaken by the polity. The enlargement of the public sphere may be an indication of an increased public concern for welfare—or (as in the United States) of the breakdown of market mechanisms for the production of necessities. Quantitatively and qualitatively, conceptions of necessity alter. We can say that the chances of a new politics lie not simply in the public insistence on the public production of necessities, but in a public demand for participation in the planning and execution of the policy. It is in these relationships that technocratic power can be challenged and possibly diminished. The challenge will entail the development of a set of standards, or values, by which different groups can adjudicate their differences: it would be absurd to suppose that the process can be free of conflict. The point lies in the reappropriation of conflict by the parties to it.

That process would require the development of democratically constituted planning agencies at different levels. It would necessitate the continuous control of expertise by public representatives—and the development by technical experts of a rigorous public ethos in the exercise of their competence. We should have to invent new forms of social organization, to replace the organized and spurious randomness of the market—organized and spurious because used (and now calculated) to perpetuate exploitation and inequality. The protests against these, however, have usually called into existence systems of quantitative reallocation dominated by technocrats. What producers have reclaimed as consumers, they have lost as citizens. The empirical justification for our present mechanisms of reallocation is that these alone can perform the tasks of coordination in a situation of extreme complexity. Suppose, however, that the complexity is in part a result of a system of domination? Marcuse has told us of "surplus repression" and it may well be that a new campaign, against "surplus complexity," is in order.

One of the fatalities of current political discussion is that some of the assumptions built into it foreclose alternatives. A central assumption of this kind is the acceptance, sometimes covertly, of the theorem of cultural exhaustion. The fecundity of Western culture, we are told, is over—particularly with respect to larger social and cultural ideas. We are left with systematic introversion or the desperate search for escape. Another theorem with negative consequences is the doctrine of arcanae: some knowledge is important, but its importance is in direct proportion to its esoteric quality. Access to knowledge is given by meritocratic means, so that the group in possession of it is open: knowledge remains something in the possession of an elite. In brief, there are no new ideas which could shape a new public. There are techniques and applications of codified knowledge, but these are administered for the public, not by the public.

Weber observed that the religions of privileged strata emphasized what they were; the religions of underprivileged strata insisted on what they would become. The theory of cultural exhaustion is a form of spiritual self-congratulation by contemporary elites: their claim is to have seen it all, and by extension, to know it all. Are there rising strata or classes which could promulgate their own ideas? None seem visible—yet despite the theory of cultural exhaustion, despite the oligopolistic claims on knowledge of a cultural elite closely associated with technocratic domination, we cannot deny a large cultural ferment, even some excitement. From where does it come?

Touraine is entirely correct to insist, in his essay, on the resonance in the capitalist societies of the Chinese Cultural Revolution. No matter that we are ignorant of China: if the Cultural Revolution did not exist, we should have to invent it. Leave China to the Chinese; our problem is the social control of knowledge, the democratization of culture. The cultural effervescence of the capitalist societies is the consequence of the extension of education. It seems impossible for any educational system to produce intelligence precisely to measure. As production (and administration) become more technical, an educated labor force cannot be educated to the limit of the functions it will exercise. These are in any event difficult to predict with exactitude. More importantly, a labor force capable of adapting to changed techniques in the sphere of work requires a general education at some level. It is inevitable that a large number of citizens will be "over-educated." They will be given specific skills which may or may not be employed, owing to cyclical fluctuations in the labor market. They will have general levels of cuture which may conflict with the fragmentation of their existence as citizens, consumers, workers. In this period of economic regression, we hear rather less about investment in human capital and the like: was it not even a half-decade ago that thinkers as little subject to illusion as Galbraith were proclaiming as a discovery the contribution of education to economic development? Let us examine a rather different assumption, that the indefinite extension of education makes impossible economic development in terms consonant with the old politics of capitalist society.

For decades the socialist movement has been the one group in society which took bourgeois culture seriously. In part this is a direct legacy from those radical German democrats, Engels and Marx. In part it is connected with the aspirations of millions of working-class families: accession to bourgeois culture meant in their view accession to a more developed, a fuller humanity. We can understand bourgeois culture as having two elements: tradition and function. Tradition entailed the incorporation of values, a sensibility, a view of the past, derived or distilled from the Western experience with a large component of secularized Christianity at the center of this vision of life. The vision, in turn, was continuously revised to serve a function: the production of individuals suited by character and choice, temperament and intellectual predisposition, to play a role in the orderly working of bourgeois society. Two things have destroyed that synthesis. The first was the autonomous development of culture itself: a new view of human nature, the predominance of the natural sciences, a critical account of our own history. The second was a change in the organization of bourgeois society, the replacement of autonomous individuals (in theory and in fact) by technocratic functionaries.

It is a commonplace of conservative cultural criticism today to argue that the avant-garde has now fused with the public, that a democratization of culture equivalent to its vulgarization has occurred. It is argued, further, that the hedonism, the anti-bourgeois values of the modernist movement are now common property of the educated. This argument is most pathetic in the United States where, a high culture having been established with some difficulty, its votaries were understandably disturbed by challenges to their monopoly of it. What kind of society would we have if everyone could read Shakespeare and Joyce, look at Rembrandt and Pollock, listen to Mozart and Stockhausen? Fears of the obliteration of boundaries on this account seem highly premature. Furthermore, the argument that the central theme of post-bourgeois culture is the acting out of the fantasies of the modernist movement is a caricature. Most members of our society are too busy with their daily lives to try to convert these into a systematic bohemianism.

The difficulty, or difficulties, lie elsewhere. There is a larger educated public—but there is little sign that it is able to relate those fragments of cultural tradition it possesses to its daily existence, or to the polity, in a systematic or satisfying way. We know, of course, about plenty of periods of historical dissonance among a culture, a polity, and a society—but we also know that in situations of this kind, new relationships, new configurations and meanings, have developed. It is no answer, then, to assert that our culture (or what there is of it) and our other orders of existence are at odds and that this is likely to continue indefinitely: the conclusion (voiced most recently in America by Bell) is another form of the conservative use of the theorem of cultural exhaustion, and may well express a fear as well as a skepticism about new possibilities. The situation of the educated, further, has its counterpart in the position of those who cannot call to their assistance the resources, however attenuated, of the tradition of high culture. Subjected to the assault of the cultural industry, millions have had to mobilize in defense the bonds and values of family, locality, community, region, and religion. The recrudescence of ethnic and national demands in western and southern Europe may be understood in the same fashion.

Socialism has long understood itself as the repository of the universal principles of the French Revolution. It has abandoned to the right the defense of tradition, family, and the other concrete patterns of existence which expressed rootedness. Not quite imperceptibly, but rapidly, a change has occurred. Universalism in the form presented by the cultural industry can be seen as the ideological servitor of centralized domination, as a mode of imposing administrative standardization in the wake of the market. The psychological search for identity, in its political form, has led to a singular reversal: radical, even revolutionary, demands are conjoined to positions that once were the exclusive property of the right. If technocratic capitalism has indeed succeeded in decomposing the opposition of a unified working class, it has—by pushing the fragmentation of a familiar opposition to extremes—called into existence a multiplicity of oppositions.

The multiplicity and diversity of the oppositions, the very fact that we may use the plural, calls attention to a weakness as well as a strength of the forces which would change society. Their strength is the specificity of their existence. Their weakness is the absence of a unifying idea, which at first glance appears to condemn the opposition (or oppositions) to a permanent guerrilla war, to opposing the center from the margins.

A new culture need not precede a new politics, but it is impossible to imagine a new politics without the concomitant development of a new culture. This cannot be invented: a new sensibility, a new set of values, new ideas of human nature and community cannot be summoned into existence. Yet as our historical experience becomes more dense, our knowledge of traditions broader, our critical capacities more acute, our ability to synthesize experience and tradition should increase. The cultural inequalities which result from the class structure, however, deny to a large part of the population the capacity to synthesize their personal experience with a coherent and realistic view of the movement of society. Moreover, our cultural elites are themselves often in bondage to technocratic thought—disguised, well or poorly, as technical and scientific knowledge. We can best describe technocratic thought by the discrepancy between its claims and its consequences. It claims to be full description of reality, but its consequences frequently entail a systematic inhibition of the moral imagination: other institutions, other values, are difficult to envisage. In other words it arrests history—for better or worse.

The problem, then, is one of both access and creativity. Under what conditions can significant numbers of persons accede to the cultural means to creativity? The socialist movement's respect for bourgeois culture has been combined with ideas of equality of opportunity. Given the high probability of the indefinite continuation of a social hierarchy expressed in part by differences of education, socialists have advocated making education more available on meritocratic criteria. The broader issue of an educated citizenry, and the less tangible but pervasive one of the kind of culture a society both democratic and industrial could have, has frequently taken second place. Ideas of permanent or recurrent education (provided that this consists of something more profound than technical and vocational retraining) clearly provide a mode of entry to high cultural tradition for groups hitherto excluded from it. That high cultural tradition, however, is itself in profound disrepair, indeed, decomposition. It does not follow that we are in a state of cultural exhaustion, at the end of history—even if we are at the end of an historic period.

The cultural protest at the margins of our society has frequently taken anachronistic forms: systematic returns to particularisms which appear to constitute regressions. In another view, there may well be method to these revolts. Tradition can be understood as a constraint, frequently oppressive. It can also be understood as a repository, a historical reservoir, of alternative values—to be evoked or summoned when the society's predominant culture offers unsatisfactory solutions to problems which do not go away. The counter-culture of the educated, particularly in the forms espoused by the student and youth movements which now seem so quiescent, appeared regressive in another sense. Instant utopias, total attacks on reunuciation, demands for the immediate termination of hierarchy, appear to belong to the realm of play, not politics. However, playfulness often has serious implications: this revolt had points of convergence with the working-class movement's recourse to ideas of participatory democracy. Three themes, then, give us some of the elements of a new cultural synthesis—or rather, their ends: the integrity of communities, the fulfillment of the self, the extension of economic autonomy.

These ends do come from the concrete experiences of marginal groups threatened by centralized domination, of younger persons in search of cultural forms for selfhood, of workers seeking to alter the forms of exploitation. Historically, it has fallen to intellectuals to fashion cultural syntheses—but inflated accounts of the importance of intellectuals exaggerate because they overlook the extent to which the intellectuals draw the material of synthesis from the society around them. Our present situation is unique because the intellectuals (in a larger sense of the intelligentsia) play an important role in administration and production. Again the idea of "over-education" comes to our aid. Even technocratic apologists cannot forever speak the language of system, regulation, and consensus—there is too much dissensus in the society, indeed, systematically engendered by it. Perhaps only fragments of cultural tradition remain, but these too may function as sources of desire—activating a demand for cultural coherence, for a society in which the spirit may feel at home. Where the inarticulate quest for a new culture moves so many, the intellectuals cannot complain that they lack synthetic tasks.

Is this a return to Mannheim's version of the flight from politics,

his idea of a "free-floating" intelligentsia, above the battle, charged with reconciling the antagonisms of a society in conflict? The idea is, in our situation, entirely unconvincing. Throughout Western history, cultural and political conflicts have been fought out among intellectuals—not resolved by them. Our society may be less complex than its present rulers in self-serving fashion claim. Its actual complexity and opaqueness may well be reduced by a new politics. For the moment it is in any historical comparison complex enough, and it is not surprising that its intellectuals should be divided as to how they view it. We can say that it is in the cultural realm that an entire series of political conflicts will have to be fought out before and as these take political form. The intellectuals, then, will differ strenuously among themselves: we can expect no monolithic party of enlightenment to emerge, and we can take such consolation as we wish from the recollection that the contributors to the Encyclopedia were often at odds.

Where, in all of this, is the promised union of quantitative and qualitative politics? Union, perhaps, is too strong and premature a term: let us explore systematic connections. What is striking about the political demands of modern populations, recently, is their qualitative nature. We can take for granted the continuation of quantitative demands: it is difficult to imagine a time when "des sous" will not be a political slogan. The context of quantitative allocation has recently, however, come under scrutiny—and some popular demands are simply not translatable into numbers. Of course, most persons would not talk in terms of these antitheses, or distinctions. We can say, however, that the extension of technocratic control has led to a heightened awareness, however limited its articulation may be at present, of severe deficiencies in the cultural and political resources available to most persons. What had originally been intended to reconcile citizenship and production, to provide a protected space for personal development, now seems to infringe upon all three spheres—while driving them apart. Technocratic mediation, in other terms, mediates not at all.

The possibility of a political alliance between classes, in a traditional sense, has been enlarged by this development. Most members of the intelligentsia, most intellectuals, are in fact employees. The free professionals face bureaucratic integration. At the summit, no doubt, some in these categories enjoy the status of technocratic controllers—but these are few in number. Those in intermediate positions suffer not from a bad conscience but from the society's inability to give them a good one: cultural incoherence has become a political fact. Those in the larger ranks of the educated increasingly recognize themselves as parts of a working class.

The defection from technocratic capitalism in a number of Western societies of what we once thought of as the middle class does not mean that a new historical bloc has emerged. The idea of a historical bloc is indeed a modification of simple notions of the antagonism of two classes: perhaps, in a situation of surplus complexity, simpler notions still have their uses. What we confront is a superimposition of conflict. The effort to regulate market struggles at times encapsulates class conflict, at times joins to it—in no simple or clear fashion, to be sure—structures of technocratic domination. The idea of a revolution or of a revolutionary politics pursued by a new historical bloc is often interpreted to mean that the means of production, the commanding heights of the economy, the centers of power, and the system of administration can somehow be possessed as a preliminary to their transformation. The very enumeration of the objectives of a politics listed with an increasing degree of vagueness suggests that the way in which power is exercised serves to consolidate it. In our society power is both concentrated at the center and suffused throughout the society: attacked in one place, it defends itself in another.

We face neither an invincible system, however, nor a demonic machine. The modern West is a historical structure like any other, and its transience is certain. What will succeed it is a factual question. Who will make the transition is a human one. Some of the elements of a new politics exist; others remain to be invented. The process of invention is also a process of education, an effort to find new limits and new forms for a humanity more that necessarily out of its spirits, true and unhoused. These notes are intended to evoke the dimensions, the difficulties, of the project.